BULLDOGS FOREVER

A HISTORY OF
ALBUQUERQUE HIGH SCHOOL
AND
A MEMOIR OF THE CLASS OF 1954

BY

H. L. (BUSTER) QUIST

"Bulldogs Forever," by H.L. Quist. ISBN 1-58939-638-3.

Published 2004 by Virtualbookworm.com Publishing Inc., P.O. Box 9949, College Station, TX 77842, US. ©2004, H.L. Quist. All rights reserved. No part of this publication may be reproduced, stored in a retrieval system, or transmitted in any form or by any means, electronic, mechanical, recording or otherwise, without the prior written permission of H.L. Quist.

Manufactured in the United States of America.

TABLE OF CONTENTS

PREFACE

"Bulldogs Forever" records and preserves memories and events of Albuquerque High School from 1879 to 1951, while at the same time this book pays a tribute to those notable individuals who formed the building blocks of our traditions at AHS.

The period of 1951-1954 is written as a memoir, which, by definition, is a narrative that the writer has lived through—an autobiography. In this case, however, it should be viewed as an experience that all of us who attended high school in the "fabulous Fifties," can share and enjoy, as we all relive our own version of those "happy days."

Those in high school during the late Forties to the mid-Fifties were born in the depths of the Great Depression, and many of us sold seeds as grade schoolers for "Victory Gardens" as our nation united and rallied to win World War II. These two catastrophic events, The Depression and the War, were, perhaps, the two most defining moments in 20th Century America. They unquestionably defined who we were as children purportedly of the greatest generation.

As the Fifties unfolded we were fascinated with a new entertainment medium that introduced us to the comedic antics of Uncle Miltie and a zany redhead by the name of Lucy. Our value systems were challenged by those iconoclastic screen rebels Marlon Brando and James Dean. A curvaceous and vulnerable blonde by the name of Marilyn aroused our sexual curiosity while the tightly-knit code of moral conduct of our era suppressed our libido.

So much in our era centered on athletics. Athletics for America's youth was a phenomenon detested by some but enthusiastically supported by most as part of a social ethic stressing team work that gave those who accepted it a sense of pride, togetherness and belonging. This book, written by someone who experienced the joy of victory as well as the disappointment of defeat, also seeks to recognize those athletes that made their marks before us in the uniform of Green and White.

"Bulldogs Forever" attempts to re-create life as it was during the Fifties—principally through a narrative amongst its principal characters from the class of `54 who, for the most part, have been interviewed. To those who are inaccurately portrayed in some way or have been omitted, I extend my sincere apologies. Memoirs are intended to preserve memories. Some will make you laugh and some will make you cry. Our grandchildren, some of whom are getting their first tattoo or their body pierced, can read about our good old days and they just might say, "Hey dude, you guys were pretty cool!"

Acknowledgements

This writer is deeply indebted to Jim Hulsman, who was not only the inspiration for this book but was also the primary resource for all the factual data so vital to this project. Without Jim's meticulous accumulating and cataloging and preservation of most of the information used here about Albuquerque High School, its students, teachers, coaches and administrators, "Bulldogs Forever" would not have the depth and scope to serve as a true historical document.

Jim's tenure as a coach at AHS for 48 years is legendary in itself, especially when quantified in wins and losses. His true value to the institution, the City, and the students he served is immeasurable. This writer never watched this coach work his magic on the hardwood, but while working on this project I believe I discovered a vital secret to his success. No one could have devoted so much time and effort in his lifetime to preserve the history of his school without a deep and bonding love of people as well as the institution. His players had to know that the team's success enabled each one of them to "find that spring in their step" so vital to life's journey. There will always be a very special place in Bulldog lore for Jim Hulsman.

To me, Bobby Santiago was pound for pound (all 130 of them) the toughest, the hardest-hitting and the most durable running back in AHS history and quite possibly in New Mexico high school football. Bobby was All-State his senior year in 1959 and was chosen to play in the All-American High School game. He was equally successful at the University of New Mexico, making the All-Skyline Team his sophomore and junior years and selected to the All-Western Athletic Conference Team as well as third team NCAA All-

III

American his senior year. Bobby capped his brilliant football career, from which he never missed a game due to an injury, by playing for the National All-Stars in the Southwestern Challenge Bowl. This true AHS icon was inducted into the UNM Hall of Honor in 1988.

Ed Garvanian, the Bulldog's Assistant Football Coach and Head Track Coach during the Fifties was not only Bobby's coach, he was his mentor and friend. Ed's constant encouragement to the diminutive athlete that "you have the potential" to be a winner was the message that inspired Bobby to believe in himself. It was Bobby's reciprocation to his mentor that was the genesis of the Albuquerque High School Alumni Association. Bobby and Ray Etherley were the Co-Founders of a scholarship fund as a tribute to Ed Garvanian.

Bobby's tireless efforts have made the Association a success by reuniting seven decades of students and athletes that had seen their memories fade with the demise of the "old school." Our rebirth has been an inspiration for *Bulldogs Forever.*

Also, to Jack Stromberg, who became my closest friend from our first day at Washington Junior High School, this writer is sincerely grateful for his collaboration on my memoir in which he plays a pivotal role. Jack's constant admonition to the author — "let the facts speak for themselves and exercise humility" — may have invoked a strict adherence to the former but less to the latter. My apologies to my friend if the author's literary license was overly exercised;

To Gloria (Glo) Hanawald (Cantwell), my girlfriend and most avid cheerleader for over four years, my most sincere appreciation to allow the reader to experience the agony and the ecstasy of our relationship as a mirror into their own;

To Al Beebe, '52, who dubbed Jack Stromberg and this writer the "Blond Bookends," for lending his professional sportswriting and journalistic skills in editing the work of an amateur; and to all those Bulldogs from years past who shared their time and a part of their youth with the author, which truly made this two and one-half year project a labor of love.

DEDICATION

To the Bulldogs of the past, present and future, may our traditions and memories last forever.

CHAPTER ONE:
CULTURE AND HISTORY

AS I RECALL, MOST OF THE AMERICAN HISTORY that I learned in elementary, junior high and high school during the Forties and Fifties focused on the discovery and settlement by northern Europeans of the eastern area of the new land, which would become known as the Thirteen Colonies. It generally ignored the southwest where the origin and development of its culture was dramatically different.

Our textbooks, principally written and published by eastern scholars, made much of the Pilgrims landing on Plymouth Rock in December 1620 and the establishment and colonization of America,[1] while Spanish explorers Alvar Nunez Cabeza de Vaca and missionary Father Marcos de Niza made expeditions into what is now New Mexico one hundred years prior to the Pilgrims landing in Massachusetts. The area near Albuquerque (Isleta) was inhabited by Pueblo people, descendants of the Anasazi culture, as early as AD 1300. In 1540 Francisco Vasquez de Coronado discovered the Seven Cities of Cibola — actually the pueblo communities of the Zuni people — but he did not find the rich treasure of gold that he was seeking.

In 1595, Juan de Onaté, who was born in New Spain (Mexico) and related by marriage to the Aztec ruler Montezuma II, won a contract (royal grant) to settle the area that we know as New Mexico and claim the territory for the King of Spain. Reaching a pueblo near the spot where the Rio Grande and the Rio Chama join, he built the capital of New

---

[1] Microsoft® Encarta® 98 Encyclopedia© 1993-1997 Microsoft Corp.

Mexico, calling it San Gabriel.

Onaté's discovery of the Rio Grande Valley will be commemorated over four hundred years later by one of Albuquerque High School's most distinguished alumni, Betty Sabo, '46. Thirty life-sized bronze figures entitled "La Journata" (The Journey) sculpted in collaboration with Renaldo (Sonny) Rivera, will depict this historic event that founded a culture so unique to our area.

Ultimately and unavoidably, there was a clash of cultures. The Spanish missionaries often imposed Christianity on the Native Americans. When priests tried to prevent native ceremonies, a revolt occurred in 1680. The missions were destroyed and the priests and many Spanish colonists were killed. The Spanish however, returned in force and by 1696, reconquered the entire area. Although many of the Native Americans remained hostile to the Spaniards, intermarriage increased and the origins of a mixed heritage and culture began.

In 1821, Mexico won its independence from Spain, and Nuevo Mexico (New Mexico) was a part of that new country. Ironically it was that same year that William Becknell brought a pack train from Franklin, Missouri, to Santa Fe along a route that would come to be known as the Santa Fe Trail. The trade immediately created friction between the European-Americans who spoke mostly English (Anglos), the Native Americans and the Spanish who spoke their own languages.

The friction between the three groups came to a head when the United States declared war on Mexico in 1846 and President James Polk sent General Stephen Watts Kearny to invade New Mexico. Kearny took Santa Fe without a shot being fired, and claimed New Mexico for the United States on August 18, 1846. The United States-Mexican War ended in 1848 with the Treaty of Guadalupe Hidalgo, and Mexico ceded New Mexico to the United States. The Congress of the United States formally created the territory of New Mexico in 1850, but statehood did not come until 1912 "... partly because of prejudice against the predominantly Spanish-speaking, Roman Catholic population of the territory" and, "... opponents also characterized New Mexico as an inhospitable land of uneducated settlers and wild Native Americans."[2]

Robert Werstler, one of our history teachers, would approve of this brief history as informative, but the reader might rightfully ask, "what purpose does it serve in a book devoted to our high school?"

A good question. I hope I have an equally good answer.

Perhaps nowhere in America did three distinct and diverse cultures create such a colorful tapestry — the social fabric that molded our formative years. Our art and architecture was as distinctive then as it remains visible today. A traveler driving by car through New Mexico will experience talk radio and music in Navajo, Spanish and English. Our community property law is based on Spanish rather than English Common Law. When purchasing a tract of land research may find the original title in Spanish as part of a grant from the King of Spain. Like a biotapestry hung on a castle wall in Europe depicting historical events, our unique culture formed the backdrop to the years remembered here.

As the Spanish incursion of almost 500 years ago created a conflict and planted the seeds of mistrust with the Native Americans, so did the Anglo settlement of almost 200 years ago reap discontent with the other two cultures. An aura of anger remained etched in our tapestry during our formative years, as articulated by a 1956 AHS graduate heralded as the "Founder of Chicano Literature."

Rudolfo (Rudy) Anaya says in his 1985 autobiography: Yes, the Fifties were a good time, but one has to remember that historians do not see everything. There are huge pockets of people whose history, at any given time, is never told. The large Mexican-American population is a case in point. Moving through high school without purpose, never seeing Mexican teachers, never reading the history of the literature of the people, created in us a

---

[2] Microsoft® Encarta®, IBID.

3

sense of the displaced. We knew our worth. It was reflected in our families, in the *Barrios*, in the cities and ranches. We knew there was a long history of the Hispanic presence in the Southwest United States, but the education we received did not reflect this. Society's melting down was at work, but the idea of a melting pot was a myth. Society did not accept, as equals, the black and brown people of the country. Prejudice did exist, racism was thriving.

In *Bless Me, Ultima*, Rudy discovers his "artistic soul," and the novel's success propelled him to national prominence and a connection to the Chicano Movement which has dramatically changed the destiny of the Mexican-American people, not only in New Mexico, but in the entire U.S. In April 2002, Rudolfo was awarded the National Medal of Art in a ceremony in Washington, D.C. by President George W. Bush.

A herculean effort was made by none other than Glen O. Ream, our AHS principal from 1927 to 1956, to ameliorate Rudy's lament. Mr. Ream, who will be celebrated as a true "Renaissance Man" in this book, wrote a history of New Mexico with special emphasis on Onaté's discovery and the origins of our rich Hispanic culture. Glen desperately wanted his work to be accepted as a text book in the Albuquerque Public School System. It was unfortunately rejected.

It is important to note that this writer has elected to use the terms Hispanic for Mexican-Americans and Blacks for Negroes, even though those terms were not used in the time period of this book.

There is an interesting personal footnote to the early history of New Mexico. My spouse's family were early pioneers homesteading near the town of Eddy (now Carlsbad) in 1884. In 1916 Francisco (Pancho) Villa led a band of revolutionaries into New Mexico and raided the southern border town of Columbus, killing 18 and burning most of the town. My future father-in-law, Dean Smith, was part of the contingent of troops under the Command of General John J. Pershing sent to battle Villa's insurgents. Shortly thereafter Dean, a Major, volunteered to join the newly formed United States Army Air Corps and became the first person to fly and land an airplane in the state of New Mexico.

My family did not move to Albuquerque until 1950, when I enrolled at Washington Junior High School. Thrust suddenly into a culture so foreign to my midwestern roots I could only absorb my surroundings without a compass or a guide to its past.

Eldred R. Harrington, who allowed those of us who were his students to call him "Doc," compiled a brief history of AHS from 1879 to 1950 from which some of the following is taken. As a graduate of our beloved school in 1920 and head of the AHS Science Department for 25 years, few would be as qualified to document our past. Doc had a B.S. and M.S. in Civil Engineering; B.S. and M.S. in Geology; a Ph.D in Physical Chemistry; an M.A. in Secondary Education; was an athlete and a coach in all sports; a teacher, principal and superintendent; a prolific writer of over 250 magazine articles and author of five text books. And, most importantly, an owner of a Harley Davidson Motor Cycle! This remarkable AHS alum, was indeed, a "Man For All Seasons." The unique opportunity that presents itself here is to make our generational contact with Doc and to preserve and amplify on his last years at AHS (1954). I think he would have liked that.

Present day Albuquerque was founded in 1706 and named Albuquerque after the Duke of Alburquerque, then Viceroy of New Spain (Mexico). Somewhere in time the first "R" was dropped. I, like many of you, can recall when the contemporary Duke visited our city to celebrate its 250th birthday. Plans are now underway to celebrate the 300th. Our *Alma Mater* should play a significant role in almost one half of the celebratory period.

In 1879 the Colorado College, located in Colorado Springs, started the Albuquerque Academy which Doc declares, "... was the direct ancestor of the Albuquerque High School today." It was located on the east side of the plaza that we refer to as "Old Town." In 1886 C.E. Hodgin was the Academy principal. Those of us who attended the University of New Mexico will vividly recall Hodgin Hall named in honor of one of the State's early educators.

By 1890 the Academy had grown to 385 students and

the "New Academy," a three-story structure built at a cost of $24,000, was erected at Central and Edith Street, where a branch of the Albuquerque Public (Collections) Library now stands. One year later, the City of Albuquerque obtained legal authority to levy taxes for the support of the school. In 1891 the school formally became a part of a public system and Mr. Hodgin was the first Superintendent of Schools. Doc Harrington indicates that the City had approximately 4000 residents at that time, and the territorial legislature authorized the building of the University of New Mexico at an isolated area "way out" on the east Mesa. In 1892, AHS graduated its first class of three students. A. B. Stroup served as our first Principal from 1902 to 1905.

AHS had occupied several locations during its early years, but by 1914 the structure that we knew so well was erected at Central Avenue and Broadway. The City then had a population of about 10,000. By 1920 there was a graduating class of 65 including Doc and a student body of 400. In 1927 the Manual Arts building was erected and six years later the Administration Building and Library that would become so familiar to us were added. Construction began on the Gymnasium in 1937 and it opened in 1939. All these improvements including Bulldog field (now Milne Stadium) were completed during The Depression as projects of the Works Progress Administration (WPA).

Recalling our impressive campus brings back fond memories, but it was our administrators, teachers and coaches who provided us an essential human connection to our past, as these individuals paved the way for our future. In 1911, John Milne, who taught at AHS and who was Principal from 1909 to 1911, was selected by the Board of Education as Superintendent of Public Schools. Remarkably, Mr. Milne remained in that position for forty years—the year our class of 1954 enrolled as sophomores. Imagine for a moment the significance of the time and the events that marked the beginning of Mr. Milne's tenure.

He was teaching at AHS when "Pioneer Day" was a daily event, evidenced by a large concrete trough to water horses at Broadway and Central, and not a special day for the student body. Most men then wore the law on their hip. Aside from Mr. Milne, who drove a black Model T Ford Touring Car, few, if any, of the teachers drove an automobile as the horseless carriage was as rare as hen's teeth and were prohibitive in cost. Most of our parents were just a gleam in our grandparents' eyes, and the cry of "Remember the Maine" still echoed from the Spanish-American War.

Some of our faculty were of the same era. Florence Hickman came to AHS in 1915 and some of us were students in her English class. Lillian Keike (typing), Barbara Phillips (English) and Mary Cole Dixon arrived in 1915. Coach F. M. (Tony) Wilson came in 1923 and Glen O. Ream became principal in 1927. Miss Mary Cole Dixon became Vice-Principal in the same year. They would both serve in that capacity for an amazing thirty-two continuous years.

Miss Dixon, on the occasion of John Milne's death in 1956, said of her mentor:

I think he was an impatient man who had schooled himself to patience. Men with the vision he had are likely to be tense when confronted by what seems like stupid opposition. I have seen his temper flare, then known him later to go to considerable trouble to see that no resentment or hurt lingered. To him the task was the thing and we were all partners, each with a definite result to achieve.

The children of Albuquerque have lost in him a tireless friend who was ever active in their behalf.[3]

It was indeed the stability, consistency and capability of our school administration, coupled with the dedication of our teachers and coaches to the education of the city's youth, that created the foundation and framework of our lives at AHS. They also linked us to our southwestern culture unique to our place. Most importantly, perhaps, being a teenager in the middle of the twentieth century enabled us to see back through our teacher's eyes to the beginning of this era, and to prepare us for the monumental change that lay ahead at the turn of the next century.

---

[3] Albuquerque Public Schools Journal, Vol. XI, No. 1, Sept. 1956.

Doc Harrington pays a special tribute to two faculty members from AHS who went on to gain particular distinction. Riley B. Ruthledge left for law school at the University of California and ultimately became a Justice of the U.S. Supreme Court. Miss Erna Fergusson left the teaching of English and Spanish at AHS to become one of America's greatest writers. For an extensive list of other faculty members I suggest that you read Doc's perspective on AHS. Other distinguished grads will be remembered in this text chronologically.

Integral parts of AHS lore and its traditions are also chronicled by Dr. Harrington. The first continuous school publication was *La Reata* (the Lariat) our high school yearbook. From Jim Hulsman who has succeeded Doc as the principal AHS historian, I learned how the yearbook derived its name.

> In my freshman year, a school yearbook was initiated, and we were asked to put proposed names in a suggestion box. I submitted the name La Reata "The Lariat," and since it was the only suggestion made, it became the name of the Albuquerque High School annual—my only claim to fame. — Kenneth C. Balcomb, Class of 1912.

I'm not certain what Ken had in mind in choosing the name, but the lariat certainly captures or lassos our memories.

Doc indicated that the first yearbook appeared in 1909 when it presumably had another name. The Editor was Oliver Peterson and the first yearbook was dedicated to W. D. Sterling, the Superintendent of Schools. Several noteworthy facts grabbed my attention as I carefully turned the pages of this somewhat worn and faded gem, almost 100 years of age.

The senior class graduated eleven girls and only three boys. The girls had a basketball team in those very early years. They beat a team from the University of New Mexico 16 to 5 at the "Casino" which conjures up images of those entertainment centers so prominent in contemporary New Mexico. Who knows? Gambling was legal in New Mexico in those days. Maybe there was a casino.

Reading these treasures reveals the remarkably descriptive prose in the students writing. Covering the athletic teams one writer says, "The football progress this year was rather jerky." The team had an average weight of 133 pounds and Fred Calkins was the team captain. In all probability, Fred was the father or uncle of teammate and 1952 graduate John Calkins who starred for three years at AHS on the gridiron.

No one, it appears, has offered any information that would determine the origin of the AHS mascot, "Butch" the Bulldog. Roy A. Stamm (1893) in his autobiography, "for ME, THE SUN," recalls a report of a Bear-Bulldog match that was held in Albuquerque in front of about 300 spectators who paid one dollar each to see the "fight" in the late 1880s. He also cited that in California in the early days of Mexican and Spanish rule, "bulls and bears were often matched, with the bull usually the victor." The bulldog apparently enjoyed a reputation as a ferocious fighter in the southwestern US in this era. Was that the source of our mascot? An interesting speculation.

The first school newspaper was the *Occident*, which was started in 1902 but expired in 1907. In 1919 Miss Oliver (the records say "Oliver") Morris, an English teacher, founded *The Record*, the school newspaper which has survived to this day. One of the early issues devoted to the "Wild West" must have been a doozy. Doc says, "Fortunately no copy of this issue has come down to posterity...the staff gathered the extra copies up and burned them so that this monstrosity of imagination would not be preserved."

In 1918 the AHS printing department took on the responsibility of printing *La Reata* by purchasing the presses and equipment to do so.

Under the ambitious advancement of faculty member Allan B. Williams in 1931, *The Record* garnered national prizes for like publications for 15 years. Doc, indicative of his subtle sense of humor says, "It looked for a while that if any other American high schools won anything, they would first have to send someone out here to shoot Al. Of course Al was raised out here in the wilds of Albuquerque and with his postgraduate living out in the wilds of 'Taixus,' he might have presented a formidable obstacle for any such eradication procedure."

In 1936, the year of most of our collective births for the class of 1954, Miss Barbara Phillips, Head of the English Department, and Glen O. Ream, our Principal, saw that there was a need for a literary publication. Prior to that date poetry and short stories appeared in *La Reata*. The *Yucca* was born. Admittedly, I had no creative input to the *Yucca* other than as Co-Editor of the Art Department.

As early as 1900 there were two literary or debating societies: "The Criterion" and the "Philo-Matheans." They continued to 1918 and were succeeded by the Theodore Roosevelt and Webster debating societies. It's interesting to note that debating competition was furious in the Twenties and Thirties but apparently died prior to our era. Debating truly has become a lost art as the public seemingly wants to absorb issues in sound bites rather than by lengthy and persuasive debate.

Music has been part of the AHS tradition as far back as the origin of the school. At the Albuquerque Academy 24 lessons were available at a cost of $18. According to Doc a glee club was formed in 1901, and is one of the oldest continuous organizations surviving to the present. In 1908 an orchestra was established, and by the Fifties the music programs had been expanded to include a band, an a capella choir, girls' chorus, boys' glee club and a special Christmas Cantata.

Being situated in the "wild, wild west," drama was probably looked upon as "not being quite proper," Typical of his wit, Doc says:

"The canaries sang a deep bass in this very tough town and some of the dramas which were put on in the downtown theaters were not of the most refined variety."

Despite that perception, one of the first class plays was *Esmeralda* performed in 1915. The Spanish Play dates back to 1916, and the Latin Play which was first introduced in 1919, was probably the origin of the Latin Club. By the mid-Twenties, however, dramatic and musical productions proliferated and ambitious stage productions were highly successful. In 1930 the first Christmas Cantata was performed still popular in our era. Drama teams produced numerous plays for the student body in the Fifties. I developed an awareness of the importance that drama played in high school as I reviewed my father's thespian activities in the early 1920s, so conspicuously preserved in his yearbook.

AHS had placed a high degree of emphasis on scholarship since the Scholarship Society (which we called the Honor Society) was organized in 1920. Doc relates the story of one of his classmates who made 11 A's, 9 B's, six athletic letters, captained a debating society, headed the "A" Club and was on the staff of *The Record*, but didn't make the Honor Society. Obviously, the rigid standards must have been relaxed by the early Fifties—I made the Honor Society three years.

Other organizations and clubs that survived from the past to our day are:

The Girls League	1916
Student Council	1918
Letterman's Club	1921 ("A" Club 1928)
Kodak Club	1922 (Projector Club)
The Pepper Club	1928
The Archaeology Society	1932
The Co-Op Club	1933 (Student Activities)
Future Farmers Organization	1937
Ski Club	1938
Silver Saddles Riding Club	1945
Future Teachers of America	1948-49

Other clubs that were organized around the time that Doc completed his history (1950) were the Hobby, ONCO, Outdoor, Ice Skating, Square Dance, Tennis, Sen-Sems Tri-Hi-Y, Bowling, Modern Dance and Rollicking Rollers.

A Radio Club was started in 1932 but was discontinued, as many clubs were when a course was offered in the curriculum. What eventually evolved was AHS' own radio station, KANW which broadcast from the top of the Administration Building.

It appears that the Junior-Senior Prom, whose origin dates back to 1909, is one of the few major social events that survived until the Fifties. Other dances mentioned by Doc in his history were not part of the social calendar during our years. Events that we enjoyed such as the Military Ball, the Green and White Ball, the "A" Club Dance, and the Pepper

Club Christmas Formal were possibly overlooked or they originated around 1950. Also not mentioned was Pioneer Day. How could our noted historian forget this noteworthy and fun event when he himself gave a hilarious rendition of "Little Nell" during the assembly in 1952? Maybe it was a performance that he preferred not to recall.

Other than the Junior-Senior Prom, perhaps the most significant event of the year was Bulldog Day (also known as Homecoming). The selection of our Queen and her Court and the coronation ceremonies, the homerooms' effort in building and competing for top prize for the best floats and the parade down Central Avenue, were a part of a well-established tradition and pageantry surrounding the game of football not only of our high school but all over America. The origin of Bulldog Day was 1946, fifty-four years after AHS fielded its first football team in 1892. So much of our high school life and spirit focused and centered around not only football but the sports world. Why? How did sports become such an integral part of the tapestry that was the fabric of our life? We will explore this, what only can be termed a phenomenon, in depth as our 1954 class begins our sophomore year.

CHAPTER TWO:
THE EARLY YEARS 1879-1929

ACCORDING TO DR. HARRINGTON, it is difficult to pinpoint precisely when organized athletic teams came into existence, but for certain the Athletic Association was formed in 1892. Doc was unaware, however, that a real gem existed waiting to be mined.

Fortunately an autobiography written by Roy A. Stamm, "for ME, THE SUN"[4] (Class of 1893) brightly illuminates the earliest of days at AHS and an activity so vital to the traditions of our school.

> *When I entered Albuquerque High all the football we played was struggling to kick a round or elliptic shaped ball below or over the cross bar of your opponents' goal, depending on which way you had agreed upon. In 1892, when I became a junior, both in the High and the University, teams were formed to play the American game [of football]. Our canvas suits carried little padding except where towels were stuffed over shoulders and knees. Head-gears, nose guards, and helmets were not yet introduced and all players cultivated heavy heads of hair for protection. Then it was a really rough game and in poor repute with those conservative [in nature]. The ball was not dead until it touched the ground, and you could hurdle*

---

[4] Published by the Albuquerque Museum, 1999 p.39, 40. For a historical picture of Albuquerque during the first half of the 20th century and a fascinating personal perspective of eight decades in the life of a remarkable man, read this book.

"cleated shoes first" if you wished. Soon, flying wedges, revolving "turtle-back" plays and tandem line bucking became common. Eventually, these massed plays were forbidden by new rules but they lasted for quite a while. I had my nose broken twice and my cheek bone caved in, also a trick knee, but escaped more serious injury probably because I was compactly built.

As captain of the High School team, the Superintendent of the Indian School asked me to coach his boys which, from time to time, I did for one season. Many of these were adults not heavy but tough and hard. This school fielded four teams with several good runners among them. Not expecting to play them, I taught those braves all our best plays and threw in our signals for good measure. We met them for a practice game one Saturday and won 12-0. They gave us a good game and we should have left well enough alone; we took them on publicly two ᵎ ᵑot trimmed 20 to 0! With four teams ᵃlmost every day and their natural abil- ᵉndurance, I decided I'd coached them

I0137100

ʰ a team almost as heavy as that of the University, we played them and won 12 to 0, largely because we sprung a new play, "interference." Taught us by a Colorado College graduate, this consisted of one back running in front and the ball carrier right behind him with one hand on his shoulder!*

Later in his book Roy describes what he wore to class prior to the turn of the century.

Today [1950's], clothes are three or four times as expensive as they were in the nineties but we needed far more then to keep up with our neighbors. All I feel qualified to describe regarding girls clothing is they wore shirtwaists and long skirts; to see a girl's ankle was an accident or a special favor, a real social achievement when I was attending High!

We boys whose parents could afford it had stiffly starched white shirt bosoms and cuffs with cuff links, high white stiff collars and four-in-hand, bow or puff ties; tie stick pins also were worn. Our coats were dark cutaways with vests sporting a watch chain. We wanted our trousers striped but did not always succeed. Brooks, Lewinson and I were suspended from school one full day because we bent over and snapped our shirts' stiff bosoms in and out in unison trying to beat out a tune. Shoes were varied, with black the color favored to match our dark cutaways. Always, hats were worn, whether derby, fedora, wide brim, crush, straw or what-have-you. In fact, we aped our fathers and this imitation was carried through our Varsity years also.

It appears that the sole opponents for the Bulldog eleven were the Indian School and the University of New Mexico, a rivalry which continued up to 1906. John Milne coached the 1908 team. The 1909 squad played four games and some of the players mentioned in addition to Fred Calkins were Kenneth Balcomb, Otto Sheer, Arthur Bachechi, Charles Lembke and F. W. Otto. Some of these early AHS athletes had children who attended AHS in the Fifties and were our classmates. The Balcombs and the Bachechis were neighbors of the Quists in the North Valley.

Our early AHS athletic and school history is well documented by Doc and *La Reata* thereby enriching our heritage and establishing our traditions. The principal focus here is to recognize and pay tribute to some of those individual athletes and students who preceded us. I'm sure that those cited here do not include all those sports heroes and distinguished students that should be recognized, but as each year dims the memory of those that made their marks before us, any attempt to chronicle and to preserve their identity and their feats for posterity will be worthwhile. Perhaps someone will take up the challenge to perpetuate the second half of the twentieth century.

In November 1918, Charles Lembke's family in Albuquerque was informed that Charles had been killed in the last days of World War I. The news of one of AHS' and Albuquerque's greatest icons was not only premature, this grad survived an amazing seventy-one more years living to the grand age of 100. Charles was a great athlete at AHS, participating in every sport offered at that time, and went on to earn eleven varsity letters at UNM and was inducted into the

University's Hall of Honor in 1989. His firm, Lembke Construction Co., was one of the largest in New Mexico and this centenarian even served as Mayor of Albuquerque from 1935 to 1939. Charles is recognized as a 1909 graduate of AHS but since he attended senior classes at UNM his name does not appear on the Alumni list of 14 students compiled decades ago. No matter, "Bulldogs Forever" claims this gracious and affable man, whom this writer knew well, certainly as one of its own.

Some of the earliest athletic records preserved are from track and field although Central High School (as it was then called) hired E. C. Benson as a full-time coach in 1911. In 1913 Paul Camp won three gold medals in the State Track and Field Meet in the shot put, triple jump and long jump. His teammate, Desmond Farrell, won first place in the high jump and the 220 yard low hurdles, and under Coach M. F. Angell the team was State Champions. The 1915 Bulldog Track Team under A. P. Hutchinson must have been quite formidable, as Grant Mann won both of the sprints and Ed Clifford won the pole vault and the high jump but the team was runner-up in State. Tom Calkins was also a double gold medal winner in 1916 in the long jump and triple jump.

In 1914, the high school opened its doors at the new building located at Central and Broadway. The school board was criticized in the press for building such a large building with a capacity for 500 students and an auditorium for 850. Most critics, as always, have their eyes in the rear-view mirror and not on the road ahead.

One of "Central's" first graduates in 1914 was a young lady by the name of Henrietta M. Weiser. Through her daughter Henrietta Bebber, '35, an interesting story emerged about Tom Moran, the school's Truant Officer, or as he was fondly referred to, "Hookey Tom."

Skipping classes was one if not the most grievous transgressions in those early years that continued into the mid-Fifties as you'll soon learn. According to Henrietta, "Hookey Tom" astride a large white horse would patrol the streets and the nearby mesa in search of truant students. Tom would literally rope the miscrants and haul them back to school. He was still at his job in the Thirties but by then had traded his single horse for multiple horsepower.

Glenn Emmons was an AHS football letterman as a starting end on the 1912 and 1913 teams. He was team captain his senior year and was selected on the All-Time AHS Football Team. Glenn, a banker, is best remembered as the U.S. Commissioner of Indian Affairs appointed by President Dwight D. Eisenhower.

It is generally recognized by all those that are familiar with not only AHS but New Mexico's athletic history that Owen "Sonora" Smaulding was the greatest all-around athlete prior to World War II. In 1916 under Coach Emil Kramic, Owen scored seven touchdowns in a game against Santa Fe which AHS won 101 to 0. He played on seven AHS State Championship teams: two in football (1916-1917), three in basketball (1916, 1917, 1919) and two in track (1917-1918). He also won two state boxing titles.

In 1917 during the State High School Track and Field Championships, Owen scored 43 of AHS' 63 points and won eight out of fifteen events, including the 100 yard dash (10.4) seconds); 220 yard hurdles (27.4 seconds); 110 yard high hurdles (17.4 seconds); shot put (44'7"); pole vault (10'5"); high jump (5'5"); broad jump (20'8") and the triple jump (39'4"). His 100 yard record stood for 28 years!

Tom Calkins is mentioned above as a member of the 1915 football team that won 3 and lost 3, but perhaps his greatest athletic accomplishment came in track and field. In 1916 in the State Championship Meet, Tom set records in both the broad jump (now referred to as the long jump) with a leap of 21' 1/2" and the triple jump with a distance of 41' 9 1/2". This mark is probably the longest standing record in school history—87 years. Tom and his wife, Dovie Mae (Johnson) Calkins bravely ventured north to the frozen tundra of Alaska where Tom became Superintendent of the Southwest District of the Bureau of Education. He wrote to the staff of La Reata in 1925, "I travel approximately 1500 miles per year by dog sled, and about twice that distance by water and a little by reindeer sled." Tom and Dovie warrant a place in "Bulldogs Forever" for their pioneering spirit.

The 1917 La Reata summarized the year's football season, and several interesting items are noteworthy in the unique prose of the day. The writer refers to our school as both "High School" and "Albuquerque High School." Up to this point in time most references to our school were simply High School or Central High School. The *La Reata* article begins, "The Albuquerque High School has a team that was not defeated once during the season." I thought it curious that the writer spoke of the team in the present, though the season had passed, and the team was not defeated as opposed to being undefeated. Language and style has changed but the message from almost 100 years ago tells a story we all share.

In 1966 Doc Harrington wrote to his successor AHS historian Jim Hulsman the following "scattered notes." Doc's distinctive and colorful prose is preserved here:

FROM: Dr. Eldred R. Harrington
TO: Jim Hulsman
*   4 February 1966*

SOME SCATTERED NOTES:

Early in the work you listed the first State Champion in Tennis: <u>Merritt</u>. His name was Maxwell Merritt and he was a student of note, later becoming a Rhodes Scholar.

Note on 1917— 18 Basketball: This just for your own personal interest. In the list of games you show an AHS lost to Tucumcari Adults 36-32. I got some dope on that one in the middle 1920's in the State of Idaho. A school superintendent in Southern Idaho (gent named Wesson) told me the story. As I remember AHS was scheduled for a game at Tucumcari. AHS showed up but there had been some sort of a jurisdictional dispute between coach and team as to who was running the show. The team, in a tantrum, quit. So there was a game coming up with AHS in a few hours and Tucumcari High had no team. Being a resourceful group, as people usually are in towns of 1500, the coach and superintendent decided to field a team of the young available adults. The superintendent knew the high school Principal (Wesson) was an ex-hotshot from the U of Oklahoma; the coach was similarly a hot-rock forward of a few years before from Kansas State. The sherriff [sic] provided a real assist by releasing a disorderly cow puncher from the local bastile [sic]. Seems that he had come west to blow up with the country and, while there, had become involved with the law. In fact I got the dope that he had created a disturbance in one of the Tucumcari whore-houses and had broken through a door by the simple stunt of whirling a LOADED piss-pot around his head and firing this through the flimsy door. This had called the attention of the madam to the misdemeanor and she had called the sherriff and the gendarmes came out in force (all two of them) and our hero was subdued and lodged in the local bastile. When the local sherriff found that Wesson and the school superintendent were having some difficulty in recruiting a team for the evening's festivities he had a talk with the cowpoke who was quite enthusiastic about playing, since this gave him a chance at his favorite game and also since it canceled out about 25 of the thirty days he has been assessed by the local judge. So with this nucleus of three they recruited several additional young gents and the game went on. The adults were a pretty good crew and they beat AHS, Smaulding and all. This took some doing. Figured I would just pass the story on to you as you would be interested.

In the 1919-20 Football Team WALTER HERNANDEZ was listed as tackle. He was our number 1 fullback,—a position which he carried on for the next 5 (yes 5) years for the University of New Mexico. Walter had a fine war record in World War II and was retired a year ago as a Brigadier General. He lives at Cuba, N.M. I noted in the 1921-22 team the name of CHARLES DEARING. Chili was a singer of some note. Went to Engineering School back east; switched to Economics and later became The President of Brookings Institute in Washington, D.C. Several times during the last 20 years he has been called in by various states to take charge of their entire road building programs. One of those jobs was when he took over the State of Illinois' program for the spending of numerous millions of dollars on their Turnpike Program. Not bad for a boy who grew up on a little truck farm over in Atrisco. Noted

19

also on the 1922 and later football teams OLIVER MOORE who along towards the end of World War II made Admiral in the U S Navy. AHS's first Admiral was LYMAN THACKERY of the team of about 1915 or 1916. The most recent one was ROBERT MACPHERSON, who also was a football player, I believe, about 1926. JACK MC FARLAND who played for AHS about 1925-1926 also made Colonel and was a member of General MacArthur's staff.

David Chavez, Jr., who grew up in the Barelas neighborhood in Albuquerque, was a three year letterman in football and basketball and also lettered his junior and senior years in track and field. After graduation from Georgetown University Law School, David rose to the rank of full colonel in the U.S. Army's Judge Advocate's office. After World War II, he returned to New Mexico where, after he lost a close election for governor, he became a Judge of the New Mexico Supreme Court. A prized family picture shows David and his brother, Senator Dennis Chavez, leaving the White House in 1947 after a meeting with President Harry Truman.

Born and raised in Albuquerque, Walter O. Berger graduated from AHS in 1917. He graduated from UNM after a brief stint in the U.S. Army during World War I, and in the early 1970s founded Berger-Briggs and Co., a real estate firm. He became a Vice President of the Bank of New Mexico and later Chairman of the Board of the Bank. This writer recalls Mr. Berger as the father of my classmate, Grafton, and as an avid golfer at the Albuquerque Country Club in the 1960s and early 1970s.

The 1917 *La Reata* states that J. Buren Linthicum's favorite expression was, "A good time to stop talking is just before you have told all you know." This man of few words was reported to have said, "A guard is a player who 'takes out' the opposing lineman so that the backfield man can run where his lineman used to be standing. This makes for spectacular gains and much fame for the backfield man but it is set up by the guards who really did it." Buren served the Albuquerque Public School System for many years as Coordinator of Instructional Services. One could say that this quiet, resourceful man ran interference for John Milne, Glen O. Ream and others who were the "backfield men" in the school system.

Games were played only against teams in Albuquerque (presumably because of the war) including the Third Battalion, UNM, Menaul and the Indian School. The *La Reata* writer pays tribute to those that toiled in the trenches but never had a chance to be heroes.

The scrubs as a whole often have more nerve than the first team. If you don't think so go out and let Smaulding and Tony run over you every night, while you never get into a real game. The scrubs may use your extra pads, but they more than make up for that.

Dr. Harrington's brother, Edwin, who won three gold medals in 1920 in the shot put, discus and high hurdles, was a classmate and teammate of Smaulding. Doc, who placed second in the pole vault, saw Owen trip and fall over a high hurdle, recover and then finish runner-up in the race. Doc said of this extraordinary athlete, "He was a good student and a person possessed of great personal charm. He was the sum total of everything that one would hope for in an athlete plus a modesty concerning his accomplishments that is seldom found in great performers." Doc's tribute to his Black classmate certainly establishes that at least in one contemporary view, there was an acceptance of Blacks as equals in Albuquerque early in AHS history.

After graduation Owen played professional baseball in the Negro League for a number of years before enrolling at the University of Idaho, where he graduated in 1931. Owen was inducted, posthumously, into the Albuquerque Sports Hall of Fame in 1990. He passed away in 1961.

Overshadowed and often overlooked during this same time period was a classmate of Owen, Tonnie Pegue, who also became a professional athlete. Tonnie, at 6'1", was an outstanding basketball player. As the Bulldogs won state titles in 1916 and 1917 under Coaches Roy Repp and Emil Kramic, a scout discovered the lanky kid in Albuquerque and, without college experience. Tonnie signed on to play for the Tulsa Eagles. He also spent a number of years with the Diamond DX Oilers and Phillips 66 when corporations sponsored professional basketball teams. In 1932, Tonnie returned to Albuquerque and officiated high school and college games, along with Iggy Mulcahy. His compensation? One dollar per game.

There were other outstanding basketball players in this era including Frank Shufllebarger and Joe McCanna (1913), David Chavez (1917), William Horner (1918), and Latiff Hyder (1920).

There's an interesting sidebar to the Pegue story. Tonnie's father, J.H. Pegue, was an early Albuquerque pioneer who, prior to the turn of the century, was in partnership with the Springer family at Second and Copper Streets in downtown Albuquerque. About the time that the automobile made its appearance on the American scene the partnership split up, with J.H. maintaining the livery stable and Springer the transportation and the sand and gravel business with predictable, in retrospect, results. By 1948, however, the Pegue family, Tonnie and son Bill, would begin servicing automobiles instead of horses at their service station at the "Triangle" east of Washington Junior High School and adjacent to the Sunshine Drug Store. I remember that well. The drug store was one of my hangouts while I was at "La Wash" and I filled up my Mom's `49 Plymouth at Pegue Chevron.

Other than athletics, other notable firsts were occurring at the "High School." In 1915 *Esmeralda* was probably the first school play presented publicly. Spanish language plays began in 1916. In 1917 *The Pennant* is the first musical comedy performed at the school. In 1918 as World War I impacted nearly everyone's life and resulted in a number of young men enlisting in the U.S. Army, a Drum and Bugle Corps was formed to participate in Liberty Bond drives. All schools in Albuquerque closed for several weeks in the fall of 1918 because of the Spanish Flu epidemic. In 1919 the Theodore Roosevelt Debating Society and the Webster Debating Society were established to compete with Menaul School. By 1920 the senior class graduated 65 and school enrollment for all classes in the Central School reached 400. Albuquerque's population was 15,175.

Possibly as a result of the recognition that Smaulding and Tonnie Pegue brought to AHS, the school system hired its first full-time all sport coach, Addison S. Moore in 1919. Up to that time teachers and townspeople donated their time to organizing and training the athletes. Moore led the Bulldogs to State Championships in Track and Field four years in succession from 1920 through 1923. One can only speculate what an impact Moore's more advanced coaching skills would have had upon Smaulding's performances.

Those track and field athletes who won gold medals during these four championship seasons were:

3 Gold Medals

1920 Edwin Harrington-shot put, discus, high hurdles

1921 Bard Farrell - javelin, 440, 100

1922 Jimmy Roybal - 100, 220, long jump

1924 Frank Stortz - 220 hurdles, pole vault, high jump

2 Gold Medals

1921 Bob Elder - long jump, pole vault

1921 John Venable - discus, shot put

1923 Jimmy Roybal - 100, 220

1925 Glenn Simpson - 880, mile

It should be noted that Ed Clifford, Owen Smaulding and Jimmy Roybal were repeat gold medal winners all three years with Owen accomplishing his feat in _four_ different events. He bequeathed an amazing legacy to Bulldog lore.

As a graduate of 1919, Jose E. Espinosa was known for his versatility. He not only was an excellent student and athlete, he was a leader in school affairs, acted and sang in both drama and operetta productions as well as the leader of "Espy's Combo," a popular dance orchestra. Jose obtained a Ph.D. from Cornell University and worked as a secretary for President Herbert Hoover. He later wrote many texts and articles, and authored _Saints in the Valley_, a history of New Mexico. Few could have been as qualified as he to write this book. His family can trace its roots back over 500 years and, as one of thirteen children, his biographical sketch indicates that the Espinosa family had more college degrees than any other in the nation. One of his brothers, Gilberto, who graduated in 1916, was a U.S. Attorney.

A 1919 graduate of AHS, Charles V. Schelke went on to obtain a degree in Electrical Engineering at the University of Colorado and a job with General Electric in Southeast Asia.

Literally trapped in the Philippines when World War II broke out, Charles became a POW. His captors suspected that Charles was the master-mind behind clandestine radio messages, but their need to keep old electrical generators operating and their lack of expertise probably spared his life. Charles completed his chosen career as a Vice President of General Electric.

Although they were separated in age by one year, the Harrington brothers both graduated the same year in 1920. They also possessed the same genetic engineering genius. Eldred R. Doc Harrington is featured later as one of AHS' most inspiring and popular teachers. Brother Edwin L. Harrington is remembered here. Edwin was unquestionably the best athlete of the two brothers winning three gold medals in the State Track and Field Championship Meet in 1920. One writer rated him as "The State's greatest baseball player; a person who had real big-league possibilities." But it was the field of engineering that piqued Edwin's principle interests, and he obtained his Ph.D in Civil Engineering from Texas A&M College and he taught there for many years, except while he served in the U.S. Navy as a Lt. Commander during World War II. Edwin, like his brother, exhibited the same versatility and diversity of interests and was an accomplished guitarist.

In the year 2000 the AHS Alumni Association sponsored a Millennium Celebration for the school. One of those recognized was a 1921 graduate of AHS by the name of Ruth Owens. Ruth, as a teacher, brought education to one-room school houses in such remote places as Conchas and Adelino, New Mexico, before she moved to Florida. There she met and married Howard B. Schleeter and they returned to Santa Fe, where Howard became a nationally known artist. Ruth had a lifetime devotion to AHS, education and art and lived to age 95, just short of the Millennium Celebration. There is something almost magical as well as memorable as I peer at Ruth's two photographs. One as an attractive AHS teenager, the other a visibly vivacious woman in her nineties.

In addition to Moore's success on the track, his basketball teams of 1921 and 1922 were State Champs and in 1920 his football team was also tops in New Mexico. Coach

Moore was responsible for organizing the Letterman's Club in 1921 and forming the New Mexico Athletic Association also in 1921. He served as that organization's first president. This period, the early Twenties, was perhaps the origin or birth of what my contemporary Ralph Melbourne refers to as the Bulldog "mystique." So dominant was AHS starting in this period in all sports that our school and its heroes became a prime representation of a new paradigm shift in American idealogy which will be explored later.

Old time followers of AHS sports remember Robert M. "Bob" Elder as a Track and Field athlete who was the State Champion in 1921 in both the pole vault and broad jump. In that meet he set a State record of 11' 2" in the pole vault, with a bamboo pole, that stood for 13 years. Most Albuquerque residents will remember Bob as a banker associated with the Albuquerque National Bank, then Sunwest Financial Services, Inc. now, Bank of America, where he started as the Bank's thirteenth employee in 1926, and as a 25-year member of the Albuquerque Public Schools Board of Education. This writer remembers Bob as an enthusiastic supporter of AHS and UNM sports, an avid golfer at Albuquerque Country Club, and a person who followed this writer's career with sincere interest.

In only two years after Owen Smaulding graduated, AHS and Coach Moore were blessed with another outstanding all-around athlete by the name of Malcolm Long. Exhibiting both durability and versatility, Malcolm lettered and starred all three years in both football and basketball from 1921 through 1924. He was a member of the State Champion Basketball Team in 1922 making the All-Tournament second team in 1922 and 1923 and first team in 1924. Malcolm was honored as first team quarterback on the AHS All-Time Team in 1939 as well as the All-Time Basketball Team.

This outstanding athlete continued his successful sports career at UNM, where he lettered in football all four years (1924-1927) and was selected to the All-Southwestern Team for three of those years. He was the star quarterback on the unbeaten 1927 Lobo team, and was inducted into UNM's Hall of Honor along with his championship team of 1927.

One of Malcolm's teammates was Charles Renfro ('23)

who had the unique distinction of lettering in football, basketball and track all three years at AHS. Charlie, indeed, could do it all and well deserved his place in the AHS Hall of Fame. At the University of New Mexico he continued to excel in athletics, and upon graduation returned to AHS as head track coach in 1934. In the next ten years, his track teams would win the State Championships seven times.

Arthur H. Bryce, better known as "Chili," graduated from AHS in 1924. He lettered in both football and basketball while a Bulldog, but his place in history was etched in the sands of White Sands Proving Grounds in 1945 when the first atomic bomb was detonated. Chili's father organized Albuquerque Foundry and Machine Works in the early 1900s and Chili started work with the firm in 1931. Called on by the government to supervise the building of a steel tower in the desert, Chili had no idea that the structure would be used to change the world as he knew it. President Truman awarded Arthur a Presidential Citation for the work his company did for the War effort.

Few athletes can be recognized for their accomplishments by more than one high school. Both St. Mary's and AHS can claim John Dolzadelli as one of their own. John was an outstanding halfback on the St. Mary's football team for two years prior to transferring to AHS in 1924 for his senior year where, playing under the tutelage of F. M. "Tony" Wilson, John was selected All-State. He also starred as a forward on the 1925 Bulldog basketball team that beat Menaul School for the State title and was named to the All-Tournament Team. He also ran the 440 yard dash on the track team. All of his teams were coached by Tony Wilson.

John, known as the "Flying Wop," went on to become a star performer at the University of New Mexico where he was twice named to the All-Southwestern Team and was selected to play in the East-West Shrine Game. He was a teammate of Malcolm Long. I knew John best as the Business Manager for the University of New Mexico Athletic Department. He along with Pete McDavid were directly responsible for my transfer to the University in 1955. John was always a positive, upbeat and gracious person even when faced with the unenviable task of approving my questionable travel ex-

26

penses.

Another 1920's athlete who would become an Albuquerque icon was Babe Parenti. In 1923 he became a starting end on F.M. (Tony) Wilson's first football team at AHS and lettered all three years. What made Babe's accomplishment remarkable is that in Coach Wilson's lexicon of rules, as you'll soon learn, sophomores never (or hardly ever) played on the varsity much less earned a letter. What we don't know is, did Coach Wilson develop this rule later, or was Babe so good, the Coach had to play him? We do know that Babe was an outstanding field goal and extra point kicker which may have made him invaluable.

Apparently without a college degree and University athletic experience, Babe became the Head Coach in all sports at St. Mary's High School in 1927. He would remain there, remarkably, for forty consecutive years until the school closed in 1967. One highlight of Babe's career was that his team won the State Championship in baseball in 1949 featuring star pitcher Pete Domenici, who would become a U.S. Congressman and Senator for nearly as long a tenure as his beloved Coach at St. Mary's.

Another exception to Coach Wilson's rule of relegating sophomores to the "Bullpup" or "B" team was Mannie Foster. This stocky, "hard as a rock" lineman lettered all three years in football starting in 1924. He also lettered all three years in basketball and had the distinction of winning the Hexathon, a competition consisting of a composite scoring of six track and field events. Pentathlons (5 events) and Decathlons (10 events) were popular in that time, but Mannie's win in this obscure event may forever remain a record.

As a testimonial to Mannie's exceptional talent and durability as a guard, he was selected All-Southwest Conference while at the University of New Mexico all four years. A very rare honor. He was also selected to play in the East-West Shrine Game but couldn't participate.

Few readers will recall that scholarships, whether they were athletic or academic, were unavailable in the Twenties in all but the major universities. As a testimony to Manny's determination, he worked a number of jobs in order to complete his college education at UNM. One, he worked at the

College Inn on Central Avenue for $.25/hour.

Mannie returned to AHS as Tony Wilson's assistant football coach from 1931 to 1938, during the height of The Great Depression. He was wounded in the Battle of the Bulge during WWII and received the Purple Heart.

Lee E. Farr, '24, received his B.S. degree from Yale in 1929 and his M.D. in 1933. Dr. Farr was the creator of the Neutron Capture Technique for the treatment of brain tumors. At the University of Texas he became the first full professor of Nuclear Medicine in the U.S., and is prominently recognized in Who's Who in America and American Men of Science.

1924 also produced another giant in the field of medicine, W. Randolph Lovelace. Randy received his M.D. degree from Harvard University School of Medicine and took his profession to new heights. Albuquerque's Lovelace Clinic and the Lovelace Medical Foundation became one of the foremost research organizations in aviation medicine. Dr. Lovelace tested a special oxygen mask himself, free falling 40,000 feet before opening his parachute. The Albuquerque clinic examined and tested America's first astronauts. Randy's brilliant career, that brought international recognition to Albuquerque in the Fifties, was cut short by a tragic airplane accident (recalled in Chapter 6).

In 1921, the just-formed New Mexico High School Activities Association initiated an All-Tournament Basketball Team after the tourney was completed. Those that were selected during the 1920s that haven't been previously mentioned were:

1921 Max Salazar and Ely Glassman
1922 Lynn Hammond and Nathan Glassman
1923 Wilbur Wilson
1924 Frank Stortz and Creighton Foraker
1925 Art Trauth
1926 Walter Bellman and Dick Vann
1927 George Mossman
1928 Fred Montoya
1929 Ray Barton
While his parents resided in Madrid, New Mexico, Mar-

shall J. Wylie arranged to live in a boarding house in Albuquerque so that he could attend AHS. Starring in football, he graduated in 1925. According to Carlos Salazar, the Albuquerque Tribune sportswriter, Marshall had the distinction of playing football at UNM in 1926 and 1927, then played at Southern California for one year before returning to play for the Lobos and graduating with a Civil Engineering degree in 1932. After serving as an officer with the Seabees in the Navy in World War II, he returned to Albuquerque and formed Wylie Brothers Construction Co. with his brother Claude in 1946. Marshall's generous devotion of his time to the United Way, the Southwest Golf Association, the Four Hills Country Club, the Airport Authority Advisory Board and numerous civic activities certainly warrants his recognition as one of AHS' most distinguished graduates. This writer remembers Marshall admiringly as a distinguished gentleman both on and off the golf course.

Robert J. Nordhaus, who is one if not the oldest living graduates of AHS (1926) as of this writing in 2003, is also tied to one of the oldest pioneer businesses in New Mexico. The Charles Ilfeld Co. saga began in 1865 in Taos, New Mexico, when Charles, who was Max Nordhaus' (Bob's father) brother-in-law, opened his mercantile store. The Albuquerque store opened in 1916 on First Street and Bob became President of the Ilfeld Company in 1960.

Bob, who graduated from Yale Law School in 1935, was assigned to the Mountain Training Center in Colorado during World War II. He became one of the original organizing officers of the 10th Mountain Division known as the "Ski Corps." It must have been this early introduction to the thrill of skiing that led Bob, with partners Ben Abruzzo and AHS grad Jerry Martin, to build the Tram at Sandia Peak. This writer had the good fortune of knowing Bob and his family extremely well. We were next door neighbors on Rio Grande Boulevard, and we all shared a passion for the exhilarating sport of skiing. Bob, appropriately, appears later atop his favorite mountain.

Tom Reid was a double gold medal winner in the State Track and Field Meet in 1928 in the 100 and 220 yard sprints. His brother, Howard, would duplicate that feat in

1934, demonstrating that fleetness of foot is hereditary, as we will soon learn with the Henrys and the Dunlaps.

Few educators anywhere in the U.S. could have had the enormous impact on their community and their school as did Glen O. Ream. This stocky and sturdily built, handsome man with a resolute face and demeanor arrived in Albuquerque in 1922 and became the director of the YMCA only a couple blocks from where he would frame his school as well as his legend.

Mr. Ream, as all of us students as well as teachers called him, began his career in the Albuquerque Public School System when he became the Principal at the new Lincoln Junior High School, and by 1926 he transferred to AHS to teach Mathematics and English. Mr. Milne chose Mr. Ream to be Principal the following year perhaps in part because of his Masters degree from Yale University and the leadership qualities he demonstrated as a Second Lieutenant in World War I.

Virtually every AHS alum who graduated between 1926 and 1956 will undoubtedly recall the formidable but fair Glen O. Ream. Many of us have our favorite stories about their Principal and some will be told here, but most former students will not know some of the significant contributions this magnificent man made to not only our school but to the community of Albuquerque. The following is taken from the August 4, 2000 Millennium Celebration Program:

The AHS Art Collection
Excerpts taken from the AHS Collection/
Albuquerque Museum Art Book

Under the direction of Principal Glen O. Ream, a body of significant art was accumulated over the years.

In 1926 the first major painting was acquired, *Sandias at Sunset* from a prominent local artist, Carl Redin. Also in 1926 the art editor for the *La Reata* was Hope Wiley. He would later attend the NY School of Design. His painting *Subway in New York* was presented to the school by the Class of 1933. The senior classes continued to present paintings like Brooks Willis' *Aspen in Fall* and Wayne Hornbakers' *Still Life* and *Art Nouveau*.

By 1941 the AHS art collection was significant. Glen

O. Ream was well aware of the renowned artists of Taos. He established an art center at AHS dedicated to the Taos artists. There the students could study and appreciate the works of the artists. Also, the four founders of the Taos Art Colony, Ernest Blumenschein, Oscar Berninghaus, Bert Phillips and J. H. Sharp were still alive and painting. Over the next few years there were many trips to Taos and a growing rapport between the Taos artists and AHS. Blumenschein took the lead by selecting *Star Road and White Sun* to sell to the high school and persuaded other members of the Taos Art Colony to select their works for sale to the school. By 1945, Berninghaus agreed to sell the painting, *Pueblo Indian Woman of Taos* to the school. *Star Road and White Sun,* were also gifts of the senior classes of 1943, 1944, 1945 and presented to AHS in October 1945.

By the late 40's and into the 50's former students, who achieved artistic recognition such as Betty Sabo, Walter Bambrook and Sam Smith, came to play an important role as contributors to the collection.

Betty Sabo, cited earlier in the Preface of *Bulldogs Forever,* has indicated that this collection, started by Mr. Ream, is now worth in excess of one million dollars. Betty, as well as many other AHS art students, must have been inspired by these works that adorned our hallowed halls. Do you remember seeing them?

Mr. Ream was instrumental in the formation of the Archaeology Society in 1932. Writing in the October 1940 issue of "Progressive Education" Mr. Ream said:

"In 1932, armed with pick, shovel and wheelbarrow, the boys and girls of the Archaeology Society turned their first shovel of dirt at Tunque, a large ruin an hour's ride north of Albuquerque, New Mexico High School. The young people were members of an extracurricular club interested in using New Mexico's countless abandoned villages to study at first hand the story of an ancient people...two years ago the Archaeology Society outgrew its "extra-curricular" garb. Today...Albuquerque High School gives full credit for a semester course covering its activities..."

In addition to the Archaeology Society, Mr. Ream started the Military Science program and the Astronomy Club at AHS. It is generally thought that Mr. Ream also initiated "Distributive Education" where students were placed with employers to learn vocational skills.

One of the best examples of Mr. Ream's desire and resourcefulness to create a learning experience for everyone presented itself when a student, Jack Bordenave, advised his Principal that nothing at school interested him and he wanted to quit. His only interest it seems was the study of small animals. Mr. Ream responded by converting a janitor's closet into a biology lab and the light went on for Jack. Not many years later Jack Bordenave rewarded his Principal with the discovery of a new species of salamander that now bears Jack's name. This story was recalled by Beverly Ream, Glen's daughter who received a prized gift from Jack—a stuffed owl.

At the completion of Mr. Ream's first year as Principal in 1927, an extraordinary student, May Stirrat graduated. Those of us who attended AHS in the Thirties, Forties and Fifties remember this exceptional history teacher as Mae Klicker. The Millennium Celebration program says of Mrs. Klicker, "Mae's greatest contribution to the students and faculty of AHS came during her term of Assistant Principal. She demanded academic excellence from the faculty." I might add as her student in 1952-53, she demanded the same standards from me and my classmates. Mrs. Klicker piqued my interest in and love of history which, in part, may have inspired me to write this book.

Like many of the teachers of this period, Mae and her husband Bob would never miss a Bulldog football or basketball game. It has been reported that the couple often served the faculty and the athletes treats at their home after the games. The Klicker's support of athletics offers evidence that high school sports were a major form of national as well as community communication that created a feeling of togetherness, belonging and spirit within our school. We will explore this phenomenon more thoroughly in Chapter 6.

Lillian Pegan Dolde, who graduated from AHS in 1928, became the first woman Vice-President of Albuquerque National Bank. While working for the bank for fifty years she perhaps created more goodwill in her chosen field than anyone in the banking industry. Lillian was an accomplished pianist and served as Chairwoman of the Albuquerque Symphony Board as well as being active in the June Music Festival, Chamber Soloists and other musical activities.

Ralph Loken must have begun working for the Public Service Co. of New Mexico while a high school student — an article written by George Baldwin in 1992 says that he started working for PNM "66 years ago," and Ralph graduated from AHS in 1928. Ralph says in the same article, "I was hired as an office boy at $25 per month." This "office boy" eventually became the Executive Vice-President of the company and a member of the Board of Directors. He maintained a journal documenting the growth of his company covering almost 50 years which is an invaluable piece of Albuquerque history.

Edna Tuttle Hooks, who graduated in 1928, gained her place in Albuquerque history as the woman who stared down a robber and refused to give him the money. Edna and her husband Johnny Hooks founded Hooks Variety, a general merchandise and grocery store near the intersection of Atrisco Road and Central Avenue on the west side of Albuquerque. After Johnny died in 1956 this stalwart woman operated the store for 23 more years on her own, and it was during that period when she confronted the would-be robber proving that Bulldogs are indeed tenacious and brave fighters.

A 1928 grad of AHS, Robert MacPherson, went on to graduate from the U.S. Naval Academy in 1933. A carrier-based Navy pilot, he fought heroically in the Pacific Theater in World War II. A recipient of numerous medals and citations, this highly decorated hero capped his meritorious career as an Admiral and returned to his *Alma Mater* to deliver a memorable commencement address.

This era produced a bevy of strong, independent and successful women, at a time when it was not fashionable. Another such person was Victoria Page Romero who graduated in 1928. Married at the age of 15 when a junior at AHS, Victoria continued her education and with her husband

Matty Romero, formed Matty's Construction Co. Later they opened Matty's Trading Post on Islela Boulevard as well as several restaurants. Central to the success of each business was the administrative and management skills that Victoria contributed to the various enterprises. Barbara Page, Victoria's admiring niece, said of her aunt, "She was an independent thinker and doer in spite of society's attempt to lessen the role of women."

Byrnes (Bernie) May, '28, could have been the original band leader from the hit movie *Music Man.* While attending UNM Bernie formed a dance band featuring vocalist Vivian Vance, also an AHS grad who became better known as Lucy Ricardo's landlady in the sit-com, "I Love Lucy." In 1932, in the depths of The Depression, Bernie began traveling the State calling on high schools promoting the sales of musical instruments. By the mid-Thirties, despite the fact that schools had meager funds for any activities, 58 high school bands had been organized. Bernie himself, was a member of AHS' first band in 1928 that was led by bandmaster William Kunkel. May's Music Co. has been in tune with the growth of Albuquerque for over five decades.

CHAPTER THREE: THE DEPRESSION YEARS 1930-1940

THE 1930S PRODUCED A WEALTH of athletic, business and professional talent, although specific information on the exploits of our AHS heroes is as scarce today as cash flow was during the depths of The Great Depression. H. L. "Hickum" Galles as a 1930 graduate made his mark as a 195-pound All-State tackle in football and went on to become a two-time All-Border Conference selection at the same position while at the University of New Mexico and a member of the 1934 conference championship team. The Galles name has been established in the automobile and auto racing business in Albuquerque since the 1920s and has been responsible not only for the promotion of Albuquerque athletics, but Hickum also has been a positive force in the explosive growth of Albuquerque over the past 70 years.

We share a rare circumstance in common. We both use the initials H.L. and not our first name (Herbert) and we both have used nicknames for so long we wouldn't respond if called by our given name.

One of Hickum's teammates was Guyton "Sheep" Hays. Given his distinctive nickname by Coach Wilson because he worked for a time as a sheepherder, Hays was tough, but at the same time as good natured as one who would protect those vulnerable little lambs. But on the football field, Sheep was as rugged a competitor at fullback as AHS has ever fielded. His 1930 team went 9-0 and won the State Championship and in 1939 he was selected on the All-AHS Football Team by the *Albuquerque Tribune*.

Sheep also excelled at track and field. He set the New Mexico State record in the mile run in 1931 with a time of 4:46.2 and the half-mile in 2:07. He went on to set records in these two events in the Border Conference while he starred at the University of New Mexico. He was inducted into UNM's Hall of Honor in 1992 earning seven letters during his college career.

There's an interesting sidebar to Sheep's story. He met and married Marie Jenson, who attended high school in Estancia, New Mexico, a small farming and ranching community east of Albuquerque. Marie was an excellent athlete in her own right (as she demonstrated later at the University of New Mexico) and starred on her school's basketball team. Desperately in need of uniforms, her school prevailed upon Iggy Mulcahy (M&W Sporting Goods) to provide the women's basketball team with suitable attire. The flashy, bright red, satin uniforms finally arrived. But—they were for boys! Short shorts, of course.

Undeterred, the Estancia girls proudly introduced their new uniforms at a game in Santa Fe against Loretto Academy, a Catholic girls school. The sisters were in shock. The public display of "leg" and girls in shorts was as unholy as it was unfathomable. Loretta wanted to cancel the game. More tolerant heads prevailed, however, and the game went on and new ground was broken. As an eighth grader in Green Bay, Wisconsin, in 1950, twenty years later, the girls basketball team at my school wore "bloomers" which few readers will be able to imagine or recall. I had the good fortune of attending one of the most rigid, authoritarian junior high schools in the country, where the principal's code of conduct was early 20th Century, but that is another story and another book. I vividly remember the "bloomers" complete with black stockings. Attractive? Not MTV material!

Randolph V. (Randy) Seligman's family immigrated from Germany and started the Bernalillo Mercantile Co. in the late 1880s. As a young boy Randy ventured out making house calls in Sandoval County with a local doctor. This experience must have mapped his life's journey. At the end of his career an article stated: "It was a beginning of a career that would make him, upon his retirement 46 years later, New Mexico's longest-practicing native-born physician." This writer remembers this 1930 AHS grad as an easy "pigeon" on the golf course at the Albuquerque Country Club, but a sly old "owl" at gin rummy after his round.

Some records indicate that Aldo F. Vaio graduated in 1930 and his obituary written in 1995 by Carlos Salazar states that Aldo finished his schooling at AHS in 1931; regardless, whatever year is correct he deserves to be recognized here.

Aldo was one of the key lay persons, along with Brother Mathias in 1951, who founded the Little Brothers of the Good Shepherd Refuge in Albuquerque. The refuge was a way station for "soldiers of the highway" as Brother Mathias called the homeless that society had forgotten. Given Aldo's background in the grocery business as part owner of Vaio & Sons Grocery, downtown, he was successful in obtaining contributions of food from wholesalers, restaurants and businesses for the Refuge.

The Bulldogs also fielded a girls basketball team in 1931 coached by Helen Harrison. Their only loss was to UNM but they didn't travel outside Albuquerque for any games. Girls tennis did compete on a state-wide level and three tournaments were held prior to the state meet. Standout players for the lady "Dawgs" were Betty Gill, Lois Blair and Ruth Haywood, but the state championship went to Carlsbad. Girls soccer was also popular during this period.

Boys tennis in the early Thirties featured AHS' Bob Chacon, who was the state runner-up in 1930 in singles and doubles with Jack Conroy and who returned in 1931 to win the state individual title in singles and the doubles with Clark Petit. There were no team champions in the Twenties and the Thirties.

As I reviewed the 1931 *La Reata* page 25 grabbed my attention. Pictured as "candidates for Graduation" were five Black girls, Exerlona Clayton, Mildred Clayton, Myrtle Redford, Carrie Holley and Thelma McDonald. What is significant is that these five girls were pictured on a separate page and not amongst the other students. So, it appears, some degree of segregation existed at our school during the Thirties but quite unlike schools in southeastern New Mexico, which didn't permit Blacks to attend public schools. This issue will clearly come into focus in the Forties and Fifties as our AHS administration takes a firm stand on segregation and in part is responsible for a break in the color line in New Mexico.

Another member of this illustrious group of athletes in the early Thirties was Ralph Bowyer who, at this writing, is alive and well at the ripe young age of eighty-nine. His recollections are as memorable as his athletic and coaching records. Nicknamed "Corpse" by his teammates (because he always seemed to be asleep), Ralph came alive when the whistle blew to start the game. He excelled as an end on the Bulldog State Champion football teams in 1930 and 1931.

The 1931 team was undefeated and cocky. They traveled to Arizona to play Phoenix Union High School in their first night game. The Bulldogs kicked off to PUHS and tackled the ball carrier on the two yard line. Deep in their own territory, the Phoenix quarterback barked out the first play without a huddle. Frank Byers, playing linebacker, yelled to the signal caller: "Hey! Why don't you run through here?" Frank pointed to a position between guard and tackle.

The QB changed the play and yelled new instructions to his teammates. Phoenix snapped the ball. The ball carrier dove into the line exactly where Byers had instructed. The clash of leather resonated loudly along the line in the Phoenix heat-baked night. Arms and legs flailed, grasping and kicking. Grunts and groans of the combatants echoed from the trenches amidst the dust. Byers, flattened by an aggressive block, looked up from his prostrate position to witness the opponents halfback disappearing into the darkness, 98 yards to a touchdown! He turned to his teammate Emilio Lopez, also recovering from a hard knock, and said:

"Guess I shoulda kept my mouth shut!"

Phoenix Union 41, Bulldogs 0.

Byers, a fullback when he wasn't a wiseguy, had another memorable line. I asked the 1932 grad if he lettered all three years.

"Heck no! No way," he said, "We all played on the "B" team as sophomores. We called ourselves "The Chinamen."

"The Chinamen?" I responded almost guessing what the answer would be.

"Yeah. We had a Chinaman's chance in h... to play on the varsity. That was one of Coach Wilson's rules. You hadda wait and earn your way on to the team."

In 1935 when the Bulldogs were suffering through their worst football season, winning only one game, Coach Renfro's "B" team was embarrassing the varsity. Charlie pleaded with Tony Wilson:

"Coach? Why not bring some of my best kids up. They could really help the team."

"Charlie? It's not their time," Coach Wilson replied. And none played until the next year. Definitely a different time, a different code.

Bowyer, along with Al Zachmann at the other end, had the good fortune to be the target of probably the school's best passer, Abbie Paiz. This small, 150 pound tailback was uncanny in his accuracy as he led the Bulldogs to the two State Championships in 1930 and 1931. Abbie was All-State both years. At the University of New Mexico Abbie switched to quarterback and led the Lobos to an 8-1 record and the Border Conference crown under Coach Gwinn Henry in 1934. Remarkably, Galles, Hays, Bowyer, Paiz along with star half-back Bill Brannin, all who could have attended major schools, decided to stick together and played for Henry at UNM. "The secret to our success," Galles said, "was that we were very close. We all had Albuquerque ties."

Bowyer also starred on the basketball team that lost to Raton in the finals of the State Tournament in 1932. Ralph remembers that game well despite the fact that it was 70 years ago.

"The Raton fans were riding us unmercificiously. The fans and the players were trying to get to us and they did. One of our stars, Rudy Heller, hit one of their guys with his fist and the refs threw him out of the game. We lost. Boy, did that game teach me a lesson," Bowyer relayed to me.

There indeed was a valuable lesson learned from this experience. The Bulldogs were undefeated in 20 straight games against New Mexico opponents in 1932 before the State Tourney. Their only loss was to a Phoenix team they had beaten 40 to 22 the night before. In one game, the AHS five beat St. Mary's 23 to 2 and during the season outscored their opponents 652 to 295. Not winning the State Championship after dominating their opponents all year was an opportunity of a lifetime lost. A lesson Ralph never forgot.

Perhaps one of life's most important lessons came from a sign on Coach Wilson's desk:

"We may reach immortality by the example we set."

That admonition functioned as Bowyer's beacon and served him well in his incredible career. Ralph recalled another incident during a basketball game in Belen. The undermanned opponents strategy was to stall. They simply held on to the ball. No dribbles, no passes (no shot clock). Nada. First quarter, AHS 2, Belen 0.

Emilio Lopez, the Bulldogs star player, who along with Ralph would be selected on the All-Tournament State Championship Team, grabbed a newspaper from a fan who, presumably, was bored by the lack of the game's intensity. Emilio read the paper while standing under the basket! Final score? AHS 8, Belen 4. A barnburner.

Another member of that year's basketball team was Bob Scott, best known for his exploits after graduation. During WWII in the Pacific theater, Lt. Scott and the men under his command were charged with the responsibility of taking the Munda Airstrip held by the Japanese in the Solomon Islands. The enemy's counterattack overran Scott's platoon's position, but despite being outmanned and wounded Lt. Scott held off superior numbers and protected his men until reinforcements arrived. Bob received the Congressional Medal of Honor for his heroism and retired as a Colonel.

In addition to football and basketball, Bowyer also participated in track and field and baseball. He was a member of the Bulldog Baseball Team as a centerfielder that won the New Mexico American Legion Baseball Championship in 1932. Ralph is remembered best perhaps for his incredible coaching record which spanned more than 30 years. It began, however, unremarkably. In fact, worse than any football coach would expect. No wins and not a single T.D. all season! It couldn't get any worse than that. He had to improve on that record. And he did.

It was at Grants, New Mexico, that Ralph made his debut as a high school coach. On the very first play in his very first game his team allowed the Albuquerque Indian School to fall on the kickoff in their opponents end zone for a T.D. and it was all downhill from there. In his five years at Grants his football teams did improve and Ralph enjoyed some success in basketball, but it as an inauspicious start on an incredible career. A short stint followed at Belen before he moved on to Carlsbad where an icon was born.

Had Ralph been coaching at Grants during the Fifties, his experience could have been dramatically different. Why? Uranium. Grants became a boom town and miners came, in droves, to the formerly small farming and ranching community, which also served as a pit stop on old Highway 66. Not only did the population increase but miners and their kids were generally tough and rough and ready characters. Football was a perfect sport for those who harbored aggressive personalities. In Carlsbad, a large percentage of the fathers worked in the potash mines and as roughnecks in the oil and gas business which worked to Ralph's success.

In examining New Mexico football, little has been made of the fact that the teams that would become football powerhouses beginning in the late Forties (Hobbs, Carlsbad, Artesia, Roswell and Farmington) were mostly oil towns. Roughnecks got that handle for a well-deserved reason. Their jobs were tough and dangerous and their lifestyle was often a mirror of their work ethic. High school kids often worked during the summer in the oil fields. They fought each other at work. They fought at night in the streets and in the bars. Football is a game of aggression. It was a perfect outlet for roughnecks. I know. I almost got blown away by a dynamite explosion while working during the summer in a mine and jousted with the roughnecks while I worked in construction in Farmington—but that's another story.

Back to the dire days of The Great Depression: I asked Ralph Bowyer what the kids did for entertainment in those days.

"There was no money, you know? The only time we went to the movies is when we did 'snake dances' through the Kimo Theater. And we'd stand on Central Avenue by the 1st National Bank and look up at the tallest building in New Mexico and everyone would stop and look up to see what we were looking at. We'd laugh. It worked all the time. We didn't realize that we were poor even though we wore the same pants all week and then washed them on the weekends. We all hung out together and when we graduated there was ten of us who met every two months and had a lunch. We (their athletic prowess) got better, of course, every year and after each lunch ˋole Sheep would get a kiss from the waitress. He was a handsome guy, you know?"

Ralph's group is blessed to have four out of the "group of 10" still together at the time of this writing in 2003. Their memories, from a time when poverty and despair were everywhere, are as precious as gold.

The one dominator that all of the above recognized athletes from 1923 to 1947 have in common, as the reader has experienced, is their coach and mentor F. M. (Tony) Wilson. Tony wasn't a graduate of AHS but he had such a positive and lasting impact on Bulldog pride and tradition his record must be mentioned here. J. D. Kailer, who as a writer has covered the Albuquerque sportsworld longer than anyone, wrote in a tribute to Coach Wilson in 1995:

> From 1923 to 1945, Wilson's Bulldog football teams won 136, lost 58 and tied 15. He coached seven state championship clubs — 1925, '28, '30, '31, '36, '40 and '42. In basketball, Wilson compiled a 476 win, 149 loss mark that produced state championships in 1925, '37 and '46 over a 24 year span. His track teams (1934-45) capped two state crowns in 1925 and 1945 and his baseball clubs won state titles three years in 1942, '43 and '46. Dr. Harrington says of Tony in his history, "In a field marked by fine men, I have rated his coaching in the same class as Owen Smaulding's competitiveness.

Yes, Tony was tough and often inflexible but he molded young boys into men.

In 1963 the Albuquerque school system named the Wilson Stadium in his honor. In 1974 Tony was inducted into the Albuquerque Sports Hall of Fame. I remember Coach Wilson best as our enthusiastic and supportive Athletic Director and having an avid interest in skiing. As our ski coach he appears in this memoir on a most memorable trip to Flagstaff, Arizona.

Robert Heron, '31, was called "one of the greatest tramway and ski-lift engineers of the past 50 years and honored as one of the 13 Founders of Skiing in the USA." From 1945 to 1979 Bob's companies designed and installed 78 ski lifts and aerial tramways around the world. One of his first projects was Lift No. 1 at Aspen Mountain which, when this writer first rode the single chair in 1952, was a marvel of engineering and helped establish an old mining town into the ski capitol of the U.S.

Joe Roehl, '32, was the Managing partner of Modrall, Sperling, Roehl, Harris and Sisk, one of New Mexico's most prestigious law firms from 1954 to 1972 and was active in the firm until his death in 1996. Most Albuquerqueans will remember Joe as a trial lawyer, but few will recall that he was a business owner (Gas Palace), a sportswriter and a sports announcer on radio station KOB. In fact, he did New Mexico's first play-by-play announcement of a World Series baseball game created from a wire teletype. In his later years Joe contributed his time and expertise to represent the poor without a fee.

It is quite possible that none of "Johnny" Walker's '32, nor any New Mexicans, for that matter, ever new this high profile person's first name, Elzer. Most knew that his initials were E.S. but who would recognize Elzer S. Walker as a two term member of the New Mexico State Legislature and member of the United States House of Representatives. Johnny also served four two-year terms as Commissioner of Public Lands and was Commissioner of the New Mexico Bureau of Revenue.

Despite the fact that there was probably only one golf course (Valley Country Club, now Albuquerque Country Club) in the city during the Thirties, several AHS golfers gained a notable level of excellence in an era when the sport was being popularized by Bobby Jones, Walter Hagen and other legends of the links.

In 1931-32 Vern (Spec) Stewart, who was also Senior Class President, won the New Mexico State Amateur and the Southwestern Title both years. Skip Schreiber was the State Champ in 1935 followed by Joe Cooper in 1935, Zeke Gutierrez in 1938 and Gilbert Sanchez in 1939. In the mid-

Thirties, Elenor (Chief) Jones won the state and Southwestern Championship and reached the finals of the boys match play tournament before losing 2 to 1—almost 70 years prior to Annika Sorenstam's foray into the men's world of professional golf. As a fourteen year old I have a vague recollection of an exhibition match between Spec Stewart and "Slammin' Sammy" Snead at the Albuquerque Country Club. My father told me that Snead had the best swing in golf. Unfortunately, this event didn't inspire me to play the game. It wasn't a part of the "Holy Trinity" of sports. You'll understand this reference as we explore the history of sports—later.

The class of 1932 also produced a well-known singer, Adelina Puccini, who after studying music in Italy became a member of the Rome Opera Ballet which toured numerous countries. She married Nicolai Timofeyew, a heroic tenor of opera who performed throughout the world. Arthur Loy, who was editor of *The Record* in 1932, must also have been a singer of note. He starred as the Captain in the operetta *Joan of the Nancy Lee*. One of his classmates and actor in the operetta wrote in Arthur's *La Reata*:

> "I wish I could begin to tell you how much I enjoyed your singing and acting in the operettas. I have had the pleasure of being with you..." — Libby Zimmerman '32.

As a testimony to the significance of sports and its place in society in this era the 1932 *La Reata* was dedicated to F. M. (Tony) Wilson, "...as an expression of our appreciation for his example of that true sportsmanship which transcends the bounds of athletics and wins the admiration of the entire school and community."

In addition to the above dedication, Walter Biddle and his *La Reata* staff paid special attention in the Foreword to recognize 1932 as "the year of sports" with the Olympics being held in Los Angeles for "A creation of goodwill and a more friendly feeling between the nations." Taking this theme to a local level to be experienced and shared by the student body, Biddle adds:

> Our sport name, "Bulldogs," not only stands for the sports which we enter, but also for school loyalty, sportsmanship in life, and a feeling of friend-

ship among the students...The staff wishes, in using this Bulldog theme that you will use these fine qualities of the Bulldog in your own lives ...

Many AHS students followed Biddle's admonition as evidenced in "Bulldogs Forever."

The Valliant Company's roots in Albuquerque date back to 1918, and it became one of the City's largest job-printing plants. George P. Valliant, '33, took control of the family business in the early 1950s. George, as a Captain in the U.S. Army during World War II, commanded the 45th Calvary Reconnaissance Squadron in the South Pacific and returned home to run the business until he sold it in 1993.

Betty Huning Hinton, '33, was one of Albuquerque's most recognized teachers and inspired students at Rio Grande High School for 25 years. Betty would have been an excellent candidate to write a history of our beloved AHS. She authored a number of books on prominent women such as "Lena Clauve, UNM's First Dean of Women," Marion Herlihy, "Fifty-Two Years in Banking," Martha Campbell Rehm Brown, "A Modern Florence Nightingale" and others.

The eve of the Class of 1934's 50th Reunion in 1984 produced some interesting memories of the perilous times. Dorothy Sabino recalled, "We were Depression kids. We walked a lot. We'd pool our money and go to the drive-in or get a Coke. Most everybody made their own fun."

The night before the homecoming game Bill Sievert recalled, "We'd always had a big bonfire and wood was scarce that year. I had a Buick touring car and we took it down to Old Town and snitched all the outhouses and kicked them in for a big bonfire." Leslie Linthicum, an *Albuquerque Tribune* staff writer, wrote as a follow-up to Sievert's story, "With the fire roaring at Central and Broadway outside the hulking brown and grey AHS building, hundreds of students formed a conga line and danced west on Central to Eighth Street and back."

The football season was shortened that year. Two games were cancelled due to a quarantine for polio. Further evidence that those days were indeed, difficult, the school system could only afford new uniforms for eleven players. Those days were bleak but spirits weren't. As Henrietta Bebber stated, "Heck, we were all in the same boat so we just had fun."

Henrietta, who graduated in 1935, had a sister Marilyn 18 years younger who graduated in 1953 and was a senior when this writer was a junior. Henrietta (aka Marie) who married Arthur Loy cited above, furnished some true gems to add to AHS lore.

The Sons of Poncho Villa (SOPV) headed by Tony Armijo as their President was a club formed to "stimulate sincere and unvarying ideals of gentlemen." The members were supposed to act as hall monitors, but unfortunately they managed to create disorder out of order rather than accomplish their mission. Fortunately, the club was mercifully "killed" (the term used in *La Reata*) at the end of the year. Henrietta must have approved of the wording. She was the editor.

A straight "A" student and member of the Honor Society, Henrietta proudly wore her gold "A" pin on her blouse everyday. Seated alphabetically, she always sat next to Ed Black (who later would become noted as one of Albuquerque's foremost car dealers), but his classmates knew him best as a prankster and musician who headed up a swing band known as "Ed Black and His Dukes." He competed with Lesman Chavez for school "gigs."

"Who was the toughest disciplinarian during the Thirties? Mr. Ream?" I asked Henrietta.

"Oh, no. It was Edith Norton. She was in charge of study hall and was responsible for checking out our books. If you didn't return your books or if they were torn, you didn't get a report card. She ruled study hall with an iron hand. We were there to study, she would always say. No monkey-business and no comic books," Henrietta reported.

As this writer looks at a photograph of a stern-faced woman with pursed lips and upside-down smile, it's not difficult to imagine that study hall was a quiet place.

"And," Henrietta continued, "Gladys Bass, Mr. Ream's secretary, was one tough cookie. She was the one who really ran the school." Henrietta offered some keen observations on her day.

"I don't think there was discrimination at AHS. Frances Washington, who was a Black girl, worked with me on *La*

Reata and we were good friends. Florence and Irene Hashimoto were popular girls. Albuquerque was different than the rest of the state," Henrietta offered.

"Why?" I asked.

"One thing. The Country Club kids didn't go away to some eastern school. They came to AHS because it was such a good school. Albuquerque High then was a mix of kids from all over town. We all got along very well," she added.

Henrietta became a teacher in the Albuquerque schools. Not many will recall that teachers took the census for the government. Assigned to the Barelas area, Henrietta took one of her bi-lingual students with her. Continuing her census taking on south First Street, she couldn't understand why all the single girls on the second floor were wearing "nighties" in the middle of the day. "I was pretty naive," Henrietta admits.

Caira (pronounced Kay Ira) May Cook was a classmate and friend of Henrietta's. She admits that the primary reason that she played the violin in the orchestra was that she had a secret crush on Carl Cramer, her teacher.

Caira, whose family came to the U.S on the Mayflower and who was a member of that distinguished club, recalls the bank closings while in high school. Her father worked for the Santa Fe Railroad in the mail car. "Dad was always concerned that someone would try to rob the train during those tough times but fortunately it never happened."

One of the perks her family enjoyed was dinners at the Alvarado Hotel at the depot. She always ordered a Monte Cristo sandwich. Kay recalls that Sunday dinner after church was .75¢ apiece in the mid-Thirties at the best restaurant in town.

Kay's brother, Zenas, got a job at Penney's downtown when jobs were hard to come by. Mr. Ream, acting on a rumor that Zenas was working during the afternoons, marched down to the store and escorted the surprised lad back to school. Depression or not, an education took precedence over everything.

Kathy Finley, '60, wrote a superb tribute to Hosier Benton (H.B.) Horn in the Spring/Summer edition of "The Dawg," the AHS Alumni Association Newsletter. H.B., '34, is a true "rags to riches" story, Kathy opined. After losing his father at the age of six and his mother soon after, he graduated from AHS when the country was still suffering under The Great Depression. H.B. built his first gas station, with his brother Calvin, on Isleta Boulevard when he was in his early twenties. He continued to expand Horn Oil Company buying more land and building more gas stations until he amassed 28 of them and sold out to an oil company. This writer vividly recalls that on several occasions the Horn Oil Co. station on North 4th street extended a fellow Bulldog credit for gas in the early Fifties in order to get to school or keep a date.

H.B., as Kathy reports, has given extensively to the community. He has served on the YMCA Metropolitan Board, Executive Committee of the UNM Foundation, Director of the Albuquerque Chamber of Commerce and has been active in the First Baptist Church for over 70 years. H.B. has also been a member of the Ballut Abyad Shrine and served as Potentate and on the Board of Governors of Shrine Hospital for Crippled Children in Los Angeles.

"Bulldogs Forever" salutes this remarkable man.

Wesley Robert Hurt, '34, must have been inspired by the interest in archaeology promoted by Principal Glen O. Ream which led to the formation of the Archaeology Society in 1932. Wesley's contributions to Paleo-Indian studies had a profound effect on the study of prehistoric peoples in the Americas. So much, in fact, that Mark G. Pew featured Wesley in his book "Exploration in American Archaeology: Essays in Honor of Wesley R. Hurt." More than 85 articles, books and reports by Wesley have been published.

A classmate of Wesley Hurt's, Carolyn Miles Osborne, followed a similar career path and became a noted anthropologist. Along with her husband, she excavated Mesa Verde and Wetherill Mesa sites. New Mexico was, indeed, fertile ground to explore the evolution of man.

The mid to late 1930s produced some talented young men that would contribute greatly to Albuquerque and the City's public school system.

One of the greatest athletes of this era was James F. (Jimmy) Pappan who graduated in 1937. Records are incomplete but it appears that Jimmy accumulated six letters in three years in three sports. This Native American member of the Pawnee Tribe of Oklahoma is recognized on both the All-Time AHS Football as well as Basketball Teams and in 1937 was State Champion in the pole vault in Track and Field. Jim also had a very successful athletic career at Eastern New Mexico University and was employed by the Bureau of Indian Affairs most of his working life. He also coached baseball and basketball at the Albuquerque Indian School.

Tom Hogg was a senior on the Bulldog Basketball Team that lost only one game all season and won the state title. Incredible as it seems today, the rules of that day permitted the team to have only nine men on its roster for the State Tournament. Tom, unfortunately, was the one player left off the team. He turned his disappointment to motivation and returned to the sport he loved to coach at Highland High School for 24 years from 1957 to 1981. His team won the State Championship in 1972 and he was New Mexico Basketball Coach of the Year twice. His teams also were State Champs in golf (3 times) and swimming (2 times).

Two sets of brothers, the Darrows and the Dunlaps, made their marks at AHS. Floyd Darrow was the center on Tony Wilson's 1936 football team that rebounded from the Bulldog's worst season in 1935 to win the State Championship one year later. He was also a guard on the 1937 basketball team that won the State Championship and made the All-Tournament Team. Perhaps the most outstanding athlete on the football team was Harlan Morris who was selected All-State at quarterback. Harold Wickham, despite being color blind, was very effective at tailback if he didn't throw the ball to an opponent. George Crow was the team's outstanding 245-pound tackle for three years. Carol Dunlap was a starter on the 1936 basketball team.

Clyde Dunlap and Bart Darrow competed during the years 1936 through 1939, both following in their older brothers' footsteps. Bart, who made first team All-State in football, especially recalls the 1939 Basketball Team.

"Almost all of us played together since junior high; Mickey Miller, Arnold Loken, Manuel Rico and Ezekiel Duran. We should have won state. We had beaten Lordsburg during the regular season despite the fact that three of our players fouled out and we only had seven on the trip. We finished the game with only four on the floor. I guess we were overconfident when we met Lordsburg again in the finals and they beat us."

Bart added:

"Hobbs had the best team in the state but the officials found out that there were three players who had already graduated from high school, so they had to play in the State Tournament without them."

The fact that Hobbs was allowed to play in the tournament, given the magnitude of their transgression, is remarkable.

Bart recalled that Manuel Rico was probably one of the two best athletes at AHS during this period. He was All-State in both football and basketball and along with their good friend and teammate Mickey Miller, the baseball program was re-activated. Bart had a "Wilsonian" experience also. He asked Coach Wilson why he and the regulars on the Baseball Team didn't receive their "A" letters. Coach's reply was, "You got one but you didn't get one." Bottom line, in the midst of The Depression, the school simply didn't have the funds to purchase the letters. AHS didn't own, or charter, a bus for team trips either. Parents and friends drove the players to games.

At this time in our school's history, AHS began to produce a number of graduates that were appointed to both military academies (Robert MacPherson had been appointed to Annapolis in 1928). One of these students was Carl W. Stapleton, who graduated in 1935. Carl received his wings at Roswell AFB in 1942 and became a fighter pilot in World War II, flying 113 combat missions in Europe. He also served in the Far East after the Korean war. At the rank of Major General, Carl was awarded the Distinguished Service Medal at his retirement in 1973.

James Samuel Shortle, known to his '35 class as "Sam," played both football and basketball at AHS and UNM and obtained his MD in 1942 from the University of Maryland. He served in the U.S. Army during World War II in the medical corps and obtained the rank of Captain. Sam enjoyed a productive and successful career in medicine in private practice in Albuquerque.

An AHS classmate of Carl Stapleton in 1935 was Nathan L. Krisberg. Both of them were also at West Point together. After a 21-year career in both the U.S. Army and the Air Force during which Nathan obtained a Ph.D in Physics and did post doctoral work at Cal Tech, he held key aerospace positions at the Boeing Co. as well as General Electric.

In that same letter cited earlier which Doc Harrington sent to Jim Hulsman in 1966, he included the following. The reader can only imagine this writer's surprise when he discovered that he was included in Doc's recollection of AHS notables. Thanks Doc. I hope that I've given you the space you well deserve.

Note that on the football team of 1931-2 ELZER WALKER. He is now known as JOHNNY WALKER and is one of New Mexico's representatives in the U S Congress. In the old 1915 days GLEN EMMONS was an AHS athlete. He was for about four years the U S Indian Commissioner. He is a banker over in Gallup and is still active in politics,—that is, as active as a Republican can be. Note that in the 1930-32 years the name of VERNE STEWART. He was a basketball player and he also won several state golf tournaments. Verne later went to Stanford and while there won two of the National Golf Championships. For a few years following this he also won the Southwestern Golf Championship,—even as he did while a junior at AHS. Verne showed real National class but he got to hitting the bottle and that killed him about 15 years ago. Noted the Tennis group about 1935-6: NATHAN KRISBERG. He went to West Point. At end of World War II he was a chicken Colonel. Left the Army to become a physician. A real smart kid. The football and basketball teams of the 1936-7 days include CLARK CHILDERS. He is a four-stripe Captain in the US Navy; graduate of Annapolis and is the number-one man for the Polaris nuclear missile shooting submarine program. I noted that in the 1946-47 football team. JOE TISDALE. Joe was a good boy; not as hot as some in high school but he went to town a few years later for USC where he starred in two Rose Bowl encounters. Letterman BUSTER QUIST of the 1951-54 crew was an All-American javelin thrower while attending UNM. Buster is now one of the national hot-shot salesmen for one of the investment businesses, I believe. Well, am just passing these observations on for your own personal edification.

— E R Harrington

H. B. Horn, cited above, once said of his brother Calvin Horn, a 1935 grad, "Calvin and I have been as close as brothers could get." A life-long friend, Jim Toulouse, said of Calvin Horn, "Calvin was more than a successful business-man, historian, author, book publisher and politician. He was a man of strong moral character and a great public leader.

Calvin founded the First Baptist Church's Noon Day Ministry and raised the first $100,000 to support the home-less. Another project which was intended to help preserve both the Hispanic and Native American Cultures was a pub-lishing company that reissued 60 out-of-print classics. Cal-vin also served for 10 years in the New Mexico State Legisla-ture and was State Chairman for the Democratic Party.

1935 was a prolific year for notable graduates of AHS. Among the leaders of this group of students was Ben C. Her-nandez. A native New Mexican born to a father who was the first Congressman elected after statehood in 1912 and a mother who was a suffragette, it seemed as though politics would be the principal focus in Ben's life. Actually, it was for a short while when President Lyndon B. Johnson named him to be the U.S. Ambassador to Paraguay. Ben is best remem-bered perhaps for his long stint as Chief Justice on the New Mexico Court of Appeals and his role in the famous Reies Lopez Tijerina case, which involved the land grant activists' raid on the Tierra Amarillo Courthouse in northern New Mexico.

Exemplifying the diversity of interests and talents of the 1935 class is Lucille Lattanner Reid Brock, noted artist and writer. After graduating from UNM Lucille moved to Taos where she said, "As I look back on those days as a bride in

Taos, I now realize how creative and carefree yet intellectual and stimulating those years were. How fortunate we were to live in a place where...a person's age, wealth, ethnic background and religion were of no importance." Lucille wrote a book about her experience there titled, *Taos Then-Only In Taos, Stories by a Bride Who Lived Them.*

Paul H. Barnes started his banking career in 1935, the same year he graduated from AHS. He left the city to attend the University of Wisconsin School of Banking. From an entry-level bookkeeper he rose to the position of President and CEO of First New Mexico Bankshare Corporation when it became the first New Mexico corporation with assets in excess of $1 billion. Paul served on the boards of nine banks in New Mexico and was involved in the industry for 50 years.

William E. Black, better known to his 1935 classmates as "Ed" and the leader of the popular band "Ed Black & His Dukes," was also a standout player on the State Championship Football Team in '35. His classmate Henrietta Beber also remembers him as a prankster. Most Albuquerqueans remember him as the man behind the "Blackbird," the trademark of his Chevy dealership on San Mateo Boulevard. This writer recalls Ed when he owned Oden's Chevrolet downtown on North 4th Street. Ed, a strong supporter of athletics, hired me as the night janitor while I attended UNM. Ed served in World War II as a glider pilot which, to those old enough to remember, was a one way flight that ended, hopefully, in a controlled crash landing. As one article said, "Ed Black was as classy as a '57 Chevy and the chrome still shined."

Emmanuel Schifani was one of nine children in his family, all of whom graduated from AHS. "Manny" must have been eager to join the battle against Germany. He enlisted in the Royal Air Force in England in 1940 before the U.S. had entered the War. Later he joined the U.S. Army Air Corps and flew 65 B-26 combat missions in Europe. He was recalled during the Korean War and flew 20 more combat missions there. He retired as a Lt. General and received the Distinguished Flying Cross and the Bronze Star. After World War II, "Manny" built Springer Corp into a regional conglomerate, and at one point the company was reported to be the largest private employer in the state. His tireless efforts serving on the Boards of the Red Cross, the Cancer Society, the Polio Foundation, the Nazareth and St. Joseph Hospital, the Albuquerque Chamber of Commerce, St. John's College, as well as on the boards of numerous privately held companies, reinforced his commitment to his city and his state.

Richard Kenneth Strome, '36, found a niche that few artists discover — a secure, good paying job as a technical illustrator that permitted him to also pursue his love of painting landscapes and portraits in watercolors, oils and pastels. A graduate of the American Academy of Art in Chicago, Richard returned to Albuquerque to work for Sandia Laboratories producing manual illustrations for the U.S. Atomic Arsenal. His works are included in the permanent collection of the New Mexico State Fair, the New Mexico Museum of Fine Arts and the Museum of Albuquerque.

In 1938 a Student Council was formed for the first time and due to increased enrollment, AHS took over the First Ward School at Edith and Tijeras for additional classrooms. It was re-named Kit Carson Hall.

Presumably, Harold Enarson graduated from AHS in 1936 since he obtained an A.B. degree from UNM in 1940. He received an M.A. from Stanford and a Ph.D from American University in 1951. Harold was a Special Assistant in the White House in the early years of the Eisenhower Administration, and served in numerous key administrative roles in government and industry before being named the Executive Vice-President of the University of New Mexico. His first year at UNM was the year this writer graduated in 1960. He also previously served as President of Ohio State University.

James (Jim) Toulouse, also a 1936 grad, was as combative as a Bulldog football player as he was as a trial lawyer. Unafraid of taking unpopular cases, Jim often represented minorities for little or no fee. He was quoted in a 1993 *Albuquerque Journal* article as saying, "You do service for people who need your help." Jim has always maintained that racial prejudice existed in Albuquerque, "...there was lots of discrimination and it still exists today. It's just beneath the surface more." He and his wife Charlotte received "Keep the

Dream Alive" awards in 1993 from the Martin Luther King, Jr. Committee.

Robert R. McCord, '36 became reacquainted with two of his classmates, Carl Quickel and Oscar Bleuher, during the early days of World War II. All three were Air Corps pilots ferrying aircraft across the Atlantic to England. All three became top fighter pilots during the War and McCord received the Distinguished Flying Cross and other prestigious medals for his successful service to his country and retired as a Lt. Colonel.

Jim McCahon, like so many members of the New Mexico National Guard, was taken prisoner in the Philippines in the early stages of World War II and survived the Bataan Death March. Although Jim earned a music degree at UNM, he later studied at Kansas State University and became a veterinarian. McCahon's Albuquerque Animal Hospital was a sanctuary for the city's pets for almost 30 years. Jim was Past Potentate of the New Mexico Shriners and Past President of the New Mexico State Veterinary Association.

Albert H. (Pat) Clancey, '36(?), attended UNM for one year before being appointed to the U.S. Naval Academy. Upon graduation he was assigned to a light cruiser, the USS Honolulu. His timing couldn't have been more dramatic. Pat was aboard that ship anchored in Pearl Harbor on that fateful morning of December 7, 1941. Although his ship was hit by enemy aircraft all of his shipmates survived the attack. This sailor became a Navy pilot and was flying off the carrier USS Bataan when the War against Japan ended. After World War II Pat obtained his M.A. degree in Aero Engineering at Cal Tech and in 1967 he was promoted to the rank of Rear Admiral.

The class of 1937 produced one of the foremost jazz musicians in America. John Lewis formed the Modern Jazz Quartet who were the innovators of a new style of music called "third stream" — part jazz and part concert. John played and arranged for the Dizzy Gillespie Orchestra and played with jazz greats Charlie Parker and Miles Davis. He taught at the Julliard School of Music in New York and was Music Professor at City College of New York. A graduate of UNM he has received an Honorary Doctorate from his school plus other numerous prestigious awards. He was raised in Albuquerque by his aunt Edith English, who was well-known to Albuquerqueans as the city's foremost caterer.

This writer best recalls Howard E. Cohea as his golfing partner while he was a member of the Four Hills Country Club, which he helped develop along with another AHS grad, Bill Brannin. Howard was an All-City and All-State tackle on the Bulldog football team and was a member of the 1935 State Championship squad. He served as a bombardier in both World War II and in Korea. He founded Automotive Acceptance Corp. and when his business was located on San Pedro Boulevard, in the early Sixties adjacent to this writer's office, we often shared our sport experiences at AHS.

Betty Burton Perkins was Co-Chairperson of her 1937 Class' 50th Reunion Committee. That event was an enormous success, which wasn't a surprise to her classmates given the organizational and public relations skills that Betty had demonstrated during her business career. She worked at the First National Bank in Albuquerque and in the years subsequent served on the boards of the Opera Guild, Chamber of Commerce, United Way, St. Joseph's Hospital and the Albuquerque Balloon Fiesta. Her most satisfying community service, she reveals, was serving on the Board of Directors of Hogares, an agency which provides group treatment homes for adolescents and on the Board of New Futures School, an agency which provides school program for teenage parents.

Graduating two years after his brother, Emmanuel, Frank M. Schifani also served in World War II but in the U.S. Army. He received his battlefield commission in Italy, where he was wounded and received the Purple Heart. He followed his brother to Springer Corp. after the War, where he was a Vice-President and Director for 18 years. Frank was always eager to relate the story of the beginning of his working career as a $2.50 per week stockboy at Safeway at the age of seven. One of Frank's major contributions to the city was bringing Triple A baseball to Albuquerque. A fervent collector of baseball memorabilia, one of Frank's prized possessions was an autographed baseball by Babe Ruth given to him personally by the "Babe" in 1934. Frank was actively involved in the American Legion, the Albuquerque Chamber of Commerce, the Elks Club, the UNM Booster Club, the St. Joseph's Hospital, the Albuquerque Economic Development Corp., the St. Pius High School Board, the University of Albuquerque and numerous other civic and charitable organizations.

Only three years out of high school Ruth E. Bebber joined the WAVES for three years during World War II. She taught Physical Education briefly at AHS for three years prior to obtaining her Ph.D at the University of Southern California. She was one of the early advocates of nutrition and taught that subject as well as aquatic and outdoor education at Southern Oregon University for 35 years. Ruth was very active in AAUW (American Association of University Women) and was President of the Oregon Federation of Business and Professional Women.

Donald Eugene Hurt, the younger brother of Wesley recognized above, graduated from AHS four years later in 1938. Don played a key role in the historic D-Day invasions of Normandy on June 6, 1944. Don was a weather forecaster stationed at the Pentagon while persistent inclement weather delayed the Allied strike. A math major at UNM, Don worked for 35 years as a quality control engineer at Sandia National Laboratory in Albuquerque.

Findley Harrison Morrow, '39, would undoubtedly enjoy "Bulldog's Forever" since he was a New Mexico history buff. Findley, as almost all grads of this era, served in World War II. He was a First Lieutenant in the Air Corps. After the War he was a Police Judge for the City of Albuquerque for 4 years and served as a State Representative in the New Mexico Legislature for 2 years. He spent more than 20 years working for the State Department of Education in the Vocational Rehabilitation Division.

Jim Hutchinson, '39 and his wife Betty Klentchy Hutchinson, who graduated three years later, should be recognized as a devoted team dedicating themselves to preserving not only AHS traditions but for their service to their community. Jim and Betty owned and operated for 35 years the Hutchinson Fruit Company, that was started across from Hopewell Field in 1921. Jim and Betty were on the committees to celebrate "An Afternoon with Glen O. Ream" held at the Bulldog Gym in 1972, and they hosted an event to celebrate the AHS Centennial Celebration at the KIMO Theater. The couple was active in the Optimists, Santa Maria Camp for Boys, New Mexico Boys Ranch, Albuquerque Boys and Girls Club, the All Faiths Receiving Home and numerous other civic endeavors. Hutchinson Fruit company provided all the cabbage and potatoes necessary for Brother Mathias' St. Patrick's Day dinner for the homeless from its inception until the business was sold.

Edward J.Apodaea, a 1939 grad who served in Germany during World War II, made a memorable and lasting effort to repair relations with our former enemy shortly after the War. During the conflict he met Ingelborg Ringelman and they married in Frankfurt in 1947. Ed graduated from Georgetown Law School and the couple returned to the bridegroom's roots in Albuquerque to practice law. Ed, active in politics, served on the New Mexico State Police Commission during the David Cargo Administration and became the Commission's Chairman.

In the 1930s formal recognition of the feats of athletes became more widespread. In basketball, in addition to the All-Tournament State Championship Team, recognition was given to those who were All-State, All-District Tournament and in Albuquerque, All-City. The 1937 AHS Bulldog basketball team had the unique distinction of having <u>six</u> players selected for one or more of these teams. They were: Jimmy Pappan, Floyd Harris, Harlan Morris, Barney Coe, Charlie Ortiz along with Floyd Darrow. The 1938 team had Ray Tanner, Ed Chavez and Roy Craig recognized. The 1939 team featured Arnold Loken, Manuel Rico and Bart Darrow were named to one or more of the teams. For some unknown reason one of the stars on this team, Mickey Miller, was not mentioned along with his teammates, but he most assuredly will be remembered here.

Miller ('39) has the distinction of being selected on the All-AHS team in football. He also enjoys the rare, if not unequalled feat, of <u>never</u> missing a single day of work coaching and teaching in the Albuquerque Public School system. For <u>44</u> years!

Mickey went on to the University of New Mexico where

he earned a total of nine athletic letters and was inducted into the school's Hall of Honor in 1994. Upon graduation from UNM Mickey enlisted in the U.S. Navy in 1942. So valuable was Mickey to the Navy's football program he spent most of his time playing for the Bainbridge Navy football team, which was the National Service Champion several years. Mickey turned down an offer to play for the Philadelphia Eagles to take the coaching job at Jefferson Junior High. He then became Highland High's first basketball and baseball coach in 1949, thereby positioning himself to become in league with the Bulldog's most hated rival. Mickey is mentioned prominently in my memoir during our classic confrontations with Highland High. Regrettably, our competitor and friend passed away just months prior to this tribute to an outstanding man.

Clyde Dunlap was a speedster who won gold medals in the 100 and 220 yard dash as well as the 440 yard relay in 1939, as Charlie Renfro's teams dominated the state's track and field meets. Surprisingly, Coach Renfro "requested" that Clyde not play football and risk injury, which must not have set well with Coach Wilson. Clyde recalls that Marion Plomteaux, who excelled at football and track, gave Clyde his precious track shoes when he graduated in 1938. Those men that he considered as stars on the football team were Howard Cohea, George Koury, Cleo Maddox, James Pappan and Ernest Echohawk. A third Dunlap brother, Roy, would follow in Clyde's quick footsteps during the war years.

A winner of three gold medals in the State Track and Field Championship meet in the Thirties was Emmett Miller in the discus, high jump and the long jump. Robin Knight won two golds in 1936 in the 120 hurdles and the long jump and Marion Plomteaux was a double winner in the sprints.

Robin Knight continued to have a keen interest in athletics long after his days at AHS. In particular he followed track and field and along with his son, Fred, who followed in his footsteps clearing the hurdles, Robin took a great interest in my track career. I hadn't seen Robin for over twenty years. In the mid-90s I ran into him at a golf tournament in Pinetop, Arizona.

"Buster? I hate to tell you this but Robin has Alzheimers.

He's confined to a nursing home but I brought him to the tournament because he loves to get out," my friend Les File reported to me.

Most of the participants in the tournament were sitting in the restaurant having dinner when I walked in.

"My goodness! If it isn't `old Buster Quist!" Robin shouted to everyone's amazement.

Somehow, I must have created a lasting impression on my friend. Often, our oldest memories are the most vivid in our minds, as evidenced by some of the stories remembered here.

In the late Thirties AHS dominated another sport which unfortunately received little recognition. Bob Stamm won the State singles title in tennis all three years, 1936, 1937 and 1938 and was the doubles champ in `36 and `37 which, had tennis been a team sport, would probably have given the Bulldogs claim to championships in all sports in the state in 1936.

Bob's father, Roy A. Stamm, mentioned earlier as one of AHS' first graduates in 1893, taught Bob and his brother Roy to play tennis when Bob was only eight years old.

"We played at Nordhaus Park near Central Avenue and 14th Street. Las Vegas, Clovis, Roswell and Los Alamos had tennis teams. The kid I beat in the finals in 1938 was from Los Alamos. He was good. He learned how to play in the east," Bob recalled.

Bob was also one of Albuquerque's first skiing enthusiasts encouraged by Bob Nordhaus, cited earlier, who Bob refers to as the "Father of New Mexico Skiing." Stamm reminisced about meets that their Albuquerque group had with Los Alamos. They had no tows on the "hill" in those days and the competitors had to climb to the top of the mountain to start their races. (The first rope tow in the US was built in 1934 in Woodstock, Vermont.) In a few years a formal Ski Club at AHS would be formed followed by a Ski Team.

Bob also found time to run the 440 and 880 yard runs on Charlie Renfro's track team. His senior year he won both races in the district meet. Concerned that he couldn't run in the State Track and Field Championships and play three or four singles matches, plus doubles, in the Tennis Tournament, Bob opted to play tennis and secured his spot in Bulldog lore. His coach? Tony Wilson who Bob referred to as "The John Wooden of his day—a real class act."

Few, if any grads have contributed more to the community of Albuquerque than Bob Stamm. The imprint that the entire Stamm family has left on Albuquerque and New Mexico is gigantic. Bob received a BA in Civil Engineering from UNM, did post graduate study at the U.S. Naval Academy, and retired from active duty as a Commander after World War II. He joined O.G. Bradbury, a construction firm in 1946, and became a partner in 1958. Bradbury Stamm was incorporated in 1974 and Bob remains as the CEO and Chairman of the Board. In 1999, his firm ranked number one in New Mexico in volume and listed amongst their many high-profile New Mexico projects the old AHS gym in 1938 and the new Albuquerque High School. A few of Bob's awards for distinguished service are: UNM Regents Recognition Medal, UNM Most Prestigious Zimmerman Award, 7-time winner of the State of New Mexico Distinguished Public Service Award for Most Admired Company, Presbyterian Healthcare Foundation Award of Excellence, Boy Scouts of America Distinguished Citizen Award, New Mexico Outstanding Leader in Philanthropy, Albuquerque Museum Foundation Award, United Way Lifetime Achievement Award and many other citations for this man's contributions to his community. "Bulldogs Forever" pays a well-deserved tribute to one of its most distinguished alums who has a unique tie to his *alma mater.* He met his wife Florence Bradbury at AHS and they both received their diplomas in the new gymnasium built by Florence's father's company, O. G Bradbury.In 1974 Bob's firm, Bradbury Stamm Construction, built the new AHS school on Odelia Road.

David Simms, inheriting Bob's expertise on the tennis court, continued the Bulldog reign of champions as he won the state title in 1939. David is remembered by me as well as many other grads in their future years as their dentist. Eddie Gladden picked up the tennis mantra from Stamm and Simms in 1940, but an injury suffered while high jumping probably prevented AHS' number one player from garnering the state singles title.

Mel Otero was an outstanding basketball player in 1938 and 1939 and also competed in baseball with the game's revival in 1938. After college Mel returned to the court and all sports venues as a referee for an amazing thirty-six years. According to Jim Hulsman, who watched Mel perform his duties up close and personal from the bench as AHS coach courtside, said that Mel officiated over 2,500 games in his long career. Jim called him a "trail blazer." One of Mel's highlights was being chosen to referee the 1975 basketball game between the USA and Russia.

Other basketball players that were selected to one or more of the All-State, All-Tournament or All-City teams were as follows:

1930 Jack Jones
1931 Harley Gooch
1932 Mariano Montoya, Frank Montoya, Rudy Heller (and Ralph Bowyer and Emilio Lopez previously mentioned)
1933 Richard Montoya
1934 Faustin Saavedra
1935 Eloy Springer
1936 Harold Canfield

Ironically, Mel Otero is not mentioned but his teammates attest to the fact that he was indeed a vital cog on the 1938 and 1939 teams. It wasn't the first time that sportswriters didn't get it right.

The World War II period has often been referred to by sports writers of the time as the "modern era." Looking back from the turn of the 21st Century, those days and marks look anything but modern, but it was a time when AHS athletic teams and individual heroes enhanced and capitalized on the Bulldog mystique. It was a time prior to the opening of a second public high school thereby assuring AHS a maximum talent pool in the state's largest, rapidly growing city. The "Dawgs" were a dominant power in all sports and understandably became the team to beat.

In 1940, the New Mexico High School Coaches Association initiated a North-South All Star Football game. Basketball was added in 1947. The coaches selected approximately

26 football players from all the high schools that would play a game in Albuquerque in August. The players selected from AHS for the first game from the team of 1939 for the 1940 game were Bill Jourdan and Howard Martin. In 1941, Thomas E. (Shanty) Hogan, Bill Gregg, Orville Roberts, Jim Thayer, Roger Diers and Al Staehlin were chosen.

The 1940 Bulldog football team was exceptional. Led by Captain and right tackle Orville Roberts the Green and White was undefeated, winning ten games including the UNM frosh, and allowed their opponents only an average of about three points per game. Hobbs High School and sportswriters in southeastern New Mexico referred to AHS as "mythical" champions because they, too, were undefeated, and to them football played north of Highway 66 wasn't the same caliber as the south. Seemingly, the Bulldogs 24-7 thrashing of Roswell wasn't sufficient evidence to the contrary. It would take 13 more years before this perennial argument was resolved and our team of 1953 had the distinction of participating in the first playoff for the undisputed champion.

The inspirational leader of this great team was quarterback/blocking back Thomas E. (Shanty) Hogan. Diminutive in size and only 16 years of age as a senior he was All-City and All-State. According to Shanty the best all-around athlete was (single wing) tailback Roger Diers who only played football his senior year and made All-State. Roger was also an outstanding catcher on AHS's first baseball team and went on to play professionally. Bill Gregg played center and linebacker and Al Staehlin, a real tough hard-nosed guy, played left end. Jim Thayer was also an All-Star at fullback. Shanty also starred as a forward on the basketball team that went to the semi-finals in the State Tournament. The team was led by 6'4" center Glenn Young who was reportedly the tallest player in the State that year. Roger Diers was also an important cog on the hardwood.

Glenn, who lettered in basketball his junior and senior years, and made the All-Tournament Team, recalls the 1940 state tournament:

"We lost to Las Cruces in the semi-finals because Shanty and Roger (Diers) were sick and couldn't play. George Leavitt was our captain (and All-State) and best player at guard along with Jack Hitchins and Steve Johnson but we just couldn't win without those two guys."

George Leavitt, Glenn noted, was badly wounded in North Africa during WWII, but miraculously survived and as of this writing is still enjoying life and recalling the "good old days" at AHS. Glenn also recalled his history teacher, Mr. Drypulcher, who had more influence on him than any other person in his life.

"He impressed upon us what a great country America was. I became a patriot then and have remained one." A lesson that, 60 years later, needs to become a part of our curriculum again.

Hogan, who went on to star in football and baseball at the University of Arizona, became a legend in Arizona high school coaching ranks and was noted for his well disciplined teams, says that, "It was the camaraderie that we as teammates felt and experienced that made us winners." Now in their eighties, many of these teammates still get together and share their AHS experience.

Another member of the exceptional football team of 1940 was Edwin (Bub) Johnson, son of the University of New Mexico's legendary Roy Johnson. Bub must have been an outstanding athlete. Coach Wilson, not known for bending his own rules allowed Bub to play on the varsity his sophomore year. He lettered as an end all three years.

Bub, as a testament to his all-around athletic ability, also starred on Wilson's basketball teams in 1941 and 1942 and he recalled that he was the top scorer in the city his senior year averaging "about 10 points per game." Bub along with teammates John Mayne, DeSoto Powers and Manuel Baldonado were selected to a number of All-Tournament teams. In track and field Bub threw the discus 151', an AHS record which stood for 20 years. An extreme rarity occurred when the Bulldog track team won the State Championship in 1941. All of the team's points were garnered in the field events. Bub's brother Steffan placed in the shot put, discus and javelin.

Another graduate of 1940 whose career path dawned at the birth of the Atomic Age was Floy Agnes Naranjo (Stroud)

Lee. Agnes, after obtaining her B.S. in Biology at UNM in 1945, soon found herself at Los Alamos Scientific Research Laboratory as a research assistant studying the effects of nuclear radiation. A Native American, she continued in the field of Radiation Biology and Cytogenetics (chromosome abnormalities due to radiation or birth defects) and obtained a Ph.D in Biological Sciences at the University of Chicago. She has authored or co-authored over 35 papers or books on her chosen study.

Sam L. Johnson was Vice-President of his Senior Class of 1940 as well as a star on the Bulldog basketball team. After obtaining a B.S. degree in Civil Engineering and working out of state, Sam returned to New Mexico and in 1946 became one of the initial employees in Los Alamos for what would come to be known as Sandia National Laboratories. He worked in the design and construction of Building 892 which was (presumably) Sandia's secret atomic stockpile production facility. Sam worked closely with the Atomic Energy Commission and the Air Force a number of years in remote locations and returned to Albuquerque to work for Sandia until he retired in 1985.

Another 1940 grad, Leo N. Hudleston, became a career military officer in the U.S. Navy. In fact, Leo served in three conflicts: World War II, Korea and he was Commander of Naval Forces in Vietnam in 1967 and 1968. Leo retired from the Navy after serving his country for 27 years.

After suffering a football injury while playing for the Bulldogs, William E. (Bill) Hall, Jr. decided he would best enjoy the sport utilizing his typewriter rather than his pads. Graduating in 1940 Bill went to work for the *Albuquerque Tribune* but was soon drafted into the Army in World War II. He was wounded while at the front lines in France and was repositioned to the Counter Intelligence Corps. After the War he graduated from UNM with a degree in Journalism, and after a short stint at the Tribune as Sports Editor, Bill became the first full time director of the UNM Alumni Association. He was instrumental in the building of the War Memorial Chapel at UNM. Bill later received his Doctorate of mass Communications from the University of Iowa and served as Director of Journalism at Texas Tech and the University of

Nebraska.

Edward D. "Ed" Gladden was another AHS alum whose graduation in 1940, just prior to World War II, interrupted his college studies. But the War probably opened a door of opportunity as it did for other builders and contractors mentioned above. World War II created an enormous demand for housing and Albuquerque was poised to boom. Ed joined his father-in-law Fred Mossman and formed Mossman Gladden, Inc., that would in the ensuing thirty plus years build a total of 4,500 homes throughout New Mexico. Ed recalls with pride that they started building in the Bel-Air Addition off San Mateo Boulevard. He and his wife bought a 780 square foot home there in 1949 for about $6,800 or less than $10/square foot including the lot. Ed, who served as President of the Albuquerque Home Builders Association and a Director of the National Association of Home Builders, remains active in many civic projects.

Asa B. Edwards, better known to his classmates in 1940 as "Ace," twice had a prospective career at the Albuquerque National Bank interrupted by war. Shortly after joining the bank Ace enlisted in the Army Air Corps and served in the 39th Bomb Group on a B-29 Superfortress in the Pacific. After the War he rejoined the bank but was called back for active duty during the Korean War. Ace remained in the Air Force as a career officer for 33 years and received numerous decorations for his service to his country.

Chapter One of this book briefly chronicles the origins of the three distinct and diverse cultures of New Mexico. May Simms (Denham), a 1940 graduate, is one person who exemplifies the assimilation of two cultures. May was born in Dulce, New Mexico, of Navajo and Apache parents. She was adopted and raised by a missionary family, graduated from UNM and married Roy D. Denham in 1948. May was a lifelong member of the Presbyterian Church and became an elder in that church. She also was elected to the post of National President of United Presbyterian Women. For her devotion to civic and church work May received both the Lobo Award and the James F. Zimmerman Award from UNM. She also received an Honorary L.L.D. from Central College in Iowa where she also attended school.

CHAPTER FOUR:
THE WAR YEARS 1941-1945

DECEMBER 7, 1941 WAS INDEED "a date that will live in infamy," as President Roosevelt declared in his speech to Congress the next day. The emotional impact on those young men who were graduating in 1942 must have been excruciating as the country faced its most defining moment in the 20th Century. Moved by patriotic impulse many students quit school and enlisted in military service. Many would postpone college to respond to the Nation's call. By 1943 virtually every able-bodied American male was in uniform. One very little known but poignant situation arose at our school at this defining moment.

Attending AHS during the onset of the War was a young man whose name was Richard Hashimoto. Apparently his brother Gene had already graduated by the time the War began. With paranoia running amok those of Japanese descent were herded up by the government and placed in internment camps including one situated in southern New Mexico which is a remarkable story in itself. There are several incredible twists to this story. One, according to Bob Mikkelson '44, the mother of the two young men was of Native American descent (Navajo), therefore the boys were half Japanese. From Bub Johnson ('42) I learned that Gene Hashimoto changed his last name to Hart and enlisted in the U.S. Army. Richard, with the assistance of Glen O. Ream, Tony Wilson and others was allowed to remain at AHS and his father apparently was never detained. The ultimate irony in this story, of course, is that the Navajo "Code Talkers" became the unsung (until recently) heroes of WWII.

Al Herron, '44, wrote a memoir of his days at AHS. His ruminations of those precarious but precious days are recorded here:

HIGH SCHOOL YEARS 1941-44

In September 1941, I started high school in grand style, driving four of us to school in my Model T Ford for the first few days. (The Model T is discussed in the chapter DRIVING AND CARS, but I had bought it in July for $25 and sold it in October for $20.) In those days, hardly any high schoolers drove to school because most families had only one car, and the father drove it. There was not even a parking lot at Albuquerque High...we parked on the street. Teachers mostly rode city busses. The Model T had no top and I was afraid somebody might mess with it, so took it to school for only a few days. After I sold the T a few weeks later, things settled into a routine. Until Pearl Harbor Day.

I remember that day very well, Sunday, December 7, 1941. We had just returned from church and I turned on the radio, and there it was: the Japanese had bombed Pearl Harbor with many ships sunk, including the largest battleships, and an unknown loss of life. It was terrible...partly because it was so unexpected.

The next day, all Albuquerque High students were brought together in the gymnasium to hear President Roosevelt's speech to Congress, which was broadcast worldwide...the speech where he talked about "the day that will live in infamy," and asked Congress to declare war on the Japanese. Congress soon did, and the Germans and Italians as well.

The United States had tried to stay out of the war in Europe, to the great consternation of Britain. After the Germans overran Poland, France, Belgium, Holland, Denmark, and some other countries, only Britain was left to hold off the Nazi war machine. The U.S. had been supplying the Brits with all the ships, planes, and weapons we could build, but it was not until we actually declared war that things got into high gear. The war greatly influenced everything from then on.

Soon after we got into it, rationing was instituted. That included gasoline, canned food, sugar, meat, shoes, and probably other things which I've forgotten about.

Canned food was rationed to a certain number of cans per week for each person in the family. Meat was so many pounds...something like two pounds a week per person. A similar thing for sugar and butter. It was all handled with coupons, which arrived in the mail quarterly. Every family had to fill out a questionnaire identifying all the members of the family and their ages. We would occasionally read about someone who cheated or tried to use counterfeit coupons, but I don't think that was much of a problem. Almost everybody was very patriotic and wanted to help the war effort.

Gasoline was rationed on the basis of gallons per car...I think the amount was five gallons per week per auto, but some occupations got more. We had coupon books with each coupon good for five gallons. The coupons were dated you could save them and use several at once, but you couldn't get ahead of the validity date. This meant that there was very little travel which was not really necessary. I got to use the car for dating once in a while, but not very often. There was a national speed limit of 35 miles per hour to save gasoline. In case of special need, such as moving from one city to another, you could get special coupons for that purpose.

There were no new autos for sale "for the duration" which meant until the war was over, so there were no model years 1942, `43, `44, or `45. Considerable effort was made to keep the existing cars running by making replacement parts available. Also, there were practically no new tires manufactured for the civilian population, but you could get your old ones recapped as often as necessary. The national speed limit of 35 mph undoubtedly helped keep both tires and cars running longer. Most people got to school on city busses.

Clocks ran on what was called "war time." It was

like daylight saving time only it was two hours earlier instead of one, and was in effect year around...until the war ended. The basic ideas was to have more usable daylight by moving some daylight hours from early morning to the evening. So, when we started school at eight a.m. by the clock, it was really six a.m. by the sun, and that was still nighttime for much of the school year. I took the typical courses for a sophomore: English, Spanish, World History, Biology, and Plane Geometry. In the junior year it was English, Spanish, U.S. History, Algebra II, and Chemistry. As a senior I took English, Trigonometry, Solid Geometry, Physics, Meteorology, and Air Navigation. The last two were one-semester courses which Dr. Harrington, Chairman of the Science Department, taught to help the guys who would be going into service. He wrote the textbook for both classes, but it wasn't hardback...just mimeographed. I heard that some other schools used his books to teach the same material. This wasn't an easy schedule, and to my surprise I managed to stay on the honor roll and was president of the Honor Society my senior year.

Extracurricular activities? Well, I performed in the school Operetta each year, but certainly not as a soloist. Lettered in track as a junior and senior (hurdles, relay, javelin, discus), and lettered in football as a senior ...

Something else Dad didn't like was dancing...Southern Baptists believed that dancing was sinful. The Bible tells about Salome dancing for King Herod and then asking for the head of John the Baptist on a platter as a reward. Well, Southern Baptists believe that that proves that dancing is wicked, so what dancing I did, I had to sneak off and do it secretly. Bill and Carolyn went to dances, but none of my other Baptist friends did. I went to three or four school sponsored dances, usually without a date, and never learned to dance very well. Other than the Senior Prom, I cannot remember taking a date to a dance in high school ...

I had as many dates in high school as my pocketbook would allow, but no steady girlfriend—which was typical then. Not many guys and girls "went steady." With the war on, there weren't many things to do since we couldn't drive more than a bare minimum I guess movies constituted about 90 percent of my dates, and we usually rode the city bus to get there.

Graduation was fun. We wore caps and gowns and walked across the stage to receive our diploma, and maybe recognition for some special achievement. I went to the dance afterward, and when it was over, a buddy and I drove out on the mesa and celebrated by drinking a quart of warm beer out of the bottle.

After graduating in May 1944, Uncle Sam invited me to join the Navy.

As a grade schooler in Wisconsin, I can vividly recall selling seeds for "Victory Gardens" to conserve food supplies for our troops. We brought scrap metal, rubber toys, rubber bands, rags, paper and other items to school for the all-out war effort. Bob Mikkelson recalls the huge mountain of aluminum piled in the patio at AHS. He also painfully recalls that Hugh Cooper, his best friend who joined the Navy, was lost in a typhoon in the Pacific. Gas rationing restricted team travel to sporting events. Parents pooled their gas coupons in order to make a few trips. Teams took the train to Gallup. But there was one lasting, albeit somewhat negative, impact of the war that few would recall.

"Everyone seemed to scatter with the wind," Bob observed. "The war took our guys all over. No one seems to come back to our reunions." The Class of 1943 which celebrated its 60th reunion in 2003, did return to its roots.

Mikkelson achieved a milestone (of sorts) during his two years as starting end on the varsity football team. He would have to be the only pass receiver to make the All-AHS team who never caught a pass! The teams of 1942 and 1943 must have epitomized the phrase, "five yards and a cloud of dust."

Bill Pegue held down the other end of the 1942 State

Championship Team that posted a 10-0 record. One of Bill's classmates was Carlos Salazar, who became so enamored with sports that he began compiling statistics of all the games.

Carlos, who later became an icon amongst New Mexico sportswriters as he reported for the *Albuquerque Tribune*, maintained that the `42 Bulldogs were the leading rushing team in the nation with over 500 yards per game. We know that the team rarely threw a pass so that statistic could be fact.

Bill and many of his teammates knew each other well since they played together from grade school on. "Whether it was shooting hoops or playing war games with rubber bands on wooden guns, we were always competing against each other," Bill recalled. His best friend was Jerry Gatewood.

"Jerry was our quarterback. He was the best all-around athlete at AHS. Both of us played football and basketball together all three years and then we joined the Navy together, then on to UNM. Jerry was All-Everything," Bill added. This writer remembers Jerry well. He was my next door neighbor near Altura Park when I married and acquired my instant family. One day I was a bachelor. The next day I had a bride, two children, a dog and a station wagon. Jerry would observe my workouts in the park during the early-Sixties. One day while shooting the bull Jerry said to me, "Buster, I take my hat off to you. Here you are married, got a couple kids and in your late twenties and still competing on a national scale. You're the only ex-Bulldog that I know who has done that."

I asked Bill, "Tell me who your teammates were on that great football team?"

"We had Jim (Toodles) Roberts at end. He was All-State, and our Captain. Our halfbacks were Bob Contreras and Martin Shaw. Fullback was Clarence Roberts. Some of the other guys were Clem Charlton, Duke Natress, John Giannini...those three guys made the All-Star Team in 1946 because there wasn't an All-Star game during the War. And, Louie Lutich, Phil Martinez, Bliss Bushman, Roy Touche, Ned Ross, Bill Morrow, Ernie Archuleta, Bob McDonald...Bob was killed in the War...I'm sure I've missed a lot of the guys but all of us were a close knit group," Bill said wistfully.

"One thing that still sticks out in my mind. `Ole Coach Wilson dressed in a suit and tie during every game...rain or shine or snow," Bill recalled. "And, one other thing. I remember how tough Glen Ream was. If I got outta line, Mr. Ream would call home and tell my dad and boy I got my butt whipped. I once saw Mr. Ream chase a kid down Central Avenue and he caught up to him at the underpass. Boy, did that guy get his butt kicked. Don't know what he did but I'll bet he didn't do it again," Bill said as he laughed.

Jim (Toodles) Roberts amplified on this great `42 team:

"We were undefeated and unscored upon that year in New Mexico but we didn't win State. We lost a game to North Phoenix High School but the tie game with Raton cost us the State Championship. Raton had these real big kids that were coal miners and they stopped us several times right at the goal line.[5] Carlsbad won the State Championship. They were undefeated in state too and we didn't play them."

Jim also revealed that the first unofficial game of the season was a matchup with the AHS alumni. He remembers it well because he faced off against his brother Orville, who played tackle in front of him. One of Jim's cherished possessions was a shoe string tied up in knots. It seems that Coach Wilson used to pace the sidelines nervously with the string in his hands. Each knot must have represented an offsides, a fumble or some other frustrating miscue.

The subject turned to basketball.

"Man! Did we have a great team. We had Bill Blackburn, Jack Wheeler and Jerry Gatewood, who I think all three were All-City and maybe All-State too, plus Bill Caldwell, Bill Pegue, Clem Charlton, Max Shirley, J.C Wray, Bill Morrow, Jim Roberts and that crazy Bill Gosso. And myself. We were loaded and breezed through the season and the District Tournament and were scheduled to play Navajo Mission our

---

[5] Most New Mexicans may not recall that Raton and Dawson were coal mining towns in the 20s, 30s and 40s. Another bit of evidence that mining and oil produced some pretty good hard-nosed football players.

first game. Now here was a group of short Indians that played on a <u>dirt court</u>. We took one look at them warming up and I told my teammates 'We're goin' to kill these guys.' Well, believe it or not, those little guys beat us! And, Capitan won the State Tournament and we waxed those guys earlier. I think we all learned a valuable lesson that day," Bill concluded. Numerous Bulldog teams learned the lesson of over confidence, invaluable in later life.

Samuel C. (Sam) Hicks, Jr., '41, was both an artist and a musician. He graduated from UNM with a B.A. in Art and the Julliard School of Music in New York. While at AHS Sam was a member of the Albuquerque Civic Symphony. He served in World War II in Europe with the 92nd Infantry Division and was recalled during the Vietnam war. After his retirement from military service Sam utilized his artistic talents as an illustrator for several companies.

Elsa Marie Olson (Neuman), who graduated from AHS in 1941, and this writer share a great deal in common. Both of our fathers were Swedish immigrants coming to America in the same year 1905. Her parents moved to New Mexico from Wisconsin and Elsa and her husband Bert Paul Neuman were married at St. Paul's Lutheran Church in Albuquerque, as was this writer and his spouse. Elsa served in the WAVES in World War II and obtained both her Masters and Doctorate degrees at UNM. Her entire business career was devoted to teaching in the Albuquerque Public School System and she has been recognized in Who's Who in American Women.

William S. (Bill) Horabin, like so many of his 1941 classmates, enlisted in the U.S. Army immediately after graduating from AHS. Despite the fact that he was not a member of the New Mexico National Guard, Bill found himself along with many of his fellow AHS classmates and New Mexicans in the Philippines early in World War II. His 200th Coast Artillery Unit along with the New Mexico Guard and others were taken prisoners in the spring of 1942. Bill survived the brutal Bataan Death March and 26 months of incarceration and bravely escaped from prison camp. After returning home after the War, Bill remained very active in local chapters of the American Ex-Prisoners of War.

The onset of World War II was obviously a shock to the

Nation but to Glen O. Ream and the Board of Education it must have been expected.

Amongst a treasure trove of memorabilia is a picture taken circa 1942 showing a number of AHS students disembarking from a TWA DC-3 that featured the inscription "THE LINDBERG LINE" on its fuselage. Under the photo is a very telling notation:

> *Our War classes began two years before the United States declared war. The aviation, machine, and commercial classes were started. At present our classes are going 24 hours daily—night classes being held for people outside of school.*
>
> *So, War courses are not new to the minds of Albuquerque High School.*

Then in one of the most humorous, tongue-in-cheek pieces ever imagined, a purported teacher wrote to Miss Dixon, the Assistant Principal, about the deplorable conditions at AHS during the War. Miss Dixon was at home nursing a broken foot when this letter arrived. This writer suspects that Doc Harrington's fingerprints are all over this letter but no one can confirm its source. Unfortunately, this masterpiece is cut off in mid-sentence and the balance is lost to posterity.

> *November--1st week*

Dear Miss Dixon:

> *I am an old soldier in the battle for education. I have labored long in the vineyard at the corner of Broadway and Central. If any students sought knowledge, I gave them some if I had it and there was not too much trouble attached. I have always protected the furniture in 221, insisting that any and all furniture breaking should be done only under my personal supervision. I have always been aggressively in front in movements designed to promote such fundamentals of American life as the "long noon hour", the "full dinner pail", "two chickens in every pot", "the siesta", "the Townsend plan" and the "Progressive school". Being such a staunch, stalwart, militant, upright, aggressive advancer of the American way of life I naturally am sorely grieved about the conditions at the Albuquerque*

High School. I feel that the facts concerning this social, moral, and intellectual decline have been withheld from you or you would have arisen, ere now, and tramped down there to set all aright. Loath as I am to become an informer I must do so in the name of humanity and F.D.R. here are a few of the things that are going on:

A serious moral condition has been brought on by the war. Mr. Williams is the worst offender. He never thinks of beginning a class without the presentation of a floor show. He now teaches ball room dancing instead of composition and rhetoric. His students can no longer spell, let alone read and write but they are experts on the Conga, rhumba, bunny-hug, carioca, and the Jersey bounce. In this nefarious work Mr. W. has obtained the enthusiastic help and personal assistance of Mr. Pierce and the dancing team form the Ladies of the Church adjacent to the campus. Mr. Cristy and Mr. Maxsom were heard practicing the "calls" for the square dance to the tunes of Turkey in the Straw and the Arkansas Traveler. These last two mentioned gentlemen have also taken their students on a tour of the Buckhorn and Blue Ribbon Beer Gardens and it is rumored that they are secretly preparing a course in bar tending.

The Commercial department has adopted new methods. Miss Kieke never appears before 10:30 A.M. and only then three days a week. She is teaching classes in W.P.A. demanding the standards of at least 30 mistakes per minute with strike overs and erasures thrown in. She always beats the children out of the room at the bell,—usually by at least 15 minutes. Her home room contains a large sign saying "never do today what you can put off until tomorrow". She often bars her door and refuses a duo to the hot music. On entering I was shocked to see a crap game in session. The clicking of the dice was almost deafening. A well equipped gambling salon was in full operation. Miss Hendricks had the dice as I entered. She was blowing on them and informing them that "baby needs a new *pair of shoes". I guess it was the truth too because she had just lost her shoes in the game. I saw the shoes in front of Miss Goddard who had won them on the preceding throw of the dice. Miss Goddard was saying: "Roll them bones! I'll fade you." In the southeast corner there was a roulette wheel made by Mr. Sanchez and Mr. Pierce in their aeronautics classes. It is rumored that an electrical-radio control system was put in by Mr. Maxsom so that the operator can control the winning numbers. I guess this is correct because Miss Truesdell had been working out a "system" in her Algebra IIb classes. Her system had been perfected and tested and now she had lost all her money backing it. She kept muttering: "That *__!__*__!__*outfit is crooked!" Miss Childer kept raking in the chips as she hissed: "There is no system that can beat roulette!" Miss Johnson had been more fortunate in bucking Mr. Ferguson's "black jack" game up in the art room. In fact she had busted the bank and Mr. Ferguson had to go home in a barrel to get more money. Admiring onlookers had intimated that Miss Johnson had marked the cards but I doubt this. I think she just carried the extra aces in her sleeves instead. Miss Hickman and Miss Keleher were going to take over the game and run it. They had just cleaned Mr. Tate out in the...*

The 1943 Track Team Coached by Charlie Renfro repeated as state champs. Bill Pegue recalled that he placed second in the high hurdles but Louie Lutich won the lows. Bub Johnson again won the discus.

After three years where the Bulldogs didn't have a state champion in tennis Stanley Potts won the singles title in 1943. Harold Smith, Stan's teammate, was runner-up but he teamed with Bill Caldwell to win the doubles championship. AHS fared much better in golf as Hugh Cooper, Jr., was state champ in 1942, Bart Kinney in 1943 and Roy Chavira in 1944.

From an article that apparently appeared in *The Record* in 1942, by an unknown writer, we know that AHS had formed a Ski Club. Excerpts from two articles are fun reading. Attending a meet at Aqua Piedra near Taos the reporter described in hyperbole a trail called "Downfall:"

> The Taos and Las Vegas skiers told of a hill so steep that it was impossible to turn on it. Also, it possessed a grade equal to suicide hill, three times as long, and half as wide. No one has ever been timed on it...for no one has ever finished it...visions of trees covered in blood and bodies piled at the bottom of the downfall ran through each skier's mind.

Despite the treacherous challenge apparently all the AHS participants survived. The boys competing were Don Charles, Edgar Rawls, Joe Mullings, Bob Iden, Foster Murphy, Marion Dargan, Bob Pegue and Bill Cletsoway. The girls were Betty Benton, Priscilla Newcomb and Joan Koch. The writer states that, "the very top skier AHS has to offer is Don Charles," of Gale Martin he says, "this petite miss has long been known to be one of the best woman skiers in the southwest." Foster Murphy must have left his mark also. A trail at La Madera (now Sandia Peak) has carried his name for 60 years, as you will soon discover.

Golf, tennis, skiing, wrestling, boxing and some other activities were called "minor sports" in those days. Who would have predicted then that these sports would not only warrant front page they would breed millionaires within twenty years?

The Class of 1942 also produced a young lady who rose to the top of her craft as a stage and film star. Jan Krampner (bluewombat@earthlink.net) is currently writing a book on this actress' life as "Bulldogs Forever" is also in process. The author would like to hear from Patricia Reid's classmates and friends. At this writer's request Jan wrote:

> Kim Stanley (Patricia Reid) AHS`42 was one of the greatest stage actresses of her generation. She starred on Broadway in *Picnic* (1953), Horton Foote's *The Traveling Lady* (1954), William Inge's *Bus Stop* (1955), Eugene O'Neill's *A Touch of the Poet* (1955), and Chekhov's *The Three Sisters* (1964). An acolyte of the Actor's Studio and its "method" style of acting, she was renowned for the incandescent intensity of her performances. The leading lady of 1950s live

television drama, she also starred in several films including "Seance on a Wet Afternoon" (1964). The daughter of UNM Profession J. T. "Pop" Reid, her career was cut short by drinking and personal problems.

John Porter Bloom entered military service soon after graduation in 1942 and completed his B.A. degree in Inter-American Affairs in 1947 at UNM. Focusing on U.S. History John received his M.A. from George Washington University and his Ph.D from Emory University. History would become John's life interest and he became an authority on the Western U.S., publishing "The American Territorial System" and "The Territorial Papers of the U.S." serving as Editor of the "Treaty of Guadalupe Hidalgo" for the Dona Ana County Historical Society, referenced in Chapter One. John is listed in Who's Who in America. John clearly acknowledged and recognized the uniqueness of our southwestern culture.

Jack Redman was as prominent as his Junior and Senior Class President (1942) as he would later become as an Albuquerque physician. Jack joined the U.S. Navy during World War II, was in the Navy Medical Corps during the Korean War, and was a volunteer physician during the Vietnam War. Approximately 3,000 babies came into the world delivered by Dr. Redman, but to many he was known as "the Sherlock Holmes of skin cancer." Dr. Jack founded the New Mexico Skin Cancer Project in 1977 and often politely accosted strangers in public and examined them with a magnifying glass for tell-tale signs of melanoma. Dr. Redman was one of the first doctors to link exposure to the sun and melanoma.

Carl Arvid Olson's sister Elsa (cited earlier) preceded him at AHS two years prior to his class of 1943. While Elsa was serving as a WAVE during World War II, Carl was an Ensign in the Navy in the Pacific Theater. After the War Carl returned to Albuquerque and graduated from UNM with a degree in Civil Engineering. Carl was employed during his entire working career by Robert McKee Engineering. One of Carl's most interesting jobs was working as a Operations Manager of the National Test Site in Nevada.

Georgia (Chval) Otero, '43, is indeed, a lady of many talents. After receiving her R.N. degree in 1946 she worked as a Registered Nurse before marrying Meliton (Mel) Otero, also an AHS grad, who is prominently mentioned above. The Oteros raised seven children but Georgia found time to become very active in politics working as a staff volunteer for Democratic aspirants such as Tom Morris, Gene Lusk, Jerry Apodaca, Joe Skeen and others. Georgia and Mel also operated a successful Dairy Queen franchise which she proudly recalled when she received the Eldred Harrington Award during the Millennium Celebration, "I flipped many a burger and made one beautiful banana split."

John Max Shirley, who lettered in both basketball and baseball while at AHS and graduated in 1943, would, after receiving both Bachelor of Arts and Masters degrees from UNM, become the father of adult and junior recreation for Albuquerque and Bernalillo County. "Nearly 10,000 people took part in softball, semi-pro baseball and basketball leagues at APS gyms and fields during off-hours," Max recalled in an interview with Carlos Salazar, Albuquerque's long-time sports writer. Max, who was a sergeant in the Army and was involved in the Iwo Jima campaign during World War II, also organized the Albuquerque Athletic Association which was the percussor to the Albuquerque Sports Hall of Fame. Max, who later earned his Ph.D from Northern Colorado, is remembered appreciably by this writer as a tireless worker dedicated to the development of Albuquerque's youth, of which I was just one.

Another student whose interest in art and more specifically the Taos artists must have been stimulated by Principal Glen O. Ream's collection (displayed in our hallowed halls) was Dorothy Skousen, '43. Dorothy taught her love of art in the Albuquerque Public School System for 35 years. Her Master's Thesis "Taos as an Art Colony" (1978), has often been used as a source for several books about Taos painters. Dorothy also served on the boards of the UNM Fine Arts Alumnae Chapter and the New Mexico Route 66 Memorial Monument and Museum Committee.

The 1942 and 1943 Championship Baseball teams also featured a dominating pitcher, Carl Boyer who, in the `43 Bulldog semi-finals game against Clovis, struck out 14 of a total of 27 outs in that game. The Bulldogs also featured two other aces on the mound. Jim "Toodles" Roberts was a fire baller and Martin Zamora absolutely baffled the opposing batsmen with his array of curve-balls and assorted junk. So dominating were the Dawgs in `42 and `43 that Jim can not recall that the team lost a single game. Jim indicated that one press account reported that he held the longest number of innings without giving up a hit in the State Tournament. Other members of these sterling teams were:

Marvin Boyer	Rex Miller
Con Chambers	Henry Pedroza
Ralph French	Tilden Pond
Dale Guest	James Roberts
Kelly Hallman	Ned Ross
Frank Martin	Johnny Sanchez
Phil Martinez	Max Shirley
Bill Miller	Theron Smith
	Martin Zamora

Bob Mikkelson also starred on the State Championship baseball team of 1944. Playing first base, Bob had a sparkling .406 average about the same time as Ted Williams exceeded that magic .400 number. Bob fondly recalls his teammate Bill Gosso, whose distinctive laugh still echoes across their field of dreams.

"Bill was a heckofa ballplayer but he was also a real 'nut.' He's the only guy I knew that spent five years at AHS."

This writer remembers Bill as a cigar-chomping salesman at one of the sporting goods stores. Bill didn't really care if he sold you anything. He just wanted to talk sports. Bob was accurate in his assessment. Bill was a character.

Destined to be a pilot when he started taking flying lessons at the age of 14, Russell T. (Tom) Dawe made a career out of aviation. Tom, '44, was an airplane mechanic long before he captained a 747 for United Airlines on international flights. While attending classes at AHS Tom could disassemble and reassemble an airplane engine, and often reflected back upon the hours he enjoyed in the Manual Arts Building. After a short stint in the Army Air Corps near the end of World War II, Tom taught aviation classes at Highlands Uni-

81

versity before joining United in 1953. He served 33 years with United and was Chairman of United's Airline Pilots Association. Tom considered himself a success because he made a living pursuing his passion — A message that he communicated to young people who were trying to discover their career path.

Few graduates, boys or girls, would enjoy such a multi-faceted and diverse lifetime of experiences as Lou Ann (Graham) Jones, '44. She enrolled at the Regina School of Nursing after graduation from AHS, then completed her B.A. at UNM where she majored in Physical Education and minored in Music. Lou Ann then went on to receive her M.A. in Theatre Arts at the University of Nebraska, which eventually led her to San Francisco, where she founded "The Young Conservatory of the American Conservatory Theatre" as well as "The San Francisco Attic Theatre." Lou Ann wore many hats. She was an administrator, teacher, director, script writer and actor and lists a number of TV and film roles to her list of credits. Form the mid-80s to the mid-90s while living in the south of France, Lou Ann directed and acted in "Murder Mystery Weekends" in grand hotels throughout Europe. She also worked for Berlitz teaching English as a second language.

Few people in the military rise from the rank of Private to General, but 1945 grad John K. Davis accomplished that rare feat. In fact, at the completion of forty years in military service John retired as Assistant Commandant of the U.S. Marine Corps. After a school hitch as an enlisted man at the end of World War II, John took advantage of the G.I. Bill, as many servicemen did, and enrolled at UNM. When the Korean War started John rejoined the Marines as a Second Lieutenant and he became a naval aviator in 1954. During his long, meritorious career, John flew more than 30 different aircraft, 285 combat hours and 171 combat missions. Upon his retirement he continued to serve his fellow servicemen as President of the Marine Corps Association and numerous other related groups.

Most memorable during the mid-Forties however was a kid diametrically opposite to the comedic figure of Bill Gosso by the name of Bruce Ackerson.

Tall, broad-shouldered, muscular with sharp handsome features and a raw athletic talent, he looked like "Little Abner" (who wasn't by any stretch, little) to Bob. To Jim Hulsman, if Bruce would have worn tights and a cape with an "S" on his chest, he would have been a living, breathing replica of "Superman." Bruce possessed the strength to win the state discus throw in 1944 and the speed (of a bullet) to run a leg on the winning 880 yard relay team with Bub Henry, Roy Dunlap and Lucio Valdez. What followed after graduation was even more noteworthy.

Bruce enlisted in the military service near the end of the War. He returned to Albuquerque and played football at UNM in 1945 and played in the Harbor Bowl on January 1, 1946. He then transferred to the U.S. Military Academy where he played on Army's national championship team. Against Michigan in 1950, the Associated Press named him "Player of the Week." Numerous AHS titans flourished at West Point.

This writer had the privilege of being a student during 1945 graduate Mary Lou McCollum's (Heaphy) first year of teaching. The year was 1950. The school was Washington Junior High. Unfortunately the APS system lost an excellent teacher the following year. Mary Lou married and was terminated when she became pregnant as a result of one of the few archaic and onerous policy mandates of the day, that prevented pregnant women from teaching. Students from that era may not recall that policy. Contemporary students and teachers probably never ascertained why a large number of teachers remained single during their career.

Mary Lou's disappointment must have somewhat motivated her to excellence. She became a writer, public speaker and a mother of six children while finding time to serve numerous civic and non-profit organizations as an officer and fund raiser.

Shirley Mount (Hufstedler) '45, was a pathfinder. She opened doors in a profession where few women dared to tread. A graduate of UNM, Shirley received her law degree from Stanford University and she was a member of the first Editorial Board of the Stanford Law Review and was the Article and Book Editor. She was admitted to the California

State Bar and joined the firm of Beardsley, Hufstedler and Kemble and later married Seth Hufstedler, a partner in the firm. Shirley became involved as legal counsel to the California Attorney General in connection with the Colorado River litigation, which at the time of this writing has become a critical issue for the State of California. Shirley served as Judge of the Superior Court of California and in 1966 was the Featured speaker at the AHS Commencement.

A 1945 graduate of AHS, Herbert G. Koogle, founded one of the foremost engineering firms in the southwest, Koogle & Pauls Engineering, Inc. His company pioneered the use of photogrammetry and digital terrain mapping and was responsible for mapping approximately 200 square miles in and around Albuquerque. Herbert became President of the National Society of Professional Engineers and has been a member of numerous professional groups. He has also served two terms as President of the Board of Trustees for the New Mexico Symphony Orchestra and has participated in United Fund drives. Herb is a Past-President of the Rotary Club of Albuquerque.

Robert Books, better known to his 1945 classmates as "Moe," also had the good fortune to graduate just prior to the end of World War II, and enlisted in the U.S. Navy Air Corps. Moe starred as a distance runner on the AHS State Championship Track Team in 1944 and 1945. After his tour of duty in the Navy, Moe attended UNM where he also lettered in track. After he married Barbara Gere, '47, Moe received his degree in dentistry from the Kansas City Dental College in 1960. He has practiced Dentistry his entire career in Albuquerque. Many of us that know Moe well speculate that this man of good humor missed his true calling, as a dead-pan, stand-up comedian.

CHAPTER FIVE:
THE GOLDEN YEARS
1946-1951

JACK RUSHING, WHO WILL BE PROMINENTLY PORTRAYED in this and succeeding chapters, says later that, "The Fifties were the Golden Era of Coaching."

Jack would have also included the 1946-50 post-War period in this assessment, but the end of World War II also marked the beginning of a golden era in American society. It was a period that this writer believes ended with the assassination of John F. Kennedy in 1963 which is often marked as "the death of the age of innocence."

Yes, the taboos of adultery, homosexuality, illegitimacy, alcoholism, divorce and racism tarnished the golden image, but these issues weren't discussed in our presence at home or at school. We were the innocents. Our days at AHS were simple and fun, unburdened by the unsavory.

The 1945-46 school year showcased perhaps the most outstanding all-around athlete since Owen Smaulding. John Henry (Jack) Madden did it all. He was an outstanding end on the Bulldog football team and forward on Tony Wilson's State Champion Basketball team in 1946. But, it was track and field where Jack excelled the most, where he could run the sprints as well as the mile run. He amassed a total of 29 points himself in the State Track Meet in 1945 when he won the 880 run in 2:09.6, the high hurdles in 16.0, the broad jump with a mark of 19'8½", and the high jump at 5'7". He also placed fifth in the grueling 440 yard dash. Fletcher Thompson, who had the physique and strength of Charles Atlas, won the shot put and discus. Roy Dunlap won gold medals in the 100 and 200 yard dash, as we referred to this event in those days. The Bulldogs won the State Track title four consecutive years, three while Madden was at AHS.

Coach Wilson must have felt that he had been blessed with an abundance of speed on the same team when Gwinn (Bub) Henry tied the State record in the 100 yard dash at 10.2 seconds as a sophomore. Bub's fleetness of foot was in his genes. His father, Gwinn Sr., was reported to be "the fastest man in the world" in the Jim Thorpe era. A broken leg compounded with a steel plate prevented him from reaching his full potential, but Bub articulates our legacy in part woven into the tapestry of our history when he said:

Albuquerque High School during my years as a student was the single public high school in our community. It had a multitude of races and cultures. Kids from all areas of the community. Five Points, Martineztown, Barelas and Nob Hill, altogether, professing to be Bulldogs...whether rich, poor, black or white. We had good times together. We were truly the last of the all-Albuquerque generation.

This writer recalls Bub working out with our track teams in the Fifties trying to stay in shape while lamenting, as many of us did, how injuries frustrated our dreams.

Jack Madden recalls his first track meet as a sophomore against the Albuquerque Indian School. Preparing to run his first competitive race in the 880 yard run, Coach Wilson instructed his young, eager but nervous, protege:

"Stay right behind that kid there. He's their best runner. Stay behind him and you'll finish second."

Jack, following his Coach's mandate, followed closely on the Indian's heels. Jack thought to himself, "I can pass this guy. What will Coach say if I pass him?" His competitive instinct motivated the inexperienced runner to pass the leader. Jack won. Coach Wilson? Didn't say a word.

Jack attended the University of New Mexico for two years and ran a very respectable 1:58 one-half mile under the tutiledge of the uncompromising Roy (Ironhead) Johnson.

Another teammate of Jack and Bub was S. Y. "Tony" Jackson. The 185-pound quarterback considered oversized for his position was the smallest man in the AHS backfield. Gilbert Wenk at a reported 280 pounds was an awesome force at fullback and this Bulldog team was comparable in size to most college elevens.

S. Y. recalls from the 1945 season:

We went into the Roswell game undefeated and averaging about 45 points per game but there was no way those folks in Roswell were going to let us win. We rolled up over 400 yards in total offense and every time we got near the goal line we got penalized. On top of that, Madden leveled a guy with a good clean hit and Jack said to him, 'How did you like that?' The referee kicks him out of the game and later we lost 3 more guys! We lost 33-0! How can you have that much offense and not score? To top it off we had to stay in the worst and only motel in the town that would accept our Black players. But you know what? No one complained one bit. We were a team. There was absolutely no discrimination on our team. That's what I remember the most.

(As late as 1953 our AHS baseball team suffered the same fate in Clovis as you'll soon discover but fortunately with different results.)

Some of his classmates of 1946 called him Tony. Some called him S.Y. Some of his teachers called him Sherwood. He's Sherwood Young Jackson, Jr. Tony grew up in the laundry business, and for ten of his twenty-four years with Excelsior Laundry he was the Executive Vice-President. He successfully transitioned to banking and was Vice-President of Marketing and Corporate Business Development for the Bank of New Mexico for five years. He culminated his business career as the Executive Director of the UNM Foundation. Tony has been very active in the 20-30 Club, the Sandia and Albuquerque Kiwanis Clubs, Toastmasters International (President 2 years), UNM Booster Club (President 1969), the United Way, the Albuquerque Chamber of Commerce, Goodwill Industries, the Albuquerque Museum, the YMCA and the Albuquerque Public School Advisory Board. AHS students will remember that his father served on the APS Board of Education for many years. This three-sport AHS letterman certainly has earned his place in Bulldog lore.

This formidable football team had another defeat that

certainly could be labeled "questionable." It was Pete McDavid's last year as head coach of the Santa Fe Demons, and the Bulldogs held a thin margin as the game dwindled down to its last minutes. Only a desperation pass could possibly defeat the mighty Green and White.

Al Grubesic playing end on defense saw his counterpart "Cookie" Quintana jog off the field to the sidelines close but not out of bounds by his team's bench. The Dawgs assumed Cookie was out of the game. The Demons quarterback, Bob Sweeney, lofted a pass towards the sideline. Quintana, all alone, a foot in bounds, gathered in the pigskin and scampered untouched into the end zone. The trick play crafted by the imaginative McDavid must have scored big in Albuquerque. Pete McDavid was hired by AHS for the next season and a few years later UNM hired quarterback Sweeney as their head basketball coach.

All-Stars selected from this 1945 team included S.Y., Al Grubesic and Gilbert Wenk. These three were joined by Clem Charlton, Charles (Duke) Natress and John Giannini who missed their opportunity to play in an All-Star game due to the cancellation of the event during World War II from 1942 to 1945.

The 1945 baseball team not only won the State Tournament, it had an exceptional pitcher and an unusual coach. Tony Wilson, probably overwhelmed by coaching four sports, named Bill Gosso as the team's coach while he was still a student at AHS. Bill, as mentioned earlier, was ineligible as a player and was having difficulty finding home plate when it came to his diploma. Tony recognized that Bill had a great baseball mind but one that couldn't score in the classroom.

Dick Davidson was a rare, raw talent. In the title game against the Santa Fe Indian School, which had an exceptional baseball program, Dickie struck out, incredibly, 22 batters. Only five outs were made other than by strike out in the 23-5 victory. I speculated with Bob Lalicker, who was manning second base in that game, that Dickie could have been so overpowering with his fastball that there must have been a number of passed balls on the catcher plus a few walks in order for Santa Fe to score five runs.

During the 50th reunion of the Class of 1953, the AHS

Alumni Lettermen's Association, especially acknowledged the feats of this 1945 team. Matt Schulick, who was Davidson's catcher all season and had the pleasure of being on the receiving end of Dick's masterful pitching performance in the Championship game, sat next to me at this breakfast.

"How in the world did Santa Fe score five runs when they obviously couldn't see the ball?" I asked Matt.

"I hada 'rag tag' clove. Hada buy your own, ya know? It wasn't very good and Dickie's fastball and curveball had so much movement I hada tough time hanging on," Matt replied.

I asked Dick the same question.

"Oh heck. They gotta couple guys on early in the game and this guy hits a home run. Couldn't believe it. It made me so mad as h.... I made sure that didn't happen again," Dick said, still feisty and competitive as he spoke of that spectacular day almost 60 years prior.

"Did you ever lose a game at AHS?" I asked the silver-haired man who looked like he could still throw a pretty mean fastball.

"Don't think so. If I would've I'da been devastated," Dick replied.

In addition to his prowess on the mound Dick, as a quarterback, threw a pretty accurate football also. In addition he was All-District III when the Bulldogs placed third in the State Basketball Tournament.

Another member of the `45 team, outfielder Al Grubesic, recalls that this stellar team also won the American Legion State Championship title during the summer. The four state regional playoffs were held in Austin, Texas. It was August 1945. Just prior to the team's departure to the University of Texas stadium for their first game, the nation and the world learned that the War with Japan was over. People poured out into the streets wildly celebrating the American and Allied victory. The Bulldogs and their bus were trapped in the melee. The team had to walk several miles to the stadium loaded down with their equipment.

Unfortunately, the Bulldogs couldn't continue their winning season—one of the best in AHS baseball history. For Al, however, that day was both memorable for its historic impact as well as the fact that he hit a triple and a double. Al also paid tribute to the team's sponsor, Otto Beck. Otto was the franchisee in Albuquerque for Coca Cola and many of the players worked in the plant during the summer. Their pay? About $.25/hour!

Bob Lalicker was also a member of the 1946 team that won the State tourney. I asked Bob:

"Why was AHS so dominant in baseball in the 40s?"

"A couple of reasons, I think. One, all of us played American Legion ball all summer and there were a number of great teams in Albuquerque. Another reason possibly, the southern New Mexico schools didn't play baseball. We only played about seventeen games a year. We had to take a trip to Tucson to get some stiff competition," Bob opined.

No 'bout a doubt it. The American Legion was not only responsible for sponsoring summer baseball, the Veteran's group was also responsible for the Western States Ski Championships that will be chronicled later. At age ten this writer was a bat boy for an American Legion team in Wisconsin, which unquestionably piqued my interest in the sport and opened the door to my success. Little did I know that I was following in the formidable footsteps of Carl Boyer and Dick Davidson as a "fire baller." I wish I had known in 1953 what I know today of our past heroes.

During this same breakfast meeting, Jim Hulsman, a great baseball player as well as coach, made an astute and humorous observation which echoed Bob Lalicker's earlier comment:

"The American Legion Summer League was the farm system for AHS. The Bulldogs got to pick the best players. The rest went to St. Mary's!"

Herbie Hughes, the keynote speaker at this same event, paid a tribute to Jim, his friend and his coach. One, to Hulsman for fixing him up with dates, and to Jack Rushing his coach who, Herb said, "had an amazing commitment to anyone who wanted to play."

Blasting a 3-0 pitch that would have been a home run on a field without a fence, Coach Rushing grabbed Herb as he reached first base and held him there.

"That's for not taking a 3-0 pitch," his coach and mentor

admonished Herb.

There was a message in Coach Rushing's unorthodox methods, and like most of us who played for this man, we heard it loud and clear.

The 1946 AHS Championship Basketball team was promoted by Carlos Salazar, a sportswriter for the *Albuquerque Tribune*, as "the tallest in the nation." They were also the winningest in AHS history at 29 and 5. Somewhat hyper-extended in measurement, the team consisted of: Glen Harry 6'9", Milton Mikkelson (Bob's brother) 6'6", Ed Tixier 6'4", Jack Madden 6' 3", David Ackerson (Bruce's brother) 6'2", and Richard Stockton, S. Y. Jackson, and Paul White who were at 6'0". Ralph Duran was probably the only player under 6'0". Jack Madden, who was the team's leading scorer for two years at about 12 points per game, recalled several notable events from the past.

"Ed Tixier was our 'horse.' I remember a game against Gallup when he had 27 out of our team's 31 points. The ceiling was so low we couldn't even lob a pass into our tall guys! And, at Fort Summer, Ed had so much speed on a drive to the basket that his momentum carried him into the door and out into the parking lot. He did a swan dive into the darkness and came back into the gym covered in mud and snow. In `46 we played Forrest — that little town near Clovis — for the State Championship and won. They had only seven guys on their team." (Our AHS team played a very memorable game against the same upstart team of Forrest in 1953 which is chronicled later with less favorable results.)

After a thorough blistering of the Clovis Wildcats by this marvelous Bulldog team that toiled together like a well-oiled machine, a local Clovis sportswriter wrote, "...in addition to the best talent ever seen here, the Bulldogs exhibited the best sportsmanship." Tony Wilson's team of 1946 not only won the State Championship, they won with character and class — A Bulldog trait fostered through the years by tough taskmasters who expected no less from their kids and whose mentorship served all of their legions well for a lifetime. Without exception, every athlete and student interviewed acknowledges the influential role that their AHS experience played in their life. This book is also a tribute to their coach's and teacher's devotion to their life's work.

Another member of this esteemed group that graduated in 1946 was Paul (Pablo) White. Paul, born in the wind-swept plains in ranching country near Thomas, New Mexico, unfortunately lost his father when he was only six years of age. Paul and his mother along with five siblings moved to Clayton, New Mexico, in her attempt to support their family. Paul describes their hardscrabble existence in a book soon to be published entitled *13th Disciple* which is a tribute to his mother. He can vividly recall eating young thistles and lamb-squarters (a spinach-like green weed) for sustenance.

Fortunately, the family moved to Albuquerque where Paul was able to attend AHS, where he made All-City and All-State on the `46 Championship team and graduated from the University of New Mexico. Pablo, who married Jeannie Jernigan (the 1953 Miss New Mexico from Hobbs) began a career in the oil business as a roughneck and rose through the ranks to become a Vice-President of a major oil company. He writes of his rough and tumble early years in the oil fields in his book *Blossoms of Steel*. Like so many kids that grew up in this era in poverty without government assistance, they managed to survive and succeed. They, like most of us, were children whose parents suffered through The Great Depression, and their experience fostered independence and self-reliance. Pablo firmly believes that his AHS experience gave him "the spring in his step" that propelled him to success. In particular, he cites Tony Valdez as his mentor. "Tony was the most communicative and patient person I ever knew. No matter what you wanted to know Tony was there to help me." This writer can second that. Tony was one of my favorite people.

Given the dominance of this 1946 team, it is amazing that only S.Y. and Paul were singled out for various all-team selections that year. The 1945 team had Charles Weeks, Dick Davidson and Roy Dunlap selected for special recognition and Ed Tixier, Jerry Romney and Ralph Duran were named to various all-star teams in 1947. That fact is possibly a testimony to the teams diversity of talent and on any night anyone could shine.

In addition to Jack Madden's continued dominance,

1946 produced a double gold medal winner in the State Track and Field Championship meet in which the Bulldogs were victorious. Ben Turner won both the 100 and 200 yard sprints. Ironically, it would take another nine years until AHS produced another two-time gold medal winner. Bob Schnurr, my friend and teammate both in high school and college won both hurdle events in 1955.

Another gold medal winner at this meet was the 440 yard relay team anchored by Ben. On that team was a freshman by the name of Warren Woods, who went on to become a four year letterman in track and only one of two athletes ever to accomplish that feat at AHS. How did that happen?

Only old-timers will recall that the Bulldogs conducted spring football drills and invited ninth graders from the junior highs to participate. Hundreds of young aspirants attended "spring practice." Coach Wilson called for the athletes to run wind sprints of 100 yards. Warren beat all the upper classmen and the freshman. After the workout Coach Wilson said:

"Warren? I want you to report this week to Zimmerman Field. You're on the track team."

Ecstatic, Warren complied. He made the relay team. The Bulldog foursome won the District Meet and the State Meet and Warren was awarded his letter. A rare accomplishment.

There was a sad footnote however to this story. The other relay team members, in addition to Ben and Warren, were Bub Henry and Buddy Gallegos. Shortly after the State meet Buddy was killed when he attempted to pour gasoline into the carburetor of his car after it had stalled.

P. G. Cornish, III, was not only a Co-Captain and All-Star center on the 1946 football team, he starred and lettered on the basketball, golf, baseball and ski teams. He earned five letters his senior year and a total of 11 "A"'s while at AHS. A remarkable feat. A goal that this writer hoped to achieve my senior year.

The 1946 football team was so talented that Joe Tisdale, who played fullback but didn't make the All-Star Team, later went on to the University of Southern California and played a prominent role in the 1953 Rose Bowl which game becomes noteworthy in Chapter Seven for reasons other than football.

Another multi-sport All-State athlete was Ed Tixier, who starred on both the football and basketball teams. The team however, was led by the stylistic open-field running of junior halfback Charles "Chuck" Hill who drew raves from all quarters including opponents. Ralph Bowyer, an opposing coach at Carlsbad High School, called Chuck, "the best high school football player I've ever seen."

The 1947 All-Star football team included in addition P.G. Cornish, Ed Hart, Bob Wadlington, Earl Cook and Wayne McCarty.

1946 also marked the inaugural State Boxing Championship which was won by the Bulldogs under Coach Tony Valdez. Remarkably, it was a fourteen year old freshman by the name of Rickey Stevens who provided the team's winning margin. The 108 pound Flyweight was a student at Washington Junior High and somehow (like Warren Woods earlier) was able to represent AHS and he proved to be "one of the smoothest boxers in the state," according to a newspaper article. Other Bulldog winners were Genaro Velarde (Gnat Weight), Edwin Sanchez (Bantamweight), Jeff Newbill (Middleweight) and Ed Tixier (Heavyweight).

The Bulldog boxing team won the state championship the next four years and went undefeated in 1948 and 1949. The 1950 team picture had no less than 39 competitors. For some unknown reason, the sport was discontinued in 1951. Rickey related a great story:

"We boxers were working out one day and I was paired with Tony Vigil. He was lighter than me and faster. When sparring he could really give me a good workout. We never hurt each other. I never tried to hit him too hard as I was larger than him. Coach Valdez also paired Richard Pyeatt and D. C. Coleman. Both were great athletes. D.C. Coleman was a born athlete. He traveled from first string football to number one on the boxing team. Pyeatt was no slouch, as he weighed 145 pounds and played first string football as a right guard. Pyeatt never knew what it meant to spar. He would come at D.C. as though he was going to kill him. D.C. decided that he would have to slow the little bugger down.

D.C. weighed about 160 pounds and was all man. So Pyeatt came toward D.C. throwing haymakers and D.C. leveled him with a left jab and a right cross to the chin. This slowed Pyeatt down. We all finished that round of boxing and went to the shower room. I asked Pyeatt how he was doing and he said fine. I said do you need a ride home as I had a car that day. He said "Yes but where am I?" The moral of the story is don't mess with Texas or with D.C. Coleman.

Tony Valdez was a well respected coach and father figure to all his boxers. We were all very close to him. His philosophy was "you may lose a match but not because you are out of condition." He never forgot any of us. I met him at the Country Club many years after I graduated. He came to our table and bought everyone a drink. I only ordered a Coke because when I was around Coach I always felt I should be in training.

Betty Sabo, one of the most celebrated AHS alums and unquestionably one of its heralded "free spirits," graduated in 1946. She readily admits to being insolent calling her art teacher, a balding Joe Ferguson, "Curly." Her spirit was tamed somewhat when she referred to Mr. Glen O. Ream by the same moniker.

"I beg your pardon, young lady!" Mr. Ream responded firmly, leaving no doubt that free spirits were not "fresh" in the principal's office.

Joe Ferguson was the consummate teacher for creative students. He taught the fundamentals and allowed his budding artists to explore any medium. A huge painting of Kilroy with his large schnozz draped over a fence adorned the classroom wall. For those who don't have a clue who Kilroy was, he was everywhere during the War. This comedic caricature was probably the origin of graffiti as he left his trademark "Kilroy was Here" on walls around the world.

In 1946, AHS expanded its campus north of the gym with surplus government barracks. They remained in use for many years. Glen O. Ream with his interest and devotion to art, set the tone for a healthy environment for artists. He changed the public's image of the artist as lazy, sex-crazed drug addicts to one that had to be nurtured and encouraged to pursue their dream. Betty was in a perfect place and allowed her as a teenager to recognize her calling.

Betty's friends were Camille Grantham, Barbara Ansorg, Margie Odle and Martha McCullough. The called their gang JUGS—just us girls. They went to lunch at the Alvarado every day. As the troop trains stopped and the soldiers took a break, they photographed themselves with the attractive and giggly teenagers. On one occasion after consuming Fred Harvey's famous blueberry pie, they discovered to their chagrin that their pearly white smiles were somewhat stained. Somewhere in America a WWII veteran has a photograph of an Albuquerque girl flashing a set of pearly blues.

Betty lived in a small modest home with four brothers and sisters, a grandmother, a mother and father, and an uncle and his wife. Meals were chaos. When Betty spent the night sleeping over at Martha's house it was to her like living in a castle and Martha was the princess. In one of life's strange twists, Camille Grantham would, many years later, become my cousin through marriage. Martha, too, would become a good friend and yes, she still is a princess.

I asked Betty, "Given your interest in art were you divorced from ordinary school life? What did you think of the school sports and traditions?" Surprisingly, Betty revealed: "Athletics seemed so right. It was the big thing then. Jack Madden, Bub Henry and the guys were our heroes. Winning games was very important to us girls too."

Most people, particularly today would think that there was little synergism or compatibility between both interests. Quite the contrary. To the surprise of many readers, one of this writer's favorite classes was also art, as you will discover in Chapter Six.

Albert L. (Al) Grubesic's family was reportedly one of the first from Croatia to settle in Albuquerque. With World War II over Al was able to attend college before he entered the U.S. Army. He enrolled at Riverside College in California prior to receiving a degree in Business Administration from UNM. After a short stint working for a home builder in Santa Fe, Al founded his own real estate brokerage firm and has enjoyed Santa Fe's growth for over 30 years. He served as a member of the Santa Fe City Council for four and one-half years as well as a Financial Advisory Board member for St.

Michael's High School. Al, returning to the game of baseball from his days at AHS when the Bulldogs were State Champs in 1945 and 1946, was active as a sponsor and Assistant Coach for various baseball leagues for Santa Fe youth.

Butterfield Personal Service Jewelers was founded in Pana, Illinois, in 1928 and its founder, Ernest B. Butterfield, brought his business and his family to Albuquerque in 1945. His son Bernie graduated from AHS one year later and was destined to carry on the family tradition as one of the City's most respected jewelers. At the time of this writing in 2003, the third generation of Mike Butterfield and Theresa Butterfield Moxey has continued not only the business which carries the family name, but serve the City in numerous civic endeavors. The always professional and accommodating Bernie sold this writer the wedding ring that has graced his bride's hand for 42 years.

Bruce Caird also graduated a year after World War II ended but served in the U.S. Army with the occupational force in Japan. He attended UNM for two and one-half years studying civil engineering, and left school to become a construction superintendent for the Dale Bellamah Companies as the home construction boom accelerated. In 1957 Bruce founded his own real estate firm which is now managed by two of his children. It was possibly the sale of the volcanos on the west mesa to the City of Albuquerque that was the most unique and high profile transaction in Bruce's career. He has also served the City on the Board of Governors of TVI and Goodwill Industries. Bruce was also a Past-President of the Lay Board of Doctors Osteopathic Hospital and was, for several years, a member of the City of Albuquerque's Board of Adjustment.

Despite the fact that Gwinn (Bub) Henry, III is mentioned above, special recognition needs to be allocated for this 1946 alum who, in 1964, received the Outstanding Graduate Award from AHS. In many respects Bub Henry's legacy to UNM is what Jim Hulsman's is to AHS. For 22 years Bub ran UNM's Student Union recreation and sports program and from 1968 to 1982 he served as UNM's Director of Alumni Relations. From 1982 to his retirement in 1990, this affable and ever enthusiastic Irishman was director of the Hodgin Hall restoration project and the Alumni Memorial Chapel on the UNM campus. During this period he created a pictorial chronology of the history of UNM athletics. Fittingly, Bub, along with numerous other well-deserved accolades, received the UNM Alumni Service Award. Bub and his wife Dona Lee have, five sons all of whom are carrying on the family tradition in sports.

Fern L. Guest (Hudson) was one of Glen O. Ream's office assistants who were the wily principal's "informants." Though most of her classmates will remember Fern as one of the majorettes, this 1946 grad's responsibility was to police Highland Pharmacy to report those students that were playing hookey sipping a cherry phosphate. As an Air Force wife, Fern lived in Japan, Canada, Okinawa as well as numerous locations in the U.S. She was always active in PTA, Air Force Family Services, Eastern Star, and the American Cancer Society (breast cancer survivor). In Orlando, Florida, Fern received a "Key to the City" for her community service. Amongst her cherished possessions is a book of cartoons drawn by none other than Glen O. Ream who was truly a man of many talents.

Like his fellow 1946 classmate, teammate and long-time friend Gwinn Bub Henry, Robert G. Lalicker devoted most of his working career at UNM during the school's explosive growth period from the Fifties to the Eighties. After graduating from UNM in 1950 Bob was commissioned as an Ensign in the U.S. Navy. He served during the Korean War and was awarded the Bronze Star for valor during combat. Bob returned to UNM after the War and received his Master's degree. In 1956 he began his career at UNM which included Director of Placement, Executive Director of the Alumni Association, Assistant to the President and Executive Director of the UNM Foundation. Bob received the Edna S. Fergusson Award in recognition of his distinguished service to UNM. In addition Bob has served the community of Albuquerque in many ways including the Chamber of Commerce, United Way, YMCA, March of Dimes, Red Cross, Boy Scouts of America and numerous other civic groups.

The 1946 AHS graduating class seemingly had a plethora of individuals who made an enormous contribution to the community that they loved. Rodney W. Shoemaker is another alum who richly deserved the Dr. Eldred (Doc) Harrington Award for distinguished service to his community. Most Duke City residents recall Rod's long term association as a Senior Executive with Albuquerque Federal Savings & Loan and involvement as Past-President of both the New Mexico Savings & Loan League and Albuquerque Mortgage Bankers Association. Rod has also contributed much of his time to UNM serving as Past-President of the UNM Alumni Association, the Albuquerque Alumni Chapter, UNM Foundation/Development Fund and the Lobo Club, of which he has been a member for over 50 years. He has served his community as President or Chairman of the United Way, Boys Club, March of Dimes, Manzano Senior Citizens Committee, Cerebral Palsy Telethon, YMCA and numerous other civic activities

The fact that Robert James Throckmorton ('46) earned his Doctorate of Education at the University of Southern California would in itself merit this teacher's inclusion amongst the most distinguished AHS alums. This accomplishment, however, was achieved after Robert was severely injured in an auto accident that rendered him a quadriplegic. In a feature article that appeared in the *Las Vegas Times*, someone asked Robert how he felt being in a wheel chair. His reply? "It wasn't bad since it spares me listening to sob stories about people's minor problems." "Robert's ability to laugh at life's inequities has been one measure of his strength," wrote Michael Vitto, the Times reporter. And, it should be added, strength to thousands of others that are faced with the same dilemma every year.

1947 ushered in the coaching era of Paul (Pete) McDavid, who came to AHS from Santa Fe High School after a successful athletic career at UNM. In his first year his football team was the State undisputed champion going undefeated within New Mexico. The team's only loss was to Phoenix High School 27 to 20. Pete was blessed with some very talented athletes.

Sportswriter and statisticians began keeping records about this time. In two years as an All-Stater, Chuck Hill rushed for 2,624 yards at an average carry of 9.048 yards.

During his senior year in 1947 he scored a State record 147 points and 24 touchdowns, while college recruiters were constantly buzzing around Broadway and Central. In addition, he was an outstanding baseball player on Jack Rushing's State Championship Team of 1948 and many said that Chuck could have played pro ball. He didn't and went on to complete an outstanding record in both sports at UNM and was inducted into the school's Hall of Honor. Chuck is remembered fondly in this memoir as a true hero by his teammates and those of us that followed in the Fifties, but one incident was humbling to the superhero.

Given all the accolades from students, parents, sportswriters and even opponents, it was understandable that Chuck, as down to earth a guy that he was, got a case of the "big head" according to a teammate. In one game Chuck made an offhand remark to his teammates about his indispensability. The linemen all missed their blocks on a couple of plays. Chuck got the message. There was no "I" in team.

Chuck did have a formidable supporting cast showcasing his talents as the tailback from an offense-oriented spread formation as well as the "T." The potent Bulldog attack was led by All-Staters and All-Stars D.C. Coleman (left end), Ken Carson (right tackle) and Herbie Hughes (quarterback/wingback). The team was blessed with two outstanding fullbacks, Roy Mounday and Bob Cooke, who both made the All-Star team along with Floyd Williams at guard and Phil McGahey at center.

Herbie Hughes recalls the blatant bigotry that continued in southeastern New Mexico, which cast a divisive pall on a game intended to foster good sportsmanship amongst rivals.

In Carlsbad, D. C. Coleman, Ken Carson and two other Black Bulldog players were forced to sleep on the school bus and private homes rather than the La Caverna Hotel when the team played the Cavemen. Ken Carson vividly recalls the taunts and threats against him and D.C. during the game.

It was the game scheduled with Roswell, however, that indelibly exposed the Black issue to the light of day.

J. D. Shinkle, the Superintendent of the Roswell School District, advised the Albuquerque administration against bringing the Bulldog Black athletes to Roswell "because of community threats." John Milne, the Albuquerque Superintendent, refused to play the game if the AHS Black athletes would not compete. Milne stated, "If we have to pay a forfeit fee for cancelling the game, we will gladly pay it." The coaches left the final decision to the players. They voted not to play if their Black teammates couldn't. The game was never played.

McDavid's 1947 team was probably as talented and as dominant as any team in AHS history, and Pete quite possibly knew that it would be necessary to play and beat another southeastern school in addition to Carlsbad in order to hope to claim the state championship. A game was scheduled with Hobbs, a burgeoning oil business community that enthusiastically supported its football team. Hobbs first agreed then cancelled the game in support of Roswell's position or pretense of "racial tensions."

John Milne was quoted in the Albuquerque papers as saying, "I don't know if there's anything more to say...we can't play them this year or any other year," The City of Albuquerque applauded Milne's stand. The undefeated Bulldogs claimed their right to the state crown but the south, as expected, considered it mythical.

In a current interview with Ken Carson, a key player in this true-to-life drama, he recalled:

Roswell probably figured that they couldn't beat us or had a better chance if D.C. and I didn't play. They used that threat against the four of us Black players as a ploy.

I asked Ken how the entire discrimination ordeal impacted him:

Actually it effected me more my junior year. We couldn't play at all in three games. I didn't even want to play my senior year but Coach Rushing told me that things would be different and convinced me to play. I wanted to go to UNM but Burl Huffman, the football coach, told me that since UNM was in the Border Conference I wouldn't be able to play so I went away to school.

"How were conditions in Albuquerque? Did you face discrimination there when you were in high school?"

Well, we couldn't go to the movies at the KIMO or the Sunshine. We could go to the Mesa Theater near 3rd and Central if we sat in the back. We couldn't sit at the lunch counter at Woolworths either. We could get a shake and take it out but we couldn't sit down and drink it inside the store. Yeah, there was discrimination in Albuquerque in the Forties but we tried not to put ourselves in situations where we would be rejected. That's what my parents told me. The only thing that really hurt me is that I wanted desperately to coach kids in Albuquerque. When I graduated from college there just weren't any jobs for Black coaches.

Ken's recollections are significant since they are in contrast with the generally perceived notion that discrimination only existed south of Highway 66.

Fortunately, segregation was making its last stand in southeastern New Mexico and our class of 1954 would see the walls of discrimination crumble during this historical setting event.

As an example and testimony to the strength of character of those who endured the bigotry of the southeastern New Mexico schools, D. C. Coleman became a Methodist Minister, and as of this writing is a Bishop in the Chicago area.

When he graduated from AHS in 1948 Kenneth J. Carson probably didn't grasp the significance that the Roswell Incident would have on interscholastic sports in the State of New Mexico a few years later. Handicapped with a speech impediment as well as near blindness in his right eye, this Black student overcame a raft of obstacles to be selected All-State and an All-Star football selection. In addition Ken was New Mexico State Discus Champion and AHS' best pentathlete as well as an outstanding boxer. During a career with the U.S. Postal Service, Ken was able to pursue his dream of coaching and working with youth groups. He helped organize a scout troop in the Kirtland Addition, was a PTA President at Lowell Elementary School, coached a City softball team and a Young American Football Team and was a coach, manager and Board member of Altamonte Little League Baseball. In 1992, Ken founded the Wise Men and Women

Mentorship Program for elementary and middle school high risk youth. Ken has been recognized for his contribution to his community receiving the NAACP Footprint Award, Omega Psi Fraternity Citizen of the Year Award, the Fifth Episcopal District A.M.E. Church Son's of Thunder Award, the NCNW, Inc. and Los Mujeras Award, the Albuquerque Human Rights Education Award, the Heroic Award, the Senior Hall of Fame Award and other well deserved accolades.

It was a rare occurrence that AHS would produce a couple of gems or gemologists within one year of each other and, additionally, each would succeed their fathers in the jewelry business. Coincidentally each would pass that business to a third generation. Bernie Butterfield, mentioned above, graduated in 1946. Donald Fogg graduated one year later and joined F. D. Fogg & Company which Don's father had established in Albuquerque in 1921. Don graduated from UNM in 1951 and served two years in the U.S. Army before joining the firm. He became President in 1969 and has been active in AHS activities and civic affairs all of his career.

Another grad who must have revelled in Doc Harrington's Physics class was H. George Oltman, Jr. George, who graduated from AHS in 1947 and UNM in 1950, became a research engineer primarily focused on the development of antennas for commercial and military applications. George holds eleven patents: four in vacuum tubes, microwave acoustics and light deflection, four on techniques for summing the powers of solid state sources, one in slotline couplers and two patents on mircostrip antennas. He has received the Lawrence A. Hyland Patent Award and has published more than 35 technical papers in his specialized field. He has been associated with Tecon Industries, Hughes Aircraft, TRW and Sandia Laboratories. It's quite possible that a significant portion of our present day advanced communication systems can be attributed to the genius of this AHS alum.

Peggy Piper, '47, devoted her entire career teaching in the Albuquerque Public Schools System. During the Millennium Celebration Peggy received the May Stirrat Klicker Award for her outstanding tutorship. Ironically, Peggy was not only a student of May's world history class at AHS, May

103

was Peggy's supervisor during her student teaching. Peggy, paying tribute to her former teacher, said May was "an excellent role model. She truly represents the 'best'." Peggy served the First Presbyterian Church as a Deacon/Elder and was a tutor for the Martineztown House of Neighborly Service.

Once in a decade or so we discover a giant among men. Ed Tixier, '47, was one of the few who fills those shoes. Although Ed was 6'4" and weighed 200 pounds while playing a dominant role in AHS and college athletics as chronicled above, it wasn't Ed's physical stature that made him tower above the crowd. It was his strength of character formed by his own high standards and personal values. Ed was starring at both basketball and football at West Point when the cribbing scandal created a dark cloud on the Hudson. When the authorities at the Academy learned that there was cheating on tests, all the cadets were interviewed. S. Y. Jackson, Ed's teammate at AHS recalled when they asked Ed if he was cheating, he said, "no." When he was asked if he was aware that cheating was taking place he answered, "yes." When Ed was asked to name those who were cheating, he replied, "I won't do it." The honor code at West Point required that Ed blow the whistle on his classmates. His core beliefs would not allow him to betray them. He left the Academy. A lesser man would have left the military but Ed joined the Air Force after participating in ROTC at UNM, and retired a three-star Lt. General. Ed's last tour of duty was Commander of the 5th Air Force including Japan and the Republic of Korea.

Connie Alexander ('47) was a voice known literally to millions of radio listeners. His 35-year career in sports radio announcing came about as a result of the dedication and care of one teacher. Enrolled in a bookkeeping class his senior year, Marjorie Dyer (Fox) asked Connie, "What do you want to do most in your life?" Unable to effectively compete in football because of his lanky build, Connie relayed to his teacher that he wanted to become a sports announcer. Miss Dyer referred Connie to William A. Davies, who was the Director of Audio-Visual Aids, and the rest is history. Connie handled the public address system during the last Bulldog game of the 1947 Championship season with Harry Hart and Herbie Hughes as his spotters. He later announced the play-by-play of the Albuquerque Dukes' games for the grand sum of $2.00/day. After graduation from UNM with a BA in Speech and Journalism and a four year stint in the service during the Korean War, Connie's career advanced rapidly. He did the Humble Oil "Game of the Week" for the Southwest Conference which was the world's oldest sports radio series, and moved on to CBS where he broadcast major college bowl games and NFL playoffs. For 13 years Connie was heard worldwide through the American Armed Forces Network. He advanced to the top of his vocation because of the interest of a teacher. Connie acknowledged his gratitude to Miss Dyer in her later years and gave the eulogy at her funeral.

The 1947-48 basketball team went to the State quarterfinals. The Bulldogs coached by John Caton were led by 6'6" center Bill Currie, David White, Danny Darrow and Chuck Hill. David and Chuck were selected on various All-Star Teams. Bob Sanchez, a sub on the team, recalls a humorous event. Coach Caton announced that there would be practice during the Christmas holidays. "Coach? I can't practice. I'm going skiing," Chuck Hill interjected. Coach Caton paused and pondered a moment. "Okay," Coach said. "Everyone but Chuck will practice during the Christmas vacation."

Herbie Hughes also played on the team. Herb recalls with lament that the basketball team was the only team that did not win a State Championship during the 1947-48 school year. State crowns were garnered by the track, baseball, and boxing teams in addition to the football squad. A remarkable feat for the Green and White. Actually, the Bulldogs did not win tennis or golf championships that year but they were individual events, not team championships.

Cross-country races were conducted during the Fall. The runners ran a lap in the stadium then conducted most of the race over the hilly vegetation-deprived mesa, returning to the stadium for the final lap, much like the marathon run in the Olympic games. Native Americans, mostly from the Albuquerque Indian School, dominated the grueling event almost every year in the past. When the participants returned to the stadium in 1948, however, the runner in the lead was a slightly built AHS sophomore by the name of Harrison Smith. In addition to winning many cross-country events,

Harrison won the 880 yard run all three years while at AHS. Only Ed Clifford (pole vault) 1913-1915, Owen Smaulding (100, 120 yard hurdles, shot put, pole vault) 1916-1918 and Jimmy Roybal (100 and 200 yard dash) 1922-1925 were triple champions through 1954.

The baseball team, anchored by Chuck Hill, won all of its games (17-0). Herb recalled one extracurricular event extremely well. One of Herb's teammates put "red hot" in his jock strap just prior to the team leaving by bus for a game. While Herb was desperately trying to cure his problem in the locker room, Coach Rushing, impatient and punctual as ever, ordered the bus driver to leave. As the bus pulled away from the curb Herb, trying to pull on his pants, was waving and running trying to catch the bus. He did, but the hyperactivity worsened his plight. It was an uncomfortable bus ride. It seems that every winning team has its jokers or it's easier to horse around when you're winning. There's no doubt that the 1948 team had fun and baseball seemed to promote more pranksters than other sports, as you will soon discover.

Bob Sanchez, who was introduced to the sport of handball by Glen O. Ream at the "Y" and went on to become an outstanding player, was inspired by Doc Harrington, who by 1947 was a living legend at AHS. Bob not only was a devout member of Doc's Dawn Patrol, he attended Harrington's Saturday morning experiments classes in chemistry and physics, which piqued his interest in medical science. There was a story behind every chemical compound. Like, "One day the chlorine sisters went downtown and lo and behold they ran into the sodium brothers. After mixing around for a while they developed a pretty 'salty' relationship." It must have worked. Almost 60 years later Bob knew the components of salt.

Doc, according to Bob, told his classes that he was "held back" (which was a euphemism for failed) one year in fifth grade. He would then counter by saying "It completely ruined my life for fifteen minutes!" His constant admonition to his classes was: "Live and learn or live anyway." This remarkable teacher once rigged a device on his eyeglasses in order to keep his lazy eye lid open. Those of us who were fortunate to have this unique man as a teacher were inspired by his genius and calmed by his humility and quiet demeanor.

One of AHS' best behaved and obedient students during the mid-40s was a young lady by the name of Beverly R. Ream, Mr. Ream's daughter, '47. One of her most memorable recollections of her father came when she was in the grades at Monte Vista School.

A female student failed to meet her requirements to graduate from AHS. The girl's irate father showed up one evening at the Ream home at 3333 East Monte Vista with a rifle in hand threatening to shoot the Principal. Mr. Ream faced the angry man at his front door, and then invited him into the house while at the same time asking his wife Ann and young Beverly to retreat to the bedroom. A scared young girl and a frightened wife and mother feared the worst. After what seemed to be an eternity of tension, the girl's father left. Calmly, Mr. Ream defused what could have been a tragic incident.

Bev never knew whether the girl passed or not, but she knew then that her dad was not only special, he was a brave man. In all probability the persuasive principal convinced the man that Glen did what was just and right. Glen O. Ream (the O is for Orville and few people will remember that) was not only brave and special, he was a true "Renaissance Man."

Glen, a stocky 5'9" and 180 pounds in high school, played every position in the backfield on his school's football team. He loved baseball and while playing semi-pro ball he received a letter from Connie Mack encouraging him to pursue the game. He was also an accomplished boxer, and later took up the more civil games of golf and tennis. Glen possessed an excellent singing voice and often pulled a harmonica out of his pocket and played a favorite tune.

As mentioned earlier, Mr. Ream was an avid patron of the arts and painted in his later years. He took his young daughter on fishing trips to the Jemez and traced all the constellations and the stars in the clear New Mexico sky. As a writer he wrote a collection of stories for the *Albuquerque Tribune* under the title of "Out of New Mexico's Past." First and foremost however, Glen O. Ream was an educator and a motivator. Education was the key to his student's future, and he was there at AHS to make certain that everyone attended class as testimonials that follow will attest.

Glen's first wife passed away from tuberculosis but the marriage bore a son, Glen O. Jr. Glen Jr. was attached to the New Mexico National Guard and was one of the nation's first units sent into combat at the outset of WWII. Glen's son survived the Bataan Death March and returned to Albuquerque to marry Lois Renfro, Charlie's sister. Sadly, bad health, caused by his long interment plagued the young Ream for the remainder of his life.

Beverly's mother was Ann McGuire, Glen's second wife, who was an outstanding athlete in her own right, and she coached the girls basketball team at St. Vincent's Academy. Ann is remembered as one of the top women golfers for years at the Albuquerque Country Club.

Bev and her classmates recalled their days at AHS in an article just prior to their 50th reunion written by J. Gutierrez Krueger in the *Albuquerque Tribune* on April 29, 1997. Some of the highlights are recalled here.

"It was an age of innocence, a time so unlike today that high-schoolers now would scarcely have anything in common with high-schoolers then, save for hormones, acne and a love of french fries," says J. Krueger. AHS had a population of 2,500[6] students which was one of the largest high schools in the country. It was where "...students respected teachers, where school was considered fun, where youths of all races from all socio-economic realms and all parts of the city came together under the banner of Bulldog pride," Krueger adds.

Don Fogg, one of Bev's classmates, tells a story which chronicles the students' respect for their teachers.

Miss Gertrude M. McGowan, an English teacher, "...was so quiet. She never said a mean word. Everybody just lis-

---

[6] Actual enrollment in 1948 reached 2,800 students prior to Highland High School opening in 1949.

tened to her," Don revealed. Everybody it seemed but a "big shot" whom Fogg politely declined to name. One day the big shot made a disrespectful remark in class. Miss McGowan, in a surprising display of anger suddenly shouted, "OUT!"

Don continued, "And even though he was a 'big shot,' the student was never allowed back in her class. There was no parental outcry to the school board, no threat of lawsuit by the American Civil Liberties Union, no retribution. There was a great respect for teachers, for authority. Today everybody wants to have more rights than they deserve."

Occasionally, a more stern discipline had to be administered. Bev recalls that her father possessed a large wooden paddle almost the size of a tennis racket (when they were much smaller) in the bottom drawer of her dad's desk. When a miscreant was sent to Mr. Ream's office and blame was adjudicated by the Principal, Glen would ask the guilty party, as he (or she) bent over to take their punishment:

"How many swats do you deserve?"

The appropriate number may have been debated but one thing was certain, the student acknowledged his (or her) wrongdoing and accepted their fate. Bill Pegue, who was quoted earlier said, "Kids didn't lie or try to lay blame on someone else or their abuse at home or some other dang fangled reason. They admitted they made a mistake and took their medicine."

Different strokes for different folks in different times.

I asked Bev, "What is your favorite recollection of your dad at school?" Hands down, the best story was:

"Dad would play handball at the YMCA during lunch hour. Often, when he came back to school he would walk up the steps to the Administration Building on his <u>hands</u>!"

About five years later this writer witnessed a similar feat with Mr. Ream walking on his hands up the stairs inside the Admin Building. Several of us jocks looked on in awe. Our Principal born in 1894 was almost age 60!

"There were so many school activities, so much to do," said Bev, who was a member of the AHS Ski Club, Plans and Policies, Honor Society, Operetta, Pepper Club, Yucca staff and Cantata. She was also an original organizing member of Silver Saddles with Walt Timmons and Rachel Miller in

1945. Her picture graces the front page of the "C" section of the *Tribune* riding her horse down Central Avenue during the New Mexico State Fair Parade. "There were activities for everybody, not all this polarization we have now," Bev added.

"Who were some of the other kids in your class that were popular?" I asked.

"Beatrice Hight and Bob McElheney were real good friends. Joannie Sisk who was a brilliant student and Pat Foster who was a great pianist were also great friends of mine. Sue Mullings was Homecoming Queen. Mary Ann Neff, Clarence Schols, Martha McCullough, Sam Sallie, Janie Rumble and Kenneth Hill were our cheerleaders. That was rare. We had three guys in that group. One of our favorite places to go was the La Loma Ballroom. We could go dancing there as long as we didn't drink, which few of us did anyway. The big bands came there. Swing music was in. We loved to jitterbug," Bev elaborated on those good old days when life was simpler and fun.

One of the most significant and telling moments in her dad's life came in 1956 when Mr. Ream retired as Principal at AHS. He was offered the same post at a new school, Sandia, which had just opened. Her dad declined the job saying, "Times are changing. My era is over," he said prophetically to Ann and Beverly.

Glen's assessment was correct. A major paradigm shift was occurring in America, and nowhere perhaps was it more visible than in the high schools. The baton of power was passing from the school's administration, teachers and coaches to the students and their parents, with profound ramifications for not only the schools but for society and the American way of life as we knew it.

What happened? Those of us who graduated in the mid-Fifties may appreciate, though not necessarily agree with, this writer's observations.

Although "Rock and Roll" had its origins prior to 1954, Bill Haley and the Comets truly energized teenagers with "Rock Around the Clock" that year. Within months after our graduation in June 1954, my sister Joan was teaching in an inner-city school in Denver in the fall of that year. Her students were so emotionally and sensually charged by jitterbugging during the lunch hour to "R&R" that it was virtually impossible to control them in the classroom when they returned. She was required to buy a lock for her car's gas tank as "sniffing" became a new drug *du jour*. Teenagers flocked to see *Blackboard Jungle* where revolt against the "Teach" was heroic and "Rock Around the Clock" was the provocative theme song.

To some the significance of music precipitating, or at a minimum, being a major factor in societal change may be pushing the envelope a tad but lend me your ear. Recently (2003) a research team at Dartmouth (College) Center for Cognitive Neuroscience made a significant discovery. Using functional magnetic resonance imaging, the researchers found that the ability to recognize and retain music is found in the nostromedial prefrontal cortex of the brain which also plays a key role in learning and the response and control of emotions.[7]

Virtually all eras are defined with certain types of music. Music, these researchers concluded, is the greatest stimulus of all the senses. It can have a profound impact on young people in particular and can change their attitudes, behavior and values like no other sensory stimulus. Rock & Roll propelled Bill, Elvis, Jerry Lee and a myriad of other teen idols to the top of the charts as it also began to change the conservative way of American life as we knew it. Today (2004) music combined with visual enhancements such as MTV has played a pivotal role in the degeneration of our society. Rock & Roll, to us, was new, exciting and fun and it started in the mid-Fifties. How could we have known that it would lead us to where we are today?

James Dean became the teenage idol in *Rebel Without a Cause*. Marlon Brando was a new breed of iconoclast who would battle with the establishment, whomever was in charge. All our senses were bombarded with sights and sounds telling us to discard our dull and colorless, conservative past. Elvis and Marilyn told us to let go of our sexual re-

---

[7] The <u>Arizona Republic</u>, January 3, 2003, Paul Recer, Associated Press.

straints while our parents were desperately trying to hold us back.

Yes, 1954 was a pivotal year for our class. We were one of the last classes of the "Glen O. Ream era," not yet overwhelmed by the paradigm shift that was about to occur. It arrived, of course, for most of us during our college years but left, unsoiled, our good old days at AHS.

Few of us took the opportunity to thank this wonderful man for the path that he and those who served under him paved for us at AHS for 30 years. He was tough but he was fair and as Bev says, "I have never heard anyone say a bad thing about Glen O. Ream."

May "Bulldogs Forever" be in part a tribute to this true Renaissance Man and all the teachers and coaches that devoted their lives to our future. They were successful. Whether or not we achieved our potential was up to us.

It should be of little surprise that Glen's daughter, Bev, would be honored as a "Distinguished Graduate of AHS" in 1991. She graduated with honors in history at UNM and later applied her teaching skills as an aviation instructor, obtaining her pilot's license at 7-Bar Flying Service at the same time that this writer obtained his. Bev and Joan Florence became the first licensed balloon pilots west of the Mississippi, which she proudly adds to her accomplishments. She still carries on her dad's tradition of raising "Old Glory" every morning at her home.

"Dad was a true patriot. He loved this country,"

What more does anyone need to say?

AHS had the foremost baseball program in the state in the Forties. From 1940 through 1950 the Bulldogs were state champs nine out of eleven years. Only Albuquerque Indian School in 1941 and St. Mary's in 1949 were able to dethrone AHS.

Amidst a throng of 1500 vocal partisans from each side at Tingley Field, the Bulldogs faced the Cougars (St. Mary's) in a double header that was a classic matchup between the two best teams in the state and city rivals in 1948. With Don Staggs pitching and striking out 14 batters and only allowing four hits, the Bulldogs beat the "Cougs" 3 - 2 in the first game. With Manuel (Pete) Gallegos, a tall intimidating fireballer, pitching in the nightcap, the score was tied 2-2 in the bottom of the ninth inning.

Chuck Hill led off the inning with a single, moved to second on an error and then, incredibly, stole third base. Coach Rushing called for a squeeze play. The bunt was perfectly executed and Chuck scored the winning run, thus preserving Pete's one-hitter and an undefeated season.

Fifty years later at a breakfast celebrating their championship season, Pete asked Jack to again sign his Certificate ("A" Club Letter) which he did. It was a poignant moment for Coach and player and particularly for Pete, who considered Jack a friend as well as one of his mentors.

Pete, whose recollections of the good old days were as clear and unfettered as a summer New Mexico sky, offered some meaningful insights from his youth. I asked him:

"Pete? All of the Anglos that I have interviewed are quick to point out that Albuquerque and AHS were homogeneous environments and there wasn't any prejudice against Hispanics or Blacks, but that was their view. How did you feel as a youngster growing up here?"

"Well, I'll tell you Buster. I learned something very early in life. My first grade teacher was Madge Arledge, who taught in the Albuquerque Public School System from 1900 to 1951. I could only speak Spanish when I came to school the first day. She pulled me aside that first day and told me, "Manuel. I know that you can speak Spanish. My concern is how well I can teach you to speak English."

"I got the message right there and my dad told me that my teacher was always right. I should do exactly what the teachers wanted me to do. I never questioned authority. I grew up in fear of my teachers, coaches, adults and my priest, but you know what? It didn't hurt me one bit. It was a matter of attitude. If you thought you were discriminated against, you were."

One of the stars of the championship team of 1947 was George Koenig. After graduation George was accepted at West Point. Jim Hulsman and George, school chums since the fourth grade, spent time together during Christmas 1952 while on leave. Unfortunately, George was killed 23 days before the cease fire. Another member of this class was Ed Tixier, chronicled earlier. Ed, accompanied by his wife, were in the bleachers in Cairo when Anwar Sadat was assassinated. Miraculously, both of them survived the 10 minute fusillade of bullets that left most of those present wounded or killed.

By his own admission, Jim Hulsman was not an exceptional athlete, but in 1948 he did run a 10.4 second 100 yard dash and was one of the team's top running backs his senior year until an injury forced him to miss four games. Who could have possibly predicted that this man would return to his *alma mater* in 1954 and remain as an AHS coach for an incredible 48 years! Jim, who didn't play basketball at AHS (he played in the City League), won an unprecedented 660 games and lost but 223 in 34 years as basketball head coach, winning seven state championships along the way. His nearly half century devotion and allegiance to AHS plus his tenacious discipline certainly entitles him to be recognized as "Mr. Bulldog." Of all of his accomplishments and well-deserved rewards, being inducted into the National Hall of Fame, with such notables as Hershel Walker in 2003, tops the list. As a testament to his long tenure this writer can recall this young, sandy-haired man with a crew-cut that came to AHS as Pete McDavid's assistant coaching our track team in 1954. At a point in time in 2002 when most of our class of 1954 had retired, Jim, senior to us by five years, was still hard at work motivating young men. Absolutely remarkable. And, without Jim's historical library and his invaluable input this book could not have been written.

Little known other than to those who participated, AHS produced its first ski team in 1947. Members of that team were P.G. Cornish, Raymond Sanderson, Terry Headington, Jimmy Doolittle, Jack Corbett, Charlie Nuckols, Tom Savage and Jerry Martin. P.G. was an exceptional all-around athlete as chronicled earlier. Jerry Martin was a defensive half-back on the great 1947 Championship Football team and played second base on the 1948 State Baseball Championship team. He was such an accomplished skier that Coach Tony Wilson appointed Jerry as ski coach while he was still a student. In the early Fifties, this writer can vividly recall Jerry flawlessly traversing the rocky slopes at La Madera, his skis locked closely together sculpting perfect parallel turns. His form was purely poetic. I desperately wanted to ski like Jerry.

Also in the early Fifties, this writer first met another member of this team. Jack Stromberg and I were waiting in the lift line at La Madera. A lone skier, skiing fast, slightly out of control, approached the line of us skiers guarded by a red, wooden, slat snow fence that was anchored by steel poles. The unfortunate skier crashed into the snow fence and a steel pole. Jack and I rushed to his aid fearing the worse. Fortunately, the former Bulldog, Tom Savage, was unhurt. Why then was this seemingly uneventful accident so memorable? Ironically ten years later, while skiing at Taos, this writer would meet, fall in love and marry an attractive lady by the name of Olivia Savage. It is a remarkable love story with a happy ending. And, a focus of a different book.

After a stint with the U.S. Army in Korea, Jerry Martin returned to Albuquerque and became the General Manager and Ski School Director at La Madera, a position he held when we first met. Jerry later became more than a contractor. He was truly a man of vision. He, Bob Nordhaus and Ben Abruzzo, all avid skiers, conjured up the idea to build a Swiss-style tram up on the steep west face of the Sandia Mountains that would not only ferry skiers to the top of the mountain, it would draw tourists from all over the country all year round. Jerry's firm, Martin and Luther Construction Company, built the marvel of engineering and it opened in May 1966. Jerry was quoted in the *Albuquerque Tribune*, "Everybody thinks the Swiss built it. They didn't. They provided the machinery. They can't believe a local kid did it."

Jerry, who discovered his love of building things while constructing sets for stage plays at AHS, is truly one grad who reached the top of his mountain.

After a dominating and successful year in virtually all sports in 1947-48, the following year's class had a tough act to follow. With Joe Boehning at quarterback and Seyfred Toledo, a speedster, at halfback, along with stalwarts Charles Hedman and Norman Bray anchoring a fast and mobile line, the football season began with great optimism. All four players would be named later to the All-Star team.

Early in the season, however, a devastating loss to a

strong and physical Borger, Texas, team coupled with the loss by injury to several key players, foreshadowed a season that could be best described by Joe Boehning as "disappointing." The Bulldogs lost to Hobbs 14-0. The Eagles went on to become State champions.

The basketball team, coached by Johnny Caton, featured John Gee (6'3") as its biggest player. Danny Darrow, in his second year as a starter, was the leading scorer and went on to become a star at the University of New Mexico.

Aside from Stanley Potts' singles championship in 1943 and Harold Smith and Bill Caldwell combining to win the State Doubles Championship the same year, the Bulldogs were void of any tennis titles throughout the 1940s. Often a glaring need discovers an opportunity.

In 1948 there was a determined, hard-working youngster who wanted desperately to make his mark in sports but at 5'8" tall and only 120 pounds Paul Butt's chances of finding a spring in his step on the gridiron or on the basketball court was bleak at best. Tony Valdez, however, saw an outlet for Paul's quickness and competitive nature.

One day as spring was about to be sprung, challenged of course by the afternoon winds that raised havoc with all the spring sports, Paul was scrambling around the tennis courts at Tingley Park with several players on the team when his moves caught Valdez' eye.

"Hey Paul...come here a minute," the Coach yelled. "I didn't know you played tennis."

"Geez, I don't Coach. I was just horsing around with the guys," Paul replied.

"Heck you're good enough already to play on the team. Would you like to play?"

"Heck yes. That would be 'neato,' Coach," Paul replied, beaming ear to ear.

Paul went on to become the New Mexico State Champion (post high school) nine times and the State Open Champion five times. In 1954 he was ranked number one in the Southwest Section and repeated again in 1963.

There is only one negative aspect to this success story. Paul, like many students in the fall of 1949, transferred to the new high school in the "Heights" (Highland High) because his family lived close to the school. Tony Valdez and AHS, however, can take credit for his discovery. Paul paid a tribute to his first coach: "Tony and tennis changed my life," he recalled wistfully.

Paul, like virtually all of his classmates, especially recalls Chuck Hill, whom he idolized. One day during lunch hour trouble was brewing in the patio between rival groups of Pachucos and Gringos. A bloody fight was imminent. Suddenly, Chuck Hill appeared amidst the protagonists. Without a word and without any physical action on Chuck's part, the rivals receded and disbursed. An ugly confrontation was avoided.

"Chuck had so much respect he could keep control of the kids anywhere. He was like "The Fonz" in 'Happy Days'," Paul added laughing.

Paul and I would become roommates in 1961 when he was king of the tennis courts and I was playing Zeus with thunder bolts. We both began separate professional careers that would be our life's work, while at the same time enjoying America's newest craze, "twisting the night away" with Chubby Checker. Our bachelor's pad was the envy of our peers.

Victor J. Castillo was a member of the great 1947 Bulldog New Mexico State Football Championship team and followed that up as a letterman on the 1948 New Mexico State Track and Field Championship team. In 1997, Victor achieved another major milestone. As owner of Victor's Regent Pharmacy, he filled his store's one millionth prescription serving his customers in the South Valley. Victor has been recognized by the pharmaceutical industry receiving both the Ernie Welch and A.H. Robins Awards for outstanding service in his field. A Korean War veteran, Victor also received a Distinguished Alumnus Award from UNM in 1988. Victor regards his participation in the founding of Regent Drug of New Mexico, a buying cooperative that allows independent pharmacists to get prices similar to large chains, as one of his major contributions to the preservation of small, independent drug stores.

As elucidated above, Herb H. Hughes excelled in football, basketball and baseball at AHS graduating with the Class of

'48. This multi-talented athlete became equally successful in a multi-faceted career that included coaching and teaching at the college level at Florida State University, the University of Northern Colorado, and UNM, a bank officer as well as New Mexico Commissioner of Banking, New Mexico Budget-Financial Control Chief, Manager of Human Resources for BDM Corporation and top administrator for Bernalillo County. Herb's only unsuccessful public service effort was his two-time bid to be elected Mayor of Albuquerque. He was, however, elected to the Albuquerque City Council and was also elected a Vice-President of the New Mexico Constitutional Convention and the New Mexico Public Regulation Commission.

This writer and Roland B. Kool, '48, shared much in common in addition to their friendship. Roland excelled at track and lettered on the 1948 New Mexico State Track and Field Championship team. Roland continued his interest in the sport at UNM and served as an official at college meets after his graduation, while this writer was competing for UNM. We were neighbors in the late 50s and later roommates. Roland received his law degree from UNM and joined his father's firm in 1958. He went on to distinguish himself in labor law and was selected in 1983 as one of the top labor lawyers in the country. He taught labor-management relation courses at UNM Law School and served on the boards of several Albuquerque banks. In addition, Roland served on Governor Jerry Apodaca's Council of Economic Advisors and Secretary of the New Mexico Democratic Party in the 70s, and was an informal adviser to Governor Toney Anaya in the 80s.

F. Richard Zemke, '48, enjoyed both success as an athlete at AHS as well as a businessman. He was a squad member of the 1947 New Mexico State Championship Football team, the 1948 District III Basketball Champions and the 1948 New Mexico State Baseball Championship teams. Thirteen years after Richard graduated with a B.S. in Electrical engineering from UNM, he along with George Gardner formed Gardner Zemke Company. In the late 90s their firm was the largest electrical construction company in the Southwest with a ranking in the top 100 electrical contractors in the U.S. In 1999 Richard received a Distinguished Engineering Alumnus Award from UNM for his professional accomplishments.

AHS golfers retained their dominance on the golf course after the War as the great all-around athlete P.G. Cornish III won the individual state title in 1945 followed by Sam Montgomery in 1946, Hal Ferguson in 1947 and Pat Rea, who would become a professional golfer, in 1949. Team competition didn't begin until 1958 and it shouldn't have been a surprise to schools in the state that Tony Valdez' team won the first championship.

A new activity in Albuquerque created another sport as foreign to the wind-swept plateau of New Mexico as golf was to the arctic circle. Ice Skating. 1948 marked the year of AHS' first Hockey Team. Members of that first historic team were:

Ken Hansen	Phil Davey
Chuck Thomley	Joe Chisholm
Duncan Sheriff	Bill Oldacker
Jimmy Jones	Clark Schaffner
Campbell McMardie	Joe Azar
Bob Blagg	Bob Long
	George Snelson

Like boxing, hockey as a team sport at AHS would be short-lived, but not before an interesting clash with rival Highland that took place in 1952.

As Albuquerque and the area's economy both grew so did increased revenues to the schools enable AHS to add additional activities including another team sport, wrestling. Jack Rushing, assisted by L. E. Dohner who taught Agriculture, coached the school's first team in 1948.

In only their second year AHS already carved a wide swath in this grueling, technique-requisite sport. The Bulldogs beat a highly reputed Amarillo Sandies team twice that season and won eight matches while losing only two. One loss was to the New Mexico School for the Blind whose wrestlers, despite their handicap, were almost unbeatable.

In 1950 the wrestling team possessed two athletes who would later become nationally known sports figures—the

Unser brothers. Jerry and Bob Unser were members of this team but would achieve their niche later in life in auto racing. Gladys Miller ('53) knew Jerry Unser very well.

"Jerry was a couple years older than we but we dated until he quit school and joined the Navy. When the Korean War started Jerry, Sam Large, Don Des Jardin and quite a few seniors went to Korea. Jerry was the neatest and most sincere person you would ever want to meet. He was generous and well-liked by everyone who knew him.

"One day at his shop where the Unsers worked on their stock cars that they raced at Speedway Park, Jerry smeared grease all over my face. He darn near cracked up laughing. Then he used gasoline to wipe it off. Wasn't too great for my skin but it was pretty funny," Gladys recalled.

Jerry Unser's success racing stock cars propelled him to the big time — "The Brickyard" — the Indianapolis 500 in 1959. During a practice run, Jerry's car hit the wall. The impact was not fatal but the flames that engulfed Jerry's car took a life destined for greatness. Brothers Bobby and Al courageously followed in Jerry's footsteps and brought fame and fortune to themselves, their school and to Albuquerque.

After dominating the state's baseball diamonds the year before, the 1949 Bulldogs nine failed to win the district championship. The team had several outstanding players, however, Bobby Lemmel (second baseman), who had a batting average of .429 in 1950, went on to play professional ball for the Albuquerque Dukes in 1953 and 1954. Bobby was inducted into the AHS Hall of Fame in 2003. Abbie Lopez was an exceptional shortstop. Joe Boehning played in the outfield. He recalled a memorable event.

The opposing batsman hit a long fly ball over Joe's head. While in pursuit of the ball Joe, as was a habit of many of us while we played in the sandlots, threw his glove at the bouncing ball. The umpire allowed the batter to take one more base because of interference, which gave the batsman an inside-the-park home run. When the inning ended Joe, anticipating the wrath of Coach Rushing, reluctantly returned to the end of the bench. He waited for that booming bellicose voice to single him out but...it never came. It wasn't often that any player got the silent treatment from Coach

Rushing.

Margaret McLaughlin graduated with this Class of 1949. Fifty years later, she returned for a most memorable reunion. At the Saturday evening dinner, Margaret had the pleasure of sharing the occasion with Winfred Buskirk, her U.S. History and home room teacher. The student and teacher shared many memories but the most memorable aspect of their meeting occurred the next day.

"Margaret? After I returned home I recalled that you never received your La Reata when you graduated," Mr. Buskirk said.

"Oh my gosh! That's right. My dad was disabled and couldn't work in 1949. We didn't even have enough money to buy a yearbook," Margaret responded, recalling her family's dire days.

"My wife and I are moving and I would like you to have my copy of the `49 *La Reata*," Mr. Buskirk offered.

Margaret was so touched by her teacher's thoughtfulness she wept when she examined this newly discovered treasure. Still amazed she pondered, "How in the world did he remember that I didn't have a yearbook?"

Another father-son duo that both made their marks as AHS athletes were Robert M. and Robert W. (Bill) Elder. They both also followed the same career path with the Albuquerque National Bank (now Bank of America). Bill, '49, was a member of the 1948 Bulldog football team and graduated with both a BBA and MA (Economics) from UNM. Bill, like his dad, rose from the position of Teller to Sr. Vice-President and Vice-Chairman of the Board of the bank after serving 40 years. Bill served his community devoting his time to the United Way, YMCA and Salvation Army as well as a Trustee of the New Mexico School of Banking Foundation. He was also a board member of the UNM Alumni Association and the Anderson School of Business Alumni Association.

Another student/athlete who excelled at both endeavors was Noel Sorrell, Class of '49. He was Captain of the 1947 Bulldog New Mexico State Football Championship team and also lettered in track and field. Noel didn't allow athletics to interfere with his studies. He was a member of AHS' Honor Society and must have relished his physics and chemistry classes with Doc Harrington as he went on to receive his B.A. in Chemistry at UNM. Noel received his M.D. at the University of Colorado but, rather than practice medicine, he became a medical consultant for attorneys who required interpretation of medical records and documents for personal injury cases. Noel has also enjoyed a long career as a freelance writer and editor of manuscripts.

Joe Boehning excelled at both football as a squad member of the 1947 New Mexico State Champions and an All-Star in baseball as a member of the 1948 New Mexico State Champions, but Joe may well be remembered for the sport of basketball. Not as a player but as an architect. Joe was only 35 when he was selected to design what has been for the past 37 years one of Albuquerque's most famous buildings— "The Pit." In 1999 Sports Illustrated ranked Joe's ingenious, subterranean basketball court as the 13th best sports venue of the 20th Century. "We had a low budget and that was the only way to do it. It's really a pretty humble building," Joe related to Rick Wright in a 1999 article in the *Albuquerque Journal*. In addition to designing projects all over the U.S., Joe has served Albuquerque on the Board of Standards and Appeals, Vice-President and Board member of the Boys Club, the Downtown Action Plan Committee, United Way, the Downtown Neighborhood Task Force for Historic Preservation (Chairman), the Board of Directors of the Greater Albuquerque Chamber of Commerce, the Environmental Planning Commission and other civic and governmental agencies.

Most of his classmates from 1949 will remember Dan W. (Danny) Darrow as their class Vice-President and one of the stars on the basketball teams of '48 and '49. Dan also played on the New Mexico State Championship Baseball team in 1948. He continued to excel at UNM in basketball lettering three years and finishing his senior year as the team's leading scorer. After four years service in the U.S. Air Force, he received his Master's degree in hotel administration from Michigan State University and embarked on a long career in the hospitality industry with Sheraton and Disney World. In 1994 Dan was named "Hotelier of the Year" by the Florida Hotel & Motel Association.

1949 produced another mythical football State Champion with an undefeated 10-0 record. Ironically, undercutting this label was the fact that eight players on this team were chosen to play in the All-Star game. This record was remarkable considering the fact that 1949 was the first year that Highland High School opened its doors and a considerable number of would be sophomores went to the new school. 1949 would mark the last undefeated Bulldog football team in history up to 2004.

As it turned out, there were four undefeated teams in the state in 1949. Unable to compete against Hobbs and Roswell because of the race issue, the New Mexico Sportswriters Association voted for the champion. The results were:

Team	1st Place Votes	Total Points	Record
1. Hobbs	10	246	11-0
2. Tucumcari[8]	7	207	10-0
3. AHS	4	207	10-0
4. Deming	1	166	11-0

This remarkable season deserves a game-by-game review. Ralph Matteucci, who was the outstanding All-State left guard on this team, bequeathed to us an invaluable record of Bulldog lore that commemorates this year.

AHS 27 - Clayton 6

The Bulldogs simply had too much talent against a school whose town had only 5,000 residents. Clayton, which made only 5 first downs the entire game, scored with only 30 seconds remaining against the Bulldog third team. Coach McDavid used all of his players. The game was highlighted by Roy Carroll's 80 yard run and the stellar offensive play of backs

---

[8] Tucumcari challenged AHS to a game to determine second place, but the Bulldogs declined.

Jack Ward and Don Hyder.

AHS 26 - Cathedral (El Paso) 0

This game featured the tenacious defense of Larry Forderhase, Ralph Melbourne and Ralph Matteucci which held the Texas team to only 19 yards of offense in the first half. Roy Carroll again demonstrated his explosiveness as he ran for 3 quick TDs. The Dawgs never had to attempt a single pass.

AHS 7 - Borger (Texas) 0

This game was an upset. This tough team from the oil fields of the Texas panhandle could only muster 76 net yards of offense against the mighty Bulldogs anchored by Joe Azar, Miles Britelle, Jim Henrie and Bob O'Neil. Don Hyder, a 195-pound fullback who was the biggest member of the team, was also the biggest offensive weapon along with Art Casias.

AHS 14 - Winslow (Arizona) 0

Playing Winslow on the manure-infested dirt rodeo grounds, the heavily favored Bulldogs were under-performing and tied at zero at halftime. In the locker room during the intermission the team separated only by a thin masonite wall could hear the Winslow coach chastising his troops.

"If you can't beat these (blankty-blank) Bulldogs the way they're playin' you otta quit," the coach yelled.

Pete, probably perplexed on how he could motivate his minions, listened to the opposing coach's tirade not saying a word. When the loud verbiage characterizing the Bulldogs as a bunch of wimps or worse stopped, Pete took his turn:

"I think you've heard all you need to know," he said to his team.

The Bulldogs made pussycats out of the hosts in the second half, led by Stan Tixier and a defense that stopped the opponents three times inside the Bulldog 15 yard line. Hyder, Casias and Dave Matthews led the AHS offensive attack. Pete was a master sports psychologist before there were any.

AHS 18 - Santa Fe 0

The Demons could garner only 80 yards of offense against the stalwart Bulldog defense. This game featured a first. Miles and Dick Britelle were the first brothers to start a game for AHS. The backfield trio of Hyder, Casias and Matthews scored for the Green and White. This Bulldog team averaged 164 pounds per man. Very small by today's standards but 20 pounds per man heavier than the Demons.

AHS 39 - St. Mary's 6

The Bulldogs rolled up 405 yards rushing and didn't throw a single pass in dominating this inter-city rivalry game. Roy Carroll, who Stan Tixier said was the most under-rated member of this team, scored 3 touchdowns in this rout.

AHS 7 - Carlsbad 0

The Carlsbad-AHS confrontation deserves special mention albeit for both an unexpected and expected reason. The Cavemen led by Juan Mendez, Porkey Leyva, Fred Mahaffey and coached by their master strategist, Ralph Bowyer, were undefeated coming into Albuquerque. It was during the teacher's convention and the game was moved to Zimmerman Stadium to accommodate the fans from all four corners of New Mexico. It was a classic duel of north-south titans playing before 15,000 fans. Ralph Melbourne remembers the game as if it were yesterday and his personal mano y mano battle with the opposing tackle, Ken Elmore.

Ken was a 250 pound block of granite but as slow moving as a glacier. Ralph was 165 pounds soaking wet, handicapped by near blindness and almost unable to discern friend from foe. Pete McDavid, as crafty as his erstwhile coaching opponent, designed a trap play whereby the Bulldog right tackle would vacate his position allowing Elmore to charge into the backfield. Ralph, "pulling" from his left guard position, blindsided the Caveman and leveled the hulk several times, leaving a massive hole for Don Hyder and Dave Matthews to ramble

125

through. Carlsbad was moving the ball late in the game and on fourth down in the shadow of the Bulldog goalposts, Don Pfutzenreuter rolled out on a quarterback keeper with two blockers leading interference. Don Hyder, playing linebacker and sensing a do or die defining moment, rolled into the blue and white wave sending them tumbling to the turf. Then to Don's surprise he saw Pfutzenreuter stumble over the pile of humanity falling short of paydirt.

Our Bulldogs prevailed when Jim Henrie recovered a fumble on the Caveman 11 yard line and then Bob Darmitzel snuck it into the end zone for the only score. It would be the only game that the Bulldogs were outgained, 173 to 123, in what was regarded as one of the best high school games ever played in the state.

(But Carlsbad featured another star who performed not on the field but between the player's bench and the stands. The Cavemen's head cheerleader was a perky, bouncy brunette with an hourglass figure and a wide jack-o-lantern smile. Her name? Olivia Jane Smith. Eighteen hundred miles away on the frozen tundra in Green Bay, Wisconsin, a thirteen year old eighth grader of Swedish descent was watching his beloved Packers play in near zero weather dreaming of the day he would become a West High School Wildcat. Given their distance in miles, and a chasm in years at that age, what are the chances that thirteen years later Olivia and this writer would meet much less marry and celebrate forty-two years together at the completion of "Bulldogs Forever?" Slim and none, of course, but for once slim won out against fat odds.)

AHS 26 - Las Cruces 13

After this game in which the Cruces Bulldogs were the only team to score twice against the AHS formidable defense, the New Mexico Sportswriter's Association gave Hobbs 205 points and AHS and Tucumcari (which beat Carlsbad 13-0), 202 points in what was destined to be one of the state's closest races

126

ever. Stan Tixier in one of his rare offensive appearances scored on a quarterback sneak for one TD and Jack Ward scored on two passes from Bob Darmitzel.

AHS 69 - Gallup 6

The Bulldogs must have been in shock when the Tigers returned the opening kickoff 80 yards for a touchdown, but it probably proved to be just what the doctor ordered. The opponents were on life support the remainder of the game as the Dawgs rolled up 416 yards of offense in the easy win. On one play, Dave Matthews scored only to have the play called back due to a penalty. Bob Darmitzel called the same play again. Dave scored again. Every Bulldog that suited up for this game got considerable playing time.

AHS 42 - Highland 0

This game kicked off a rivalry that has lasted for fifty-four years. A crowd of 6,000 packed Milne Stadium for the inaugural game that featured Miles Brittelle intercepting one pass and picking off a fumble in mid-air and returning both for TDs.

Relegating such a significant task to sportswriters and coaches who all had their own community bias was as controversial as it was unworkable. Without question the inability to play Hobbs and Roswell led to the lopsided vote, which was probably the result intended by the Southeastern school's ploy. Despite considerable debate, a playoff system to determine an undisputed football champion would not emerge until 1953. This writer's senior year...and what a doozy it was!

Larry Forderhase (tackle) and Ralph Matteucci (guard) were First Team All-State, and Don Hyder (fullback) made second Team. Dave Matthews (halfback), Jim Henrie (end), Joe Azar (tackle), Miles Brittelle (center) and Bob Darmitzel (quarterback) along with Foderhase, Matteucci and Hyder completed the All-Star team. According to Stan Tixier who played defensive back, Roy Carroll was a great half back overlooked by sportswriters and coaches who picked the All-Stars. Dave Matthews, who missed several games during the season with an injury, played an outstanding All-Star game. Operating at both tailback and wingback Dave caught seven passes for 85 yards, ran nine times for 68 yards and even completed three passes for 28 yards. A remarkable all-around performance. Ralph Matteucci's "line play was the best of the game" according to the newspaper account. The North and South fought to a scoreless tie thereby leaving the perennial argument unresolved.

Dave recalled several incidents involving his coaches that illuminate their distinctive personalities. Making an error in practice one day, he was pulled aside by Jack Rushing to chide him and demonstrate the proper technique. Dave, confused, said:

"But Coach, I thought..."

"If you ever thought Matthews, you'd get a headache!" Rushing replied in his inimitable way.

Using a different motivational methodology Pete McDavid told his players that anyone who tackled a Carlsbad back behind the line of scrimmage would get a milkshake. Dave nailed the Caveman star halfback Juan Mendez for a loss and, true to his word, Pete bought Dave his milkshake.

Ralph Matteucci went on to become an outstanding player at UNM and was inducted into the school's Hall of Honor with his entire team. Ralph was drafted by the Detroit Lions but declined to play. "The pay was ridiculous," he reportedly said.

Often, when a team is loaded with talent it is difficult for some players who would probably warrant considerable playing time on other lesser squads, to play a sufficient number of quarters to earn a letter. One such player on this great team was Jim "Bulldog" Drummond.

Jim, who was given his nickname from the British detective and not his classmates, earned the unique distinction of almost making a university team while still in high school! One day in the spring of 1950 Jim showed up at UNM while the Lobos were conducting spring practice. He checked out his gear and began practice. All the coaches must have assumed that Jim was a student. No one asked. He performed well despite receiving a concussion during a drill. So well, in fact, Dudley DeGroot, the Lobo coach, offered Bulldog a scholarship.

Jim never attended UNM. He played his college ball at West Point and saw service in Vietnam as an adviser. He retired as a Major General. Jim has established a scholarship fund for Jack Rushing at Bacone Indian School in Muskogee, Oklahoma.

Don Hyder's two older brothers, Charles and Dick, preceded the 1950 grad. He couldn't understand why Coach Jack Rushing would break out in an unaccustomed smile and laughter every time Don came in contact with the imposing, no-nonsense, and usually reserved coach. He finally discovered why his presence elicited a humorous reaction.

Near the Coach's office was an area where the floor had a three-foot round hole that led to the laundry room twelve feet below. Towels would be gathered up after the athletes showered and dropped into the hole to the room below. One day Charles was meeting with Coach Rushing returning a key to a peg on the wall near the precariously located hole in the floor.

"One second he was right there and the next he was gone," Coach Rushing said to Don, pointing to the corner where Charles vanished.

"Wow!" Don replied. "That's a heck of a fall. I don't remember him getting hurt."

"He landed on a huge pile of towels," Coach relayed to Don. "Otherwise it could have been a bad situation."

And, needless to say, wouldn't have been very funny.

"About ten of us from the team went to a diner in Belen for lunch. Hugh Barlow, who was Black, was with us. The manager told us that they weren't going to serve any "niggers." We couldn't believe it. It really pissed us off and we left," Don revealed.

Belen is only twenty miles south of Albuquerque. Highway 66 was somewhat of a Mason-Dixon line prior to 1953.

Rarely does any one family play such an integral role in the history and the traditions of a school than the Hyder family. Latiff Hyder, who emigrated from Lebanon without his parents at the age of ten, was an outstanding football and basketball player during AHS' early years, graduating in 1920. Latiff and his wife Lucille had three sons so close in age that they all attended AHS at the same time, graduating in the successive years of 1948, 1949 and 1950.

The eldest son, Charles, received his B.S. from UNM and obtained his Doctor of Physics and Astronomy from the University of Colorado. He gained international attention during the 1980s when he fasted for 250 days in front of the White House to protest the US-USSR Cold War. Charles ended his protest when President Reagan and Michael Gorbachev signed the Icelandic Accord.

Richard, '49, was a member of the Bulldog New Mexico State Championship Football team of 1947, and was also an excellent student winning the AHS Science Award. He was a partner in Hyder Brothers, the family investment business, and also owned his own stock and bond brokerage firm. Dick also served as Chairman of the Albuquerque Planning Commission for 7 years and was Finance Committee Chairman for Senator Pete Domenici.

Don, the youngest son, was an outstanding football player on the undefeated Bulldog team of 1949 and along with his father, was selected on the All-Time AHS Football team and is the only father-son combo to be so honored. Don also lettered in hockey and tennis which was a rare combination. Don has devoted most of his business career to real estate and has served on the Airport Advisory Board and the Board of the Downtown Association.

In another example of family cohesiveness, all three sons graduated from UNM and served in the U.S. Air Force.

Although Ralph Melbourne recalled the 1949 and 1950 football teams and events easily it was his sophomore year that was most memorable...and painful.

Ralph was off to a tough start in life (at 6 weeks of age) when he lost his father. Handicapped by very poor eyesight, Ralph once recovered a helmet thinking it was the ball, which made him the brunt of his teammate's jokes and teasing. But that wasn't the worst part. On a road trip to Borger, Ralph became the target of aggressive hazing from several upper classmen. It was called an "initiation."

In the motel room the night before the Borger game several players pounded Ralph's thighs with their fists resulting in large "frogs" (knots) on his legs. The next day they were not only tight and sore, his legs were black and blue.

"Where in the devil did you get these bruises on your legs?" Coach Rushing asked in the training room prior to the game.

"I got them in practice," Ralph replied, not wanting to reveal the true cause of his discomfort.

Coach probably didn't buy Ralph's story but he packed his thighs with analgesic balm and tape and then, probably empathizing with Ralph's ordeal, sent him into his first game. Excited as never before Ralph, ignoring his pain, ran on to the field—only to discover he had not removed his warm-up jacket!

Hazing was a problem. It was like so many other issues of the day that were ignored on the pretext that they didn't exist. Was it a necessary tradition in a right of passage into manhood? The practice continued to our day. It intimidated many. It angered some. There was a way to get even. It was a defining moment in this writer's sophomore year as you will soon discover.

Salve to soothe Ralph's wounds came in the form of being named to the 1950 All-Star team along with Jack Ward, Marlin Pound, Cliff Caster and Dick Brittelle.

The 1950 Basketball Team was led by All-Stars Dave Warren, Dan Darrow and lettermen Stan Tixier and Gordon Sammon. The team won its district title but lost in the State Tournament. Tucumcari following its best football year in history won the State Championship.

The track team was exceptional, winning the State Championship with a total of 49 points, which doubled the second place team. The Bulldogs excelled in the distance races. Harrison Smith won the 880 yard run in 2:01.0 and he was State Champ in his event all 3 years. Jimmy Brooks won the mile in 4:32.6 and Dave Matthews, according to the *Albuquerque Journal,* was the "surprise victor" in the discus with a throw of 141'½".

The 1950 baseball team was one of the most exceptional in Bulldog history. Not only did the team have an 18 and 1 record and win the State Championship, this team was probably the most prolific run-producing machine ever in the history of the sport in New Mexico. They scored over 200 runs in 19 games for an average of better than 10 runs per game according to Joe Montano, the team's center fielder. He and two other players scored more runs than any other Bulldog nine prior to 1950.

A few batting averages attest to the awesome power this group displayed. John Toledo at first base hit .508 and went on to play pro ball in the West Texas League. Joe Montano hit .448. Jerry Myers .423. Bobby Lemmel, mentioned earlier, hit .429 and was remembered by Joe when he played for the Albuquerque Dukes.

"Bobby hit a home run in the bottom of the ninth inning to win the league championship for the Dukes. The crowd was going crazy at Tingley Field and sticking so many dollar bills in the backstop fence that Bobby had to call out some of his teammates to gather in all the cash! He probably picked up 300 bucks that night. More than he made in monthly salary," Joe conjectured.

I asked Joe, "How in the heck did your guys lose a game?"

"It was up in Santa Fe against the Demons. The wind was blowing 30 to 50 miles per hour. If that wasn't bad enough there were inmates from the State Prison building a fence in the outfield, and when we came to bat they would take their shovels and throw dirt into the wind so we couldn't see a darn thing! We lost 12-8.

A rare event occurred after the Bulldogs won the State Championship with a 12-3 win over Mountainair. The team met in the locker room to turn in their uniforms.

"I got somethin' to tell you guys," Coach Rushing said. "Coach Mickey Miller at Highland has challenged us to a game. It doesn't make any difference to me. You guys have beaten them twice but they think they're better than you."

The Bulldogs had to accept the challenge given the gauntlet pitched at them. Highland had Pete Vance, Mike Hoeck and a formidable team and were playing on their field in front of a large, partisan crowd. Coach Rushing, apparently to give the Hornets a fighting chance, selected Jack Housely, the team's third starter, as their pitcher. The Bulldogs hammered HHS for the third straight time 17-8, leaving little doubt who deserved to be State Champs.

Joe also recalled a game against St. Mary's in 1949.

"St. Mary's had Pete Domenici, Mike Sanchez, Charlie Villa, Leon Palmisano, Chuck Lambert and others who were great players. They won State that year. I hit a ball to short-stop and was legging it out to first. I've got my head down running as hard as I could and look up and see Gene Carrico, the St. Mary's catcher complete with shinguards and chest protector beating me to first base!"

In the dugout Coach Rushing said:

"In all my years playing and coaching baseball I've never seen a catcher beat a batter to first base. Joe, you're the slowest kid a foot that I've ever seen."

Most readers will assuredly recall St. Mary's Pete Domenici, first as Mayor of Albuquerque and secondly as U.S. Senator, but few will remember him for his pugilism. His Republicanism, yes, but as a fighter, no.

It seems that Pete took a liking to a Highland girl at the Heights Community Center one evening and asked her to dance. Jerry Unser, mentioned earlier, also had his eye on the same girl. Jerry's brother Bobby interdicted himself and challenged Pete to a fight. The two protagonists later met up at El Sombrero Restaurant nearby and the earlier confrontation escalated. Pete, the pitcher and all-around good guy, and Bobby, the hell-bent for leather race car driver and trouble maker, duked it out in the parking lot in front of an anxious audience of their peers.

"It was a draw," Joe Montano ruled in retrospect.

There is an interesting sequel to this story.

After Pete was elected Mayor and Bobby won the "Indy 500," the ever gracious and astute politician presented Bobby with a "Key to the City." Bobby, symbolically, must have given the Mayor the key to his race car as Pete drove on a fast track to Washington, D.C. and has served as a U.S. Congressman and Senator for decades.

The 1950-51 school year and the second half of the twentieth century began with the election of Ernest Barela as President of the Senior Class, Donnie Brooks, Vice-President and Mannie Gallegos as Secretary.

With the loss of eight All-Stars and only six lettermen returning, Pete MCDavid and his football staff must have had some doubts about the prospective success of his green Bull-dogs. Duplicating the undefeated season of 1949 would indeed be a hard act to follow.

A formidable defense, anchored by linemen and Co-Captains Buddy Endsley, appropriately at end, and Marlin Pound at tackle plus returning star tackle Ralph Melbourne, Bob Cummins, Dick Brittelle, Sam Large, Lee Kolb, Larry Ross and Frank Martinez, held 10 opponents to a measly 58 points the entire season. Only a close 14 to 7 loss to Clovis and a 19 to 6 defeat to the eventual state champions Carlsbad Cavemen, marred this team's 8-2 record.

The loss to Clovis was devastating. The Bulldogs should have won handily. Coaches McDavid, Rushing and Principal Glen Ream were commiserating with each other while eating dinner after the game. Pete was really "down in the dumps." Al Beebe, a junior at AHS but also a sportswriter for the *Journal*, listened intently as the three digested their loss.

"Suddenly Coach Rushing changed the subject. He started talking about his family and growing up in Oklahoma and completely took Pete's mind off the game. I'd never seen that side of Coach Rushing before. In front of the team he was always gruff and hard-nosed. Boy, was I surprised," Al remembered.

The backfield featured Cliff Caster at quarterback, speedy Fred Leyba at fullback and Jack Ward and Donn Linberg at halfbacks. Ward, Caster, Brittelle and Melbourne would be named to the All-Star Team as well as All-City.

Perhaps one of the most remarkable happenstances occurred at Bulldog Day in 1950. There were two AHS Homecoming Queens. Not only did the two girls share the crown, they were sisters—identical twins. Jean and Jane Goodman. Their gracious attendants were Rose Apodaca and Jeanette Gonzales. Many classmates during all three years never could discern who was Jane and who was Jean. On one occasion, at least, it really didn't matter.

Another memorable event occurred about the same time during Homecoming. The Class of 1950 made a gift of the Bulldog statue that graces the cover of this book and which would stand guard in our patio for years to come.

Art Casias was a star sprinter for all three years at AHS

and in 1950, his senior year, the Bulldogs were New Mexico State Champions in track and field. Art also utilized his speed as a halfback on the gridiron on the Bulldog undefeated team (10-0) in 1949. After serving the in the U.S. Air Force, Art went to work with the Air Force Weapons Laboratory and was involved as project manager for various Department of Defense classified projects. While completing 35 years of civil service, Art was also engrossed in the passion of his youth—sports. He officiated at high school football and basketball games and was a starter for APS track meets. He coached a Young American Football League (YAFL) team, was President of the YAFL Coaches and was Head Commissioner for two years. He also was Co-Head Coach of the Albuquerque Police Athletic League and was the sprinter-relay coach for the Albuquerque Supremes Track Club which won the National AAU Youth Track Championship in 1977. Art also found time to serve as a member of the League of United Latin American Citizens (LULAC) as well as the Hispanic Chamber of Commerce. In 1989 Art became Publisher of the Albuquerque Public Schools basketball and football programs through his company Albuquerque Sports Highlites.

As children many of us were fascinated by turtles and snakes, but very few make reptiles and amphibians their life's work. Letitia Creveling (Pierce), '50, credits Maude Spencer, her biology teacher, and Doc Harrington for furthering her childhood interest in the study of herpetology. Letitia, a Gold "A" Honor Society student at AHS, was active in the New Mexico Herpetological Society for over 30 years and served as the organization's President and Treasurer. She has also served on the Rio Grande Nature Center State Park Advisory Board and the Major's Zoo Advisory Board. Letitia was instrumental in starting a docent program at the Rio Grande Zoo and served as the organization's Chairperson. In 1992 she received the New Mexico Veterinary Medicine Association's "Humanitarian of the Year" award.

Those AHS students from the class of 1950 who were acquainted with Richard E. (Dick) Ransom knew that he was programmed for exceptional achievement no matter what field of endeavor he chose. While at AHS Dick was a member of the Student Council, President of the Albuquerque Youth

135

Council, Editor of the Yucca journal, a member of the Gold "A" Honor Society, a delegate to Boys State and was a letterman in track. At UNM, he continued to excel graduating *Cum Laude* with a B.A. in Political Science. He was President of his senior class as well as President of KHATALI, the men's academic honor society. He continued his athletic pursuit and lettered in track and was a Navy ROTC Marine Corps Officer Candidate. In 1959, Dick received his law degree from Georgetown University and began a 22 year career as a trial lawyer. In 1986, Dick became Justice Ransom as he was elected to the New Mexico Supreme Court. He achieved the pinnacle of his chosen career when he served as Chief Justice from 1991 to 1994. This writer vividly recalls the inspirational and professional image that Dick projected to his undergraduate fraternity brothers at UNM. We too, knew he would rise to the top.

Following in the footsteps of a brother who left a sizeable imprint at AHS could be a difficult task, but one that J.S. (Stan) Tixier met with calm and unenviable equanimity. Stan's brother Ed was his hero and a giant among men, but Stan, '50, left an indelible mark also on Bulldog lore. Stan lettered in three sports. He was a member of the undefeated football team in 1949 and a member of the District Championship Basketball Team in 1950. Stan was selected to play in the North-South All-Star Basketball Game and placed in the State Track and Field meet in the javelin. Stan enjoyed a 32 year career with the U.S Forest Service after graduating from the University of Albuquerque. He rose to the second highest position with the agency administering 31 million acres in Utah, Nevada, southern Idaho and western Wyoming. His strength of character grounded by the Tixier values has served him well in negotiating controversial natural resource management activities. Stan has written a novel "Green Underwear" in which his fictional hero, true to his service "bleeds green" much like true Bulldogs. Also an acclaimed poet, Stan dedicated his poem "The Victory Shirt" to his undefeated '49 Team. Stan raises and trains foxtrotting horses and has become a notable, published cowboy poet.

Dorothy Lewis (Ribble), better known to her 1951 classmates as "Dottie" was, by her own admission, a late bloomer.

Although she was a member of the staff of *La Reata*, a member of the Pepper Club and the Archaeology Club Dottie blossomed while as UNM. She was a majorette with the UNM Band for 4 years, Popularity Queen in 1953 and Homecoming Queen in 1954. She was also Senior Class Secretary-Treasurer and qualified for the Honor Society as a sophomore. After graduation Dottie was very active in the Junior League of Albuquerque, President of the Albuquerque City Panhellenic and the Tri-Delta Alumni Association. She has also been active in the New Mexico Alumni Association serving as Chairperson for the 10th and 25th year reunions, as well as a Board member of Jobs Daughters and Rainbow Girls.

The 50-51 basketball team was also challenged by a lack of experience. It had no lettermen returning from the previous year, and the season record of only four wins and seventeen losses reflected that fact. Home losses to Melrose, Durango, Raton and Portales, which normally in the past would all have been "W's" must have set in motion the school's decision to replace the likeable head coach Johnny Caton. The next year, this writer's sophomore year, AHS would have a new basketball coach and renewed optimism. Ironically, at the end of the next three years the total team wins in 1954 would be the same as 1951. Something that wasn't expected at the largest school in the state with a tradition of fielding competitive teams in all sports.

This Team actually possessed some excellent natural talent though inexperienced. Tom Isaacson, a junior, would, the following year, be selected an All-Star and would also be selected years later to the All-Time AHS Basketball Team. Jimmy Williams, Dick Brittelle, Cale Carson and Wade Ullom were well over six feet tall. David Marquez, Julian Montoya and Roger Aragon were good shooters and slick ball handlers. Coaching is the key ingredient to success regardless of the level of competition, but most particularly in high school, as AHS basketball in the early 50s will attest.

Tom Issacson wasn't expecting to play in the first game against Belen. He was just thrilled to be on the team. Suddenly while Tom was sitting on the bench chewing a stick of gum, Coach Caton called out:

"Tom! Get your warmups off and get in there!"

Tom admitted, suddenly thrust into the limelight in front of a full house of fans, that he was terrified. His throat went as dry as a New Mexico June day and the gum stuck to his teeth and the roof of his mouth. He was finding it difficult just to breathe, much less get into the rhythm of the game. Somehow, like so many of us who have likewise experienced that first game, saliva returned to Tom's mouth and he found that "spring in his step" as he achieved a significant level of success in 1952 on the basketball court.

Although enthusiasm had probably waned on the hard-court, student interest in hockey was heating up on the ice. Vernon King, who had graduated in 1950 and was the star skater his senior year, was named coach. His first task was to teach some of his squad, Jerry Davis in particular, how to stay vertical on the slippery surface.

Jerry's ability to participate in both football and hockey was a minor miracle in itself.

Jerry's mother died when he was just a sophomore and he and his brother were raised by their grandmother. Someone in their family had to earn an income so both boys couldn't attend school at the same time. Jerry opted to work and landed a full time job at Marberry Construction Co. By the time his brother had graduated from Highland and Jerry returned to AHS he was age 19 and too old to compete in high school athletics. Thanks to the efforts of Pete McDavid, Jerry received special consideration from the New Mexico High School Activities Association to participate in athletics for one year. With great gusto the "old man," who was mature enough to vote for Ike in 1952, seized the long-awaited opportunity in Hockey.

Jerry may have been a little too aggressive for some of the more polished performers on the opposite teams. An article in the *Albuquerque Journal* dated January 19, 1951 stated, "A third period fight between Albuquerque High's Jerry Davis and Fred Fulgenzi of the Hill Toppers (Los Alamos) charged [sic] the game." Later in a game against hated rival Highland, a major brawl broke out on the ice which prompted Jerry's visit later to Mr. Ream's office. The Principal unequivocally stated, "Mr. Davis. If you're involved in any fight again, you won't graduate." Jerry, waiting so long to get to AHS, wasn't about to blow it. He became Vice-President of his senior class and graduated at the age of 21.

One of the stars of that year's hockey team was Dave Quinlan. Thanks to our mothers, recorded records of our accomplishments as youngsters whether it is sports, music, scholarship *et al*, is usually preserved, in this era, by Mom. Mine maintained three scrapbooks which will serve as an archive for what is soon to follow. They are shamelessly biased of course, but there are no "I"s in Team and what serves as a permanent record for one son or daughter also incorporates his or her teammates. Dave Quinlan's mom preserved some invaluable articles on his hockey exploits.

Against Los Alamos, the *Journal* article read, "Dave Quinlan's goal after four minutes of play in a sudden death overtime, gave the Albuquerque Bulldogs a thrilling 1-0 ice hockey victory over Los Alamos today." In a *Tribune* article dated 2/22/51, "Wing Dave Quinlan was the hero of the Green's last ditch assault slamming home two of the needed goals home."

In another article written for the *Journal* by Al Beebe who was a student at AHS at the time stated, "Murphy (Len) was by far the finest player on the ice, skating rings around every body and handling the puck very well." Murphy, by the way, transferred from St. Mary's so that he could play hockey. The next year the Cougars had their own team, but AHS had "Murph."

Quinlan was quick to point out that though he received little press, Marlin Pound was a "monster goalie." Dave added, "Marlin was one of the greatest all-around athletes at AHS. He was an outstanding football player and was an incredible pitcher on our baseball team. Plus, he was one of the smartest students at AHS." Marlin was selected as a member of AHS' All-Time Baseball Team.

There is an interesting personal sidebar to the short-lived hockey program at AHS. As a grade schooler in the frozen clime of Green Bay, Wisconsin, this writer learned to skate about the time that he learned to walk. I played hockey as there was little else to do outdoors in the winter and ice was as abundant as water. I was also a speed skater as my mom's scrapbook attests. How was it then that I wasn't a member of the 1952 hockey team? Had new Coach George Foehr known from whence I had come to Albuquerque, I'm sure he would have recruited this "puckster," but fortunately I had discovered a new sport, and a new mountain to climb—skiing.

Despite the fact that there were only a few letterman returning from the State Championship Baseball team of 1950, the '51 team almost won it all. In addition, the previous year's batting champ, Johnny Toledo, was injured playing football and unable to play his senior year. Losing this .500 hitter was like the Yankees losing the Babe.

Great pitching from Marlin Pound and Louie Neal and backed up by All-Time AHS Team member Dave Marquez as the team leader and catcher, the Bulldogs became as the season progressed a formidable bunch. There were moments of levity also.

For some unknown reason, Stanley High School, which seemingly would be hard pressed to find nine boys in school to field a team, was on the Bulldog schedule. Cliff Caster, who was later selected as a member of the All-Time AHS Baseball Team, remembers that game. He made the second and the third outs in one inning!

The score was about 38 to zip in the third inning. Cliff, feeling compassion for the outmanned opponents deliberately, as an act of mercy, made out number three. When he returned to the dugout Coach Rushing was angry as a bear who had just stuck his nose in a hornet's nest. The game was called at the end of the third which makes the incident even more remarkable.

Dave Quinlan was playing second base in a critical game at Highland High's field, which didn't yet have an outfield fence. The Hornet batter hit a worm killer straight at the mound, which ricocheted off the hard sunbaked surface, over Dave's head at second base, between the center and right fielders and rolled to eternity. A ground ball home run! Don't see many of those even in the "olden days." Dave recalls that the Green and White lost by that one run. And, despite the fact that the Bulldogs had beaten HHS 9-0 in an earlier game, they lost the District Tournament to Highland which went on to win the State championship. Admittedly, the Hornets had a superb team but they had extreme difficulty disposing of those tenacious "Dawgs." Later the NMHSSA would amend its rules to allow the first and second teams in the District to go to the State.

Pete McDavid's 1951 track and field team was also depleted by graduation as only four letterman returned. Fred Leyba was outstanding in the sprints and the relays as well as the javelin. Lee Kolb was also blessed with great speed in the 100 and 200 yard dashes. Bob Campbell's versatility in the broad jump, sprints, and hurdles would prepare him for attaining an exceptional feat and national honor in his senior year. John Carpenter was the epitome of hard work as he "ground it out" running the gruesome mile. These idols would be my teammates in 1952.

Probably due to the persistent efforts of Jim Stevens, who would soon earn the nickname "Fish," AHS produced its first swim team in 1951. Tony Valdez was called upon to coach a triad of teams all competing at the same time: swimming, golf, and tennis. Tony, possessed with enormous energy and interest in kids, was everywhere. Boxing was eliminated as an official team sport allowing, quite possibly in Tony Wilson's mind as Athletic Director, free time for Coach Valdez.

In this inaugural year the team worked out at the YMCA only two blocks from the AHS campus. The "Y" pool was so narrow that AHS would race two swimmers on one side of the diving board and two opponents on the other side. The pool was only twenty yards in length opposed to a regulation twenty-five and the diving board was lower than the standard, but a new activity at AHS had been born and in just one year, the Bulldogs would excel at another sport.

Despite the fact that 1951 did not produce any State Champions in golf, the team won four matches according to *La Reata*. Ted Howden, who as the tallest and most physically imposing kid in his class but was unable to compete in football or basketball due to a health problem, took up golf and took out his frustration on poor little "dimples." Leroy Weller became quite proficient at the game often playing to par. Walter Schmider, who would become this writer's neighbor in the Sixties, was also a member of the 1951 team. He had a terrific array of "junk" shots. Readers who know Walter will understand this reference.

Competing on the tennis team was Jack Bobroff, who despite the fact that he never would have challenged greats like Jack Kramer or Bobby Riggs, became the Superintendent of the Albuquerque Public Schools from 1988 to 1994. Outstanding players on this team were Don Smiley and Robert Sanchez.

Jack made several interesting observations. May Klicker was Chairperson of the Loan Committee for the Teachers Credit Union in the Fifties. She kept all the records in one drawer of her small desk at AHS. In 1999 Jack assumed the same Chairmanship. By then the Credit Union had $600 million in assets and would have required most of "Old Main" to house its records.

Jack also had a great Doc Harrington story. Doc developed a formula to determine the quantity of horsepower a human being could generate. He selected Phil Harris, who was as fine a physical specimen attending AHS as was available, and had him run three flights of stairs. By extrapolating the time it took to run the stairs and factoring in Phil's weight, the percentage grade, etc. Doc arrived at a HHP— Human Horse Power. Jack couldn't recall the number but the clever and resourceful old genius concluded that according to his formula, he, Doc, had more HHP than Phil Harris. And, he probably convinced his class that he was right!

SENIOR CLASS OFFICERS

The Bulldog-Hornet game, Junior-Senior prom, Senior week — how the year of the graduating class of 1954 flew. We no sooner had our class officers elected, when it was time to elect our Bulldog Day court. Donna Standfier, Jay Twilley and Jo Hankins were the lucky three. They had a full and exciting day.

The 1954 journalistic work was directed by other members of our Senior class. Editing the Record were Harry P. Moskos, Martha Mersman and Carol Kutnewsky. La Reata was edited by Carolyn Maciel and Betty Anne Rose. The Yucca editor was Allan Vermillion.

As the graduating Seniors of 1954 received their diplomas they knew this year would never fade from memory.

CHARLOTTE STEVENS
Vice-President

BILL McILHANEY
President

MARLENE FORD
Secretary-Treasurer

GLEN O. REAM, Principal

Mr. Glen O. Ream holds the most important position at Albuquerque High School. He is looked upon not only as a principal and advisor, but also as a friend to both the students and faculty. Serving Albuquerque High for twenty-eight years, he has accomplished much. We feel that he is the one person who best represents AHS.

MARY COLE DIXON, Assistant Principal

Assistant principal of Albuquerque High is Miss Mary Cole Dixon. She is admired and respected for her efficient work here at Albuquerque High. She has served us for twenty-eight years with her wisdom and sympathy. Throughout these many years of service she, too, has been an outstanding representative of Albuquerque High.

ADMINISTRATORS OF ALBUQUERQUE HIGH SCHOOL

Pictured above are first and second semester officers, Homer Ledbetter, President; Irene Scott, Secretary; and Bill McIlhaney, Vice-President.

The most outstanding organization at AHS is the Student Council, directed by Mr. Glen O. Ream, and Student Affairs Counselor, Jewell Brown.

The council is divided into different committees which plan activities such as Pioneer Day, Pep Rallies, and the Green and White Ball.

This year's Student Council has done a very good job and the student body owes it a vote of gratitude and thanks.

STUDENT COUNCIL

Myrle Van Atta
Secretary-Treasurer

Jerry Ginsburg
President

Carol Kutnewsky
Vice-President

HONOR SOCIETY

Glo Hanawald

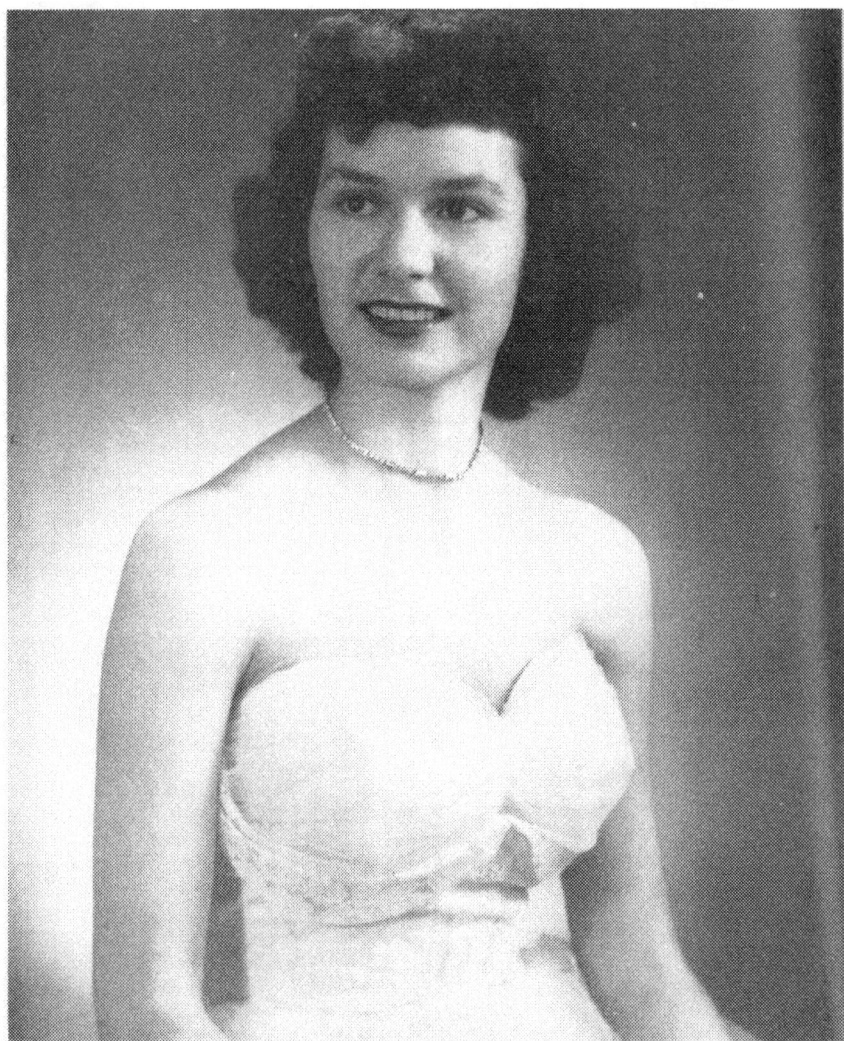

DONNA STANDFIER, Bulldog Queen

This comely brunette reigned for Bulldog Day. She was chosen from a field of twelve by the vote of the student body. She was crowned by Homer Ledbetter, president of the Student Council. While the band played and the drill squad gave salute, the applause to our queen was heard. After this glorious afternoon, she again was praised at the Homecoming game which ended her day long activities.

JO HANKINS, Attendant

JAY TWILLEY, Attendant

ROYAL COURT

The royal court is seen here watching the drill team perform during the halftime of our Homecoming game with the Carlsbad Cavemen. Our lovely Bulldog Queen Donna Standfier and her attendants Jay Twilley and Jo Hankins are shown here with their escorts. Left to right, Jay Twilley and Jack Farmer, Donna Standfier and Bill McIlhaney, Jo Hankins and John Anderson. This picture was taken on the football field during the ceremonies.

"A" TEAM CHEERLEADERS

Left to right, are Gloria Koenig, Sue Harris, Arlene Garcia (Head Cheerleader), Virginia Shaver and Joyce Campbell. They deserve much of the credit for the success of our games.

NOVEMBER

SOPHOMORE TALENT ASSEMBLY

The Sophomore class put on a talent assembly sponsored by Mr. Lacour, Mr. Thomas, Miss Trammell, and Mr. Hannah. There was a surprising amount of talent brought forward from the Sophomore class. The assembly was presented to the student body, but was made up entirely of Sophomore talent. Pictured at the left, is Betsy Bell doing her personation of the Charleston.

FOOTBALL 1953

TONY VALDEZ

ED GARVANIAN

PETE McDAVID
Head Coach
and his assistants.

JACK RUSHING

FRED RENFRO

ALBUQUERQUE BULLDOGS

First row, left to right, seated. Leonard Lewis, Sam Gardipe, Lanny Dally, Bob Stewart, Noel Baca, Mel Sedillo, Charles Salazar, Ralph Boan, Ray Dunaway, Tony Chavez, H. B. Sanders.

Second row. Stanley Williams, Dick Wilson, Bill Easley, James Morgan, Larquin Casados, Junior Gutier-rez, Merrill Rogers, Jerry Billings, Joe Shupla, Bob Apodaca, Jack Sullins, Mike Saul.

Third row, Benny Gutierrez, Gene Fox, George Hutchison, Kent Bennett, Joe Harris, Brice Day, Billy Mann, Velma Corley, Jimmie Harris, Henry Saavedra, Bob Schnurr, Jack Stromberg, Buster Quist, Dale Gallaher, Tom Neibery, Ralph Black.

RALPH BOAN
Halfback
1 Letter

Jack Stromberg (L)
H.B. Sanders (Rt)
Football Co-Captains
1953

COACH BOB HEINSOHN   COACH FRED RENFRO   COACH JOHNNY CATON   TED WATRIN, Manager

VARSITY BASKETBALL SQUAD

Below are pictured the Varsity Basketball squad, First row left to right, Eugene Agnes, Roger Montoya, Billy Barela, Allan McNamee, Sam Gardipe.

Second row, George Harris, Mike Padilla, Eddie Geis, Jack Stromberg, Lee Daily, Ambrio Villareal, Bob Fink.

ON HIS WAY: Fullback Freddie Leyba (60), moves goalward after taking a Dave Gloro pass in the second quarter of Thursday's Bulldog-Hornet game. The play was good for 36 yards and Albuquerque High's first touchdown in its 28-9 victory over rival Highland. Buster Quist (70) and Jack Stromberg (87) watch the fullback fly, while a Hornet tackler (in Leyba's shadow) fails in his attempt to bring him down.

(Laskar photo)

August 23, 1953

WHAT'S IN STORE FOR 1953: Albuquerque line coach Jack Rushing (left), Jack Stromberg, Buster Quist, and head coach Pete McDavid peer into the pigskin crystal ball, trying to see what their future will be in the AA Conference. Stromberg and Quist, both holdovers from last year, will be important cogs in the Bulldogs' machine. AHS has been undergoing conditioning drills at Hopewell Field, where about 100 candidates are trying out for the team. Albuquerque opens its campaign Sept. 18 against Gallup.

(Britton photo)

ROMP—Buster Quist finds a gaping hole and plunges for a touchdown (nullified by penalty) against Santa Fe last night, while Ray Crews makes the tackle. Watching action at left is Demon Ramon Gallegos while the referee is Billy Wood. The Bulldogs penalized 15 yards on the play above, scored on a 19-yard scamper by Jim Harris on the next play. (Russell Photo).

★ ★ ★   ★ ★ ★

Nightmare for Santa Fe — *Oct. 10, 1953*

High-Riding Dawgs Ready for Cougars; Dump Demons 52-12

Bulldogs Dominate
Nov 14, 1952
All-City Football Team

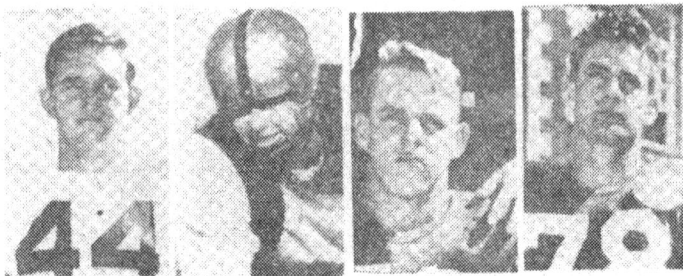

| Teddy Rhodes | John McCormack | Mike Schlick | Phil Harris |

★ ★ ★   ★ ★ ★

All-City A-Conference Team

Player and School	(Pts.)	Class	Weight	Position
Buster Quist, AHS	(60)	Jr.	170	End
John McCormack, Highland	(58)	Sr.	165	Tackle
Teddy Rhodes, Highland	(70)	Sr.	170	Guard
Mike Schlick, AHS	(66)	Sr.	164	Center
Mariano Marcelli, AHS	(43)	Sr.	150	Guard
Bob Cross, AHS	(39)	Sr.	204	Tackle
Jack Stromberg, AHS	(60)	Jr.	159	End
Davey Otero, AHS	(66)	Sr.	134	Quarterback
Tommy McDonald, Highland	(70)	Sr.	150	Halfback
Jack Brown, AHS	(53)	Sr.	165	Halfback
Phil Harris, AHS	(56)	Sr.	178	Fullback

A-Conference Second Team

Mike Hoeck, Highland	(32)	Sr.	165	End
Art Dahlberg, Highland	(38)	Sr.	172	Tackle
Jim Durrett, Highland	(39)	Sr.	145	Guard
Vern Wood, Highland	(18)	Jr.	145	Center
Anthony Simon, AHS	(29)	Sr.	157	Guard
Jack Mills, St. Mary	(37)	Sr.	160	Tackle
Vic Zurcher, Highland	(30)	Sr.	140	End
Gene Franchini, St. Mary	(31)	Sr.	150	Quarterback
Billy Wagner, Highland	(35)	Sr.	135	Halfback
H. B. Sanders, AHS	(33)	Jr.	135	Halfback
Rusty Shaffer, Highland	(54)	Sr.	150	Fullback

Honorable Mention: Ends—Maurice Herring, St. Mary 19; Irwin Thomson, Highland 9; Jerry Purdy, St. Mary 7. Tackles—Foy Graves, AHS 30; Roger Hathoot, St. Mary 17; Clemente Chavez, AHS 13. Guards—Mike Nigro, St. Mary 22; Fred Allen, AHS 19; Arnold Levick, Highland 11; Tommy Sandoval, St. Mary 8. Centers—Jack O'Boyle, Highland 11; Don DeBlassie, St. Mary 10; Monte Barton, Highland 5; Ken Martinez, St. Mary 3. Quarterbacks—David Mohar, Highland 28. Halfbacks—Dale Gallaher, AHS 14; Fred Lovato, St. Mary 10; Louie Yannoni, St. Mary 4. Fullbacks—Jackie Martinez, St. Mary 7; Dick Wilbert, Highland 4.

State Champions
1953

ALBUQUERQUE BULLDOGS: Front row, left to right: R. Lucas, D. Young, H. Cotton, R. Duran, E. Geis, D. Tenbroeck, G. Harris. Back row, left to right: Glen O. Ream, principal of Albuquerque high school, B. Day, B. Gideon, B. Stover, M. Saul, H. Saaverdra, B. Quist, B. Fink, George Foehr, coach. Seated in front: B. Young and J. Fink, batboys. Photo by Skrondahl.

AHS Wins State Legion Championship

The Albuquerque Bulldogs defeated Clovis 4-1 and 7-1 to win the American Legion Junior Baseball Tournament. Bob Stover chalked up both victories to send the winners to Regional meet at York, Nebraska.

The Bulldogs, behind Coach George Foehr, were the first AHS team to win the title of State Champs.

After defeating Highland High and Oden Motor, the Bulldogs went to Gallup to play the Regional State game there. Without wasting any time, AHS set back Gallup twice, 7-2, and 8-0.

third games. In a slugfest, the Clovis nine took a 9-6 win over the Bulldogs.

The 14 members of the team traveled to York, Nebraska, for the Regional meet. Coach Foehr and Mr. Glen Ream accompanied the team on the trip.

The Bulldogs were defeated by Hastings to knock the locals from the Tournament. The Bulldogs, behind the pitching of Buster Quist, set back Cheyenne, Wyoming 7-3, before being set back by Hastings 3-1.

Linescores—

Cheyenne   100 100 010—3 4 7
Albuq.   003 312 01x—7 9 2

Ron Mathewson and Bill Allen; Buster Quist and Ed Geis Don Tenbroeck.

First Game—
Clovis   001 000 0—1 3 2
Albuq.   100 030 x—4 7 6
Isham, Harrison (5), and Gentry; Stover and Tenbroeck
Winner—Stover. Loser—Harrison.

Third Game—
Clovis   001 000 000—1 6 8
Albuq.   140 000 20x—7 5 1
Isham, Lanier, and Howell, Stover and Tenbroeck.
Winner—Stover, Loser—Isham.

Coach Foehr
A Job Well Done

At Bell Park in Clovis the Albuquerque team won two of the three games, winning the first and

QUIST, STOVER LEADS AHS PITCHING; FINK LEADS TEAM HITTING, BATS 366

Bob Fink and Don Young were the leading batsmen for the Albuquerque Bulldogs winning team.

Fink, who boasted a 366 average, was top man for the Bulldog squad. Don Young, fast Bulldog shortstop, was hitting at the 342 mark. The only other two players over the 300 mark were first-sacker Mike Saul at 314, and ace righthander Bob Stover, who is batting at 306.

Buster Quist and Bob Stover lead the Bulldogs pitching staff with seven victories each. Quist lost only one game.

BULLDOG AVERAGES

Player	AB	Hits	Runs	Pct.
Cotton, lf	67	15	20	.223
Day, p	34	10	6	.294
Duran, of	16	4	5	.250
Fink, 2b	96	35	25	.366
Geis, c	62	14	16	.226
Gideon, rf	39	8	12	.205
Harris, 3b	87	21	21	.242
Lucas, of	9	2	3	.222
Quist, p	28	5	7	.179
Saavedra, cf	74	21	19	.276
Saul, 1b	98	31	24	.314
Stover, p	59	18	8	.306
Tenbroeck, c	33	9	7	.273
Young, ss	114	39	33	.342

PITCHING RECORDS

	G.	I.P.	H	R	W.K.	W	L	S.O.	Pct.
Day,	7	40	34	27	23	5	2	32	.714
Stover,	12	76	63	36	20	7	5	105	.583
Quist,	9	68	36	24	27	7	1	55	.875

NEW MEXICO
Magazine

FEBRUARY 1959   35 CENTS

Buster Quist
New Mexico Ski Team
1953-1954

CHAPTER SIX: SEARCHING FOR A SPRING IN OUR STEP 1951-1952

WRITING AFTER THE TURN OF THE CENTURY and looking back to the 1950's, Kathleen Parker commented aptly:

We never completely transcend our high school experience. Those who consider themselves successful in high school have a spring in their step throughout their lives, no matter how dismally they may perform later. Conversely, those who consider themselves failures in high school, no matter how much they succeed later, tend to suffer a lack of confidence.

For boys, unfortunately, success—especially a few decades ago—was tied to athletic prowess. Oh, we knew who the geniuses were, but who cared.[9]

To Parker, it is absurd to tie success to athletic prowess but we (boys), as the Fifties began, were only responding to a measurement of value placed on athletics by our parents, our peers and our past. Parker, it seems, does not understand the drama of sports, nor does she grasp the personal, social and political importance of sports in America's past and present. To those who were athletes, our personal identity, pride, self-esteem, and even our destiny was at stake in the world of sports. Richard Lipsky[10] properly frames the

---

[9] Kathleen Parker, Tribune Media Services, The Arizona Republic, November 3, 2001.

significance of this phenomenon that consumed our lives when he says, "...the Sportsworld exists as a dramatic, symbolic universe that generates an emotional impact and creates meaning for millions of people."

To Lipsky, the "holy trinity" of football, basketball and baseball became a major form of national and social communication. The emergence of a new social ethic stressing team work inherent in these three sports created a feeling of togetherness and belonging which brought about a major shift in American idealogy at the beginning of the Twentieth Century. By the time that my parents were in high school the search for human significance had manifested itself in these three sports. The sports world then contained what the real world lacked; "Charisma, magical performances, gifted leaders and intense rituals,"[11] and it still does. Athletic heroism probably best exemplified by the flamboyant personage of Babe Ruth in the golden age of sports of the 1920s, paralleled the rise of American capitalism and "dovetailed with the movement towards the nationalization of a consumer culture."[12] Without fear of overemphasizing the role of sports, Woody Hayes, the volatile coach of the Ohio State Buckeyes, is reported to have said:

"Without any winners we wouldn't have any goddamn civilization."

If we were to find a "spring in our step," in the 50s the most likely stage was the sports world. But Parker was right in one regard. Yes, we knew who the geniuses were but little value was ascribed to intellectual acumen. That day would come, of course, when we all experienced "The Revenge of The Nerds."

---

[10] "How We Play The Game—Why Sports Dominate American Life", Richard Lipsky, Beacon Press, Boston, MA, 1980, P. 144.

[11] IBID, page 62.

[12] IBID, page 113.

The Quist family moved from Green Bay, Wisconsin, in late March of 1950 to Albuquerque when my father accepted the position as State Manager for Businessmen's Assurance Co. I enrolled at Washington Junior High, or as we affectionately referred to our school La Wash, and almost immediately bonded with two of my eighth grade classmates—Jack Stromberg and Gloria (Glo) Hanawald—two friends who would almost become inseparable during out high school experience at AHS.

After graduation from La Wash in June of 1951, Jack and I had an incredible summer adventure. In possession of a driver's license for a little over one year, Jack and I (age 15) drove, unaccompanied, 1800 miles to the land of my birthplace and roots, and spent the entire summer working in Door County, Wisconsin. Exhausted but inspired by our adventure, we returned to Albuquerque two days prior to the start of football practice and two weeks before the beginning of our sophomore year.

I picked Jack up at his house to go to our first football practice at Hopewell Field, which was located "kitty corner" across from the high school. We had two practices a day before school started, one early in the morning and another at 2:00 in the afternoon. There were almost 100 aspirants that turned out for the first day of practice. The largest number were sophomores, like us, who, we would learn later, were members of the largest single class ever at AHS — nearly 1,000 students (actually 967). AHS was a big school and as the politicians like to say, a "big tent." We had the ultimate ethnic mix of students and it was generally thought that us Anglos, or Gringos, were less than 50% of the student population, but that really was of no significance to any of us.

Our head coach was Pete McDavid, who came to AHS from Santa Fe High School, where his team was State Champion in 1943. In 1947 his AHS Bulldogs were also number one. Pete was an easy going, affable man who had an uncanny ability to get the best out of his "boys" without ever threatening, intimidating or humiliating them. He always had an encouraging and motivating word even after you made one of the dumbest, bone-headed mistakes imaginable. Pete was a gem and a giant amongst his contemporaries.

Jack Rushing, who was an Indian (from an unknown Oklahoma tribe), was Pete's assistant and Line Coach. He was an impressively large man who could use the opposite tack to persuade and motivate young men. Pete's other full-time assistant was Tony Valdez, who was primarily the sophomore and "B" team coach, but very capably filled any vacancy or need Pete required of him. He was truly a player's coach. So, we had a Gringo, a Native American and a Hispanic as our coaching staff, which fairly represented the makeup and mix of our team, as well as our culture. It would take many more years before Blacks were represented in the coaching ranks not only in Albuquerque but most everywhere in the U.S.

The first couple of days were devoted to conditioning drills in shorts. Jack and I were in the group of sophomores under Coach Valdez' eye. Within a few days we became close buddies of Jim Harris, H.B. Sanders, Bill Easley, Merrill Rogers and others from the other junior high schools. Our former adversaries from Lincoln Jr. High, Joe Harris, Velma Corley and Kent Bennett who were Black, made our sophomore team an impressive group. Our former teammates at La Wash, Dick Wilson, Bob Stewart, Joe Shupla, Noel Baca, Rolfe Black, Alf Howden and many others made us a formidable team. What became obvious to all of us the first day was that someone was missing. Undoubtedly the most talented prospect and certainly the fastest runner — Ralph Boan.

"Where's your buddy Ralph?" Coach McDavid asked Jack and I in the locker room after our first practice.

"Geez, don't know," I replied. "Jack and I have been in Wisconsin all summer. We didn't have any contact with him. Jack called but his phone has been disconnected."

"Can you check it out and see what's keeping him from practice?" Pete asked, obviously concerned.

"Sure. Sure Coach. We'll go out to his house this aft," I reassured Coach McDavid. Obviously the AHS Coaches knew all about Ralph and were counting on him this season.

Jack and I went out to Ralph's house where he lived the

past year with his mom and stepfather. The house was vacant. I think Ralph's folks were renting it. Ralph's real dad, Cletus, lived at the YMCA. He had worked as a lineman for an electric company and lost the fingers on both hands when he got electrocuted back in the 40s. The accident didn't prevent Cletus from playing billiards or pool. In fact, he became so good at it that he made a living hustling bets. He lived at the "Y" so he would be close to all the action downtown. All that Mr. Boan would tell us is that Ralph had moved to Farmington, New Mexico, with his mom. What we didn't know was the financial incentive given Ralph's stepfather to move to Farmington. Someone up there knew of Ralph's talent and lured him away. AHS lost one of its most promising prospects but a bigger surprise was in store for us two years later.

Us "sophs" kept to ourselves. Hazing from the upperclassmen was getting out of hand. First it was the hiding-our-clothes trick or throwing them in the shower. Lots of penny-ante crap. The towel snapping was painful. Our protagonists would wet the corners of a bath towel then snap it as it hit you in the thigh or butt. It left a red welt. The meanest trick was putting red hot analgesic balm in your jock strap or shorts. You couldn't wash it off. It felt like you were sitting on a bed of hot coals. We didn't feel we could fight back. We were intimidated. But, the day arrived for revenge.

We were now in pads. It was a hot, humid day in late August. Everybody was "dogging it." The coaches called all the team, including the "sophs," together along the west side of Hopewell Field under the shade of a line of large elm trees. Pete called for a punting drill with the first team on offense kicking and the second team on defense trying to block the kick. Us "sophs" were spectators.

No one was making much of an effort to rush the kicker or block the kick. It looked like "touch" football. Unexpectedly, Coach Rushing yelled out:

"Tony, get some of your guys in here. Let's see if any of then want to play football. I've got a bunch of 'pussies' in here. I think they all squat to pee," which was one of Coach's oft used lines.

I had been playing quarterback on offense and end on

defense on the "B" squad. I was now over 160 pounds after eating Mrs. Thorp out of house and home in the hotel kitchen in Wisconsin, so I was bigger than most of the varsity ends with the exception of Paul Lambert. I sensed an opportunity. Also, I wanted to get even for all the hazing and this would be my chance to get the coach's eye. You don't articulate these thoughts at times like this—even to yourself, but competition naturally pricks your instincts.

Blocking my path to the kicker was Donn Linberg. Donn was a senior. A neato guy. He wasn't one of the "jerks" who harassed us but he stood between me and my objective. Donn was an excellent halfback but he was wiry and small. The program listed him at 148 pounds. He clearly wasn't ready for what was about to happen. Davey Otero, the star quarterback, was the kicker. I got down in a three point stance frothing at the bit to spring into action. The adrenaline really kicked in for the first time in my life.

Bob Cummins, the center, snapped the ball. I shot off the line like a sprinter out of the blocks. Donn was standing almost erect and was relaxed. He wasn't ready for hard contact. My shoulder hit him in the chest and my helmet caught him under his chin. Sheer force of the impact drove Donn straight back into the punter. Davey never got the kick off! Donn was dazed. Coach Rushing was ecstatic.

"Damn! We found somebody who wants to play football. Let's do'er again and see if you guys can get the kick away," Coach Rushing said, addressing and putting down the shocked first team.

The unexpected results motivated my teammates The number one guys were no longer impenetrable. But now they would be on guard.

I got ready again for my charge. On the snap, emboldened by my success, I drove off my right leg as hard as I could. Making sure I didn't hit him again full thrust, Donn got very low to block me below my waist. Too low. He tipped his strategy too soon. I leap frogged my blocker and caught the full force of the ball off Davey's foot in my chest. I smothered the kick.

"Hot damn!" Coach Rushing yelled. He ran over to where Donn was on the ground on his hands and knees still disbelieving what had just happened and bellowed his next most oft-repeated line:

"Lindberg? I don't think you can scatter s... with a rake!" Donn was embarrassed but no one dared to laugh.

But, Pete McDavid smiled.

And, Tony Valdez smiled, too. His "sophs" had made a statement.

I was elevated to the varsity. But, more importantly, I had the respect (grudgingly) of a few of my teammates, including an upperclassman, Frank Blea, a senior, who was Davey Otero's backup at QB. Frank was a short, feisty guy who had seemed to take a particular interest in me though I didn't know why.

"Pretty gutsy move there Soph," Frank said as he stared me down in the locker room after practice, with his beady, penetrating eyes.

I didn't know what to say. A pregnant silence followed. It looked like I was about to get my butt kicked by the seniors. Then Frank added:

"Yeh, you've got guts, Quist. I like that. You might be a Bulldog some day."

I had gotten even fair and square I guess. Aside from some verbal abuse, everyone left me alone from then on. This was, truly, a defining moment at a critical time in my life. It defined me as a competitor. I had to be taken seriously. As a tribute to Donn, he never held a grudge. "That's the way game is supposed to be played," he said later.

Having been on campus during pre-season football practice allowed us newcomers the opportunity to acclimate ourselves to the awesome size and grandeur of the physical layout of AHS, which would be our home for three wonderful and impressionable years. Someone arriving for class the very first day would be overwhelmed by the sheer magnitude of the campus. Finding your classes could be a test in itself, even though we had the Pepper Club, led by Jack's sister Gretchen, to assist us as Guides.

There were five major buildings, most of which were three stories high from ground level as well as a basement, laid out around the perimeter of a rectangle with a large patio situated in the middle, which served as the meeting place for the students. The architectural style could be best described as "Renaissance" according to Joe Boehning, an AHS grad and architect and athletic star from the 40s. It seemed that all schools built in the early 1900s somewhat replicated each other. Brick and concrete were the materials of choice in order to withstand an onslaught of teenagers for a hundred years. The campus was located at Central Avenue and Broadway, only a couple of blocks from downtown Albuquerque. Our school would not only serve its intended purpose for 60 years but it would enjoy a rebirth at the turn of the 21st Century.

The administration was as sturdy as the school's foundation as elucidated earlier. Glen O. Ream, our Principal, had served in that capacity since 1926 and would continue for a total of 30 years. Mary Cole Dixon, the Vice-Principal, also served in that position from 1926 and continued on for the same number of years. Given the school's consistent and capable management along with the dedicated teachers, we students had an extremely stable environment and a clearly defined system where we could learn and grow. Looking back fifty years later, Jack, who was our Sophomore Class President, said:

"There was a near total acceptance and embracing by our high school of the prevailing set of values. There was a given and established pattern. I don't remember people revolting in any aggressive way. Of course, some set out to define their own style, like the stompers or the pachucos, but this was more a gang or group mind set, not a challenge to the fundamentals. It wasn't fashionable to buck the underlying system. Most just accepted it. I guess they later called us the silent generation. But coming out after the war, with generally bright prospects before us, there were good reasons for silence. The seeds of the racial divide, and the fears of Communism that later blinded us into the tragedy of Vietnam, were certainly there, but largely unseen."

Equally defined and the most significant aspect of this new experience was the established social structure of our new community. There were three distinct visible groups: the "Rah-Rahs," the "Stompers" and the "Pachucos." The "Nerds" were not an easily definable group.

The Rah-Rahs were the athletes, the class officers, and those who were members of the Honor Society. According to Ken Skinner, who was a classmate and a Stomper, the Rah-Rahs were the kids who were "clean-cut, kept their noses clean, obeyed the rules, studied hard and acted like they owned the school." These were the kids who were "popular." And, of course, this group included the cheerleaders whose readily recognizable chant, "Rah-rah, sis-boom bah" was one of the tell-tale cheers that not only supported the "holy trinity" of football, basketball and baseball, it symbolized the new social ethic in America as described by Lipsky in his book.

Contrary to the generally accepted perception, the Rah-Rahs came from a wide range of socio-economic classes and different sections of the city. The Rah-Rahs weren't exclusively from the more upscale country club area, though Jack's family lived there. And, they weren't all Anglos. Arlene Garcia came from the Sawmill area. Dick Wilson, a Native American, lived adjacent to the Albuquerque Indian School as did Joyce Campbell. I lived in the north valley in the Alameda area which was possibly the most diverse, ethnically and economically, in the city.

Ken Skinner, who claims that the term "Stompers" originated with our class in 1951, defines who he was as a Stomper:

...our group was predominantly from the southwest valley, south of the Rio Grande river and of course, 'south of the tracks,' yet we took a measure of pride in being different.

For the most part we were the less affluent crowd. We wore skin-tight Levis, wide western-style belts with large buckles and either western-style shirts or tee shirts with the sleeves rolled up tight to show off whatever muscles we had. A few even wore western style (Cowboy) hats, but the major distinguishing part of our attire was our Cowboy boots, the fancier, the better. Mine had red wing tips against a blue background and large bootstraps down the side with my name cut into the leather...

Ken further defines the "Stompers" when they established their "turf:"

On the first day of school, we staked out our claim on

151

the High Spot Cafe and although everyone was free to come and go as they pleased, it soon became known as the Cowboy/Kicker hangout. We also staked out our 'smoking corner' across the street on the east side of school...almost all of us smoked, drank beer and strutted about as though we were tough, whether we were or not.

Lacking a "Pachuco" to define who he was or someone to admit that he was a member of that notorious gang, Ken and I developed a composite of the third of the major social groups at AHS during the early Fifties.

Although almost all the Pachucos were Hispanic very few of the Hispanics at our school were Pachucos. And, not all Hispanic groups were Pachucos and often those in the "hood" from Martineztown or Barelas would war with the Pachucos. But, despite their scarcity in members the hard core Pachucos were a very distinctive group. Their form of dress was styled after their counterparts in L.A. and the "Zoot Suiters" in New York City. According to Ken some of them wore baggy pants with pegged bottoms, thin, shiny plastic belts, loose, long-sleeved shirts, suede shoes and often sported a long chain looping down from their pants pocket. Their hair was long, slicked down with Bryllcream and combed back in a "duck tail." Most of them etched home-made tattoos into their arms and hands designating the particular gang they belonged to. Unknown to most of us at the time they got high on "weed" made of a substance none of us had ever heard of.

As ominous and intimidating as the Pachucos were, neither myself nor any of my closest friends ever had any confrontations with this group. But, we were just the Rah-Rahs. We were not the universe. A Stomper telling the story could have a totally different view as would the Pachucos and other groups, but like a painting, it is the artist's perception that molds the picture of these marvelous years of 1951 through 1954.

When the first game against Gallup at a manure-infested fairgrounds took place in a couple of weeks, I was the only sophomore in the starting lineup. Coach McDavid did not utilize his predecessor's rule prohibiting the playing of first year athletes on the varsity.

Our first team offense and defense was:

PLAYER	POSITION	CLASS
Buster Quist	Left End	Soph
Bill Tucker	Left Tackle	SR
Sid Cutter	Left Guard	SR
Bob Cummins	Center	SR
John Calkins	Right Guard	SR
Charles Barboa	Right Tackle	JR
Paul Lambert	Right End	SR
Dave Otero	Quarterback	JR
Phil Harris	Left Half Back	JR
Donn Lindberg	Right Half Back	SR
Fred Leyba	Fullback	SR

We beat an outmanned Gallup Tiger team 19 to 7 in our opener.

Our first game at home against Deming, a small town from southwestern New Mexico, was perhaps the first high school game to be televised on KOB-TV. The previous season, our family had gathered at the "Lazy Q," our ranch-styled home on Rio Grande Boulevard, and marveled at the first televised game that we had ever seen between the New Mexico Lobos and Northern Arizona University.

We were heavily favored to beat Deming but possibly due to suffering from stage fright, we garnered a not-too-impressive 36 to 24 victory.

Amongst a treasure trove of photographs is one of Donn Lindberg and me ringing the victory bell after our win over Deming. Although I can't recall doing anything exceptional, I preformed adequately enough to keep my first team job. Most importantly, I was an integral part of our team. A sense of belonging was a critical necessity at this juncture in high school. Football and athletics were our access to that end.

"Hey Buz," Jack said as I pulled up at his house on Los Alamos on our way to school. "I'm running for class president. Will you help me distribute these flyers?"

Jack had mimeographed a couple hundred of them. *No Xerox machines, of course.* It was about eight miles from our "ranch" out on Rio Grande Boulevard to Jack's house, and it was only slightly out of my way to stop and pick him up. We would usually drive up Lomas Boulevard to Broadway and then south to AHS. After driving together for over 4,000 miles it was a habit hard to break.

"Geez. Sure," I replied anxious to support my best friend.

Jack won. Arlene Garcia, from our gang at La Wash was elected Vice-President, and Mary Ann Hunt, a very attractive, olive-skinned blonde whom I thought was a "fox," was our class Secretary-Treasurer.

Our teammate Phil Harris was elected President of the Junior Class after also being President as a sophomore. Robert Vigil, who wrote in my *La Reata*, "It sure has been a thrill knowing a truly great outstanding Soph," was elected Vice-President and Sally Crook was the Junior Class Secretary-Treasurer.

The seniors, whom we looked up to with admiration, were led by Bob Campbell as President. Bob and Janet Barnes, who was the Senior Class Secretary-Treasurer, were elected to these offices all three years. They were "popular"— a very distinct designation. Jerry Davis was elected Vice-President for the first time. His arrival to this position in his class was unique and remarkable as mentioned earlier.

Perhaps the most hotly contested competition at the beginning of every year was the selection of the Cheerleaders. All five selected by the student body were seniors: Clara Lee Miller, Nancy Vann, Jane Fenley, Shirley Archibeck and Tresa Lanham. I knew Nancy well since she was one of Gretchen Stromberg's best friends and neighbor, and they were our self-appointed surrogate "mothers." They thought we needed guidance. They were probably right, as us Sophs stumbled and fumbled our way during the first month of the most significant rite of passage in our lives.

As expected given the moniker, all the Cheerleaders were Rah-Rahs with the exception of Clara Lee Miller. She was from a poor family that lived in a modest home which had no indoor plumbing, in the North Valley. She was a "country girl." And, a Stomper. Awed by the city girls, Clara Lee felt like a square peg in a round hole at AHS until she was selected by her classmates to be a Cheerleader. To be accepted was one of the most defining moments in her life and demonstrated that the holy trinity of sports could bring a spring in the step to the girls also.

Janet Barnes, who had been a member of the Drill Team for two years, desperately wanted to be a Cheerleader. She diligently trained with Jane Fenley, who had no burning aspiration to become one. Jane was elected Head Cheerleader. Janet lost out. She was devastated. She moped around for weeks but she learned from the experience. "It taught me a very valuable lesson. That dark cloud had a silver lining and fortunately, I found it," she said recalling those days a half-century ago.

Janet also recalled an event that would shortly manifest itself into a major happening. One day as the students were congregating in the patio prior to the first class, one of the boys blurted out:

"Look! Look! The Bulldog has nipples!"

Janet and her friends Gladys Miller, Helen Rogers and others peeked up at the mascot on his pedestal with disbelief. Someone had glued nipples to the Bulldog's underbelly. Draped over the neck of our symbol of male strength and tenacity was a sign which read:

"REVENGE OF THE NERDS"

The girls were embarrassed and offended. The boys were furious. Who would sully and denigrate the fighting image of our school? Who would insinuate that our heroic mascot wore a skirt? The perpetrator and an even more heinous crime would soon be revealed. Someone, obviously, that didn't subscribe to the holy trinity of sports.

Rounding out this "retinue" of support groups that were an integral part of this cultural emphasis on athletics in general and football in particular were the Majorettes, the Drill Squad and the Band.

Three girls from our gang at La Wash: Joyce Campbell, (Bob's sister), Mary Kay Hicks and Carol Jones, all sophomores, were selected as Majorettes along with Joanne Ticknor, the head of the group, who was a junior. Watching the Bulldog parade during Homecoming, Joanne reminded me of Phyllis Kessler, who performed as head majorette at Green Bay West, just two years prior. The culture in New Mexico was vastly different from Wisconsin, but the distinctly American tradition of football was the same. Not only in 1951 but thirty years prior in our parents' day.

According to *La Reata* the most prominent organization at AHS was the Student Council. This was the representational government of the citizens of our school. Although this body ran school affairs, Principal Ream, our Principal and Head Counsellor Jewell Brown had the ultimate veto power. The first semester officers were President Paul Lambert, Vice President Charles Moskos and Secretary Sally Crook. Paul repeated for the second semester and Secretary Helen Rogers and Vice President Al Beebe were newly elected officers for the second semester. Strangely, none of the elected officers were listed by their titles. As I recall Paul was President. He was well-liked and all of us who knew him regarded him as one of the hardest working and most diligent students at AHS.

I served on the Council the second semester along with my sophomore classmates Jack Stromberg, Sallie Goodrich, Jo Hankins, Harry Moskos, Gloria Koenig, Rolfe Black, Don McDonald and Dick Wilson.

The three school publications that were so popular to our every day life then and even more invaluable to us now were *La Reata,* our yearbook, the *Yucca,* our literary publication, and *The Record*, our student newspaper.

The 1952 *La Reata* with its distinctive matted, fabric cover and stylistic Latin drummer in the right-hand corner had John Johnson as its Editor-in-Chief, Marian Wiseman and Edna Ducan as Associate Editors and a staff of twenty-one students.

The Record, which was available for five cents if the students didn't have a Co-Op (ID) card, was headed by Al Beebe as Editor-in-Chief, Gordon Reiter as Associate Editor and Larry Bonaguidi as Assistant Editor. Pauline Jahraus was the Business Manager. Al, who worked for the *Albuquerque Journal* and reported on our athletic events while a student at AHS, subsequently had a long career in journalism and public relations. He was also President of the Joint Student Council with Highland High School which was the brainchild of Jewell Brown to foster better relations with what had become, in just two years, a bitter rivalry. All of the groups good effort would unravel in THE GAME with HHS two years hence.

Al was also on the staff of the *Yucca* as were my close friends Jimmie Stevens, Gretchen Stromberg, Helen Rogers, Lou Delle Fidel and Tom Isaacson. In perhaps one of the first displays of "PC" (political correctness) none of the officers were designated by their titles.

Glo was a member of the Drill Squad (90 members) which performed routines during the halftime and other events along with our Marching Band (50 members), complimented by the Honor Guard and the Color Guard. All told there were over 220 out of a student body of approximately 2000 that contributed to this spectacle and experience called football. Given this much participation and the scope and extent of the pageantry of the support groups, it is no wonder that so much societal value was placed upon this endeavor. We didn't create it. It was already in place. A natural question. How did this all begin?

The origin of football[13] can be traced back to the ancient Greeks, who played a game called Hapeston, and Italians during the Middle Ages played Calcia. The modern version of the sport, however, began in England as early as the twelfth century, but it wasn't until 1863 that the London Football Association was formed and rugby allowed the players to carry the ball for the first time.

In 1869 in the U.S. Rutgers and Princeton played an event but it was more like soccer. It was a game in 1875 between Harvard and Yale that combined the features of soccer and rugby. Walter Camp was considered the one man responsible for the formation of the American Collegiate Football Association in the same year that gave us the modern game of football.

Okay, this history is "neato" but what made this holy trinity so popular? Why did the game of football become such a dominant part of our culture and our lives?

Lipsky says, "...the high school is the foundation of the town's community identity. The importance of the team gets interwoven into the whole fabric of school and community

---

[13] Encarta Encyclopedia Deluxe Edition.

life."[14] And, he adds, "Sports is the magic elixir that feeds personal identity while it nourishes the bonds of communal solidarity."[15]

In the early Fifties, Albuquerque was the only city in New Mexico that had more than one major high school. It had three — AHS, the city's original school in the core area, St. Mary's, a Catholic high school also downtown, and Highland, a new facility (1949) in the newly developed area called Southeast Heights. There's no question that the existence of three schools (there were also two others, the Albuquerque Indian School and Menaul, a Presbyterian high school) caused a dilution of athletic talent and community identity in a town of only 97,000 residents, but it intensified an in-tracity rivalry.

After the third or fourth game Jack also made the first team at right end. Al Beebe, writing the *Albuquerque Journal*, called us the "blond bookends." We were undefeated going into the Artesia game, which was our first real competitive test although we had beaten Clovis 25 to 6 the week before.

My first class was home room. Mr. James Lacour, who taught English in room 313, was my teacher. As I looked around the room I was immediately surprised and disappointed that none of my classmates from La Wash were in the class. Most noticeably, of course, Glo wasn't there nor did I have any classes with her as I discovered at the end of the first day. Quite a change from La Wash where the same students moved together from one class to another.

Mr. Lacour was a nattily dressed young teacher with immaculately combed, long hair in a pompadour style. Like most male teachers, he wore a suit to class every day, no

---

[14] Lipsky, page 81.

[15] Lipsky, page 5.

matter if it was 90°. He stimulated my interest in literature as we read Dickens' *A Tale of Two Cities* and other classics. Wouldn't he be surprised to read this memoir? "Buster, of all kids," he would probably say shaking his head.

Glo and I would meet at the Bulldog statue that was located in the patio, if time permitted between classes and at lunch time. Quite often we would buy Mexican food from Smitty's "Tamale Cart" and have our lunch outside in the patio by the wishing well. Glo worked after school every day and on Saturdays at Korbers, and I had football practice, so we saw very little of each other during the week. At home games she performed at halftime with the drill squad and I loved to see her in her short-skirted uniform, in contrast with the almost ankle-length skirts and bobby socks. One day I suggested:

"Glo, why don't we go horseback riding on Sunday? I've got two horses now."

"That's great, Buz. I haven't ridden much. Do you think I can handle it?" Glo asked somewhat apprehensively.

"Oh sure," I reassured her. "No problem. Trigger is real docile."

It was a gorgeous fall day. The best time of the year in New Mexico. I saddled up 'ole Sparky and Trigger and we headed down through the Bosque (forest) to the Rio Grande. I wasn't about to cross the river like I did a year before with a friend of mine, but other unknown dangers were lying in wait.

The massive cottonwood trees fed by an unlimited source of underground water provided a perfect environment for a ride. There was little underbrush and the tentacle-like branches, intertwined above our heads, formed a cathedral-like ceiling. Beams of sunlight visible through the billowing dust formed a surreal aura around us.

As Glo became more comfortable with Trigger and her confidence on horseback grew, we broke out into a run. Sparky would never allow Trigger to pass him. I gained separation from Glo who was twenty yards behind me. Looking ahead, the cascading sunlight through the leaves illuminated a foreign object. A rope! Someone had strung a rope across our path, head high. I ducked just in the nick of time.

"Look out Glo! Duck!" I yelled.

"What?" Glo shouted as she rose up higher in the saddle to hear me. She didn't see the rope until the last second. It hit her arm and chest and the taut line jerked her out of the saddle, propelled her into the air, and she hit the sandy soil with a sickening thud.

I didn't know if the rope had hit her in the neck. I feared for the worst as I jumped off Sparky and ran to her side. She was frightened and crying.

"Glo, Glo! Are you alright?" I asked as I half panicked.

"I don't know. I hurt all over," she cried.

I held her in my arms. She was shaking. She sat up and began taking inventory to determine if any bones were broken. She had a bad burn on her arm where she caught the brunt of the rope. It stung and it was bleeding. She slowly regained her composure. I held her and kissed her softly. Miraculously, Glo didn't have any major injuries. Both horses returned to where they had lost their riders. Trigger put his head down as if to see if Glo was alright. She was.

It was difficult to imagine why someone would deliberately string a line across the path with an intent to injure or even kill someone. We weren't riding on private property. I climbed up on Sparky and cut the rope. Cautiously, we returned to my house and Mom fussed over Glo for an hour or so mumbling her usual, "You'll be the death of me."

Not long after that incident, I rode Sparky in the State Fair Parade which started at 10th Street and Central and ended at AHS. Somehow I coaxed Glo, who was also in the parade with the Drill Squad, to ride double with me after the parade was over. My Dad caught us on film riding around the grounds at AHS. Given what had happened earlier and that Sparky could have been spooked by a car horn or a drumbeat, it wasn't the smartest thing to do, but there wasn't an encore of Glo doing a 180° off the back of my horse. And, we rode numerous times together over the next three years albeit somewhat more cautiously.

That weekend Glo and I went to the Sunshine Theater to see *African Queen* starring Humphrey Bogart and Kathryn Hepburn. "Bogie" would get his first Oscar for his role as a captain of his own aging, steam motored, motley looking boat during World War I in the African jungle. He had to be the ugliest leading man ever in the movies but he was terrific and undeniably believable.

In one scene, Bogie has to get into the slimy, swampy water and pull his boat through the marshes. When he crawls back into the African Queen, Kate discovers that he is covered with large, blood sucking leeches. I cringed at the sight recalling those little, black "blood-suckers" that my brother Terry and I encountered on the rocky beaches in Fish Creek, Wisconsin.

More memorable, however was Bogie's performance a couple of years later in *The Treasure of Sierra Madre*. He played a desperate, greed-crazed gold miner who is attempting to find his way out of the mountains in Mexico with his fortune when he encounters a group of "banditos" posing as police.

"Whatya mean you are the police?" Bogie says addressing the ragged and dirty desperadoes. "If you're the police, show me your badges."

Then, in one of the greatest movie lines of all times the jefé (leader) of the banditos says (with appropriate accent):

"We dun't need no stinkin' bages."

And, with that, they kill poor ole' Bogie and take off with his ill-gotten gold.

Bogie, Spencer Tracy, John Wayne, Marilyn Monroe and others—they were the celebrities and the stars of the Forties and the Fifties. Today, they're classic icons. Some historians say that a true icon must have tragedy or mystery in their lives. A mysterious death, a suicide or assassination certainly enhances an icon's image but there's another key element. A true icon's image never changes in their lifetime and never changes through time. John Wayne's image of a strong, uncompromising, independent hero never changed. Marilyn was a tragic character—a vulnerable victim of the Hollywood system that molded her image, but she will remain forever in character, in life and on film.

In contrast, will the stars of recent times become classic icons? Madonna, whose luster has already faded, has had so many makeovers, the public can't identify who she is. Will Denzel Washington, Tom Cruise or Tom Hanks become, in time, classic icons? Only time will tell, but the Fifties fostered a wide array of memorable classic icons. Maybe it's simply an era that we, who lived it, recall with a sort of reverence that others don't share. Flawed or not, they were our heroes, then and remain so today.

Artesia was now the home of my Grandmother Quist and Uncle Robert as well as my Aunt Fre and Uncle Mel King and cousin Don who was my age. Dad had recruited Mel to represent BMA in Artesia. Dad and Mom were at the game with the whole "fam-damily."

After our second touchdown, I raced down the field on the kickoff like a Kamikaze pilot with reckless abandon seeking to destroy the ball carrier. My target was Larry Beadle, Artesia's star running back, who was listed at 180 pounds but he looked much bigger. I don't think he ever saw me coming as I drove my shoulder into his stomach going full speed head on. Dad said it was one hell of a collision. Mom cringed. Larry got up and staggered off the field. I couldn't breathe. I was gasping for air and was writhing in pain on the field as Coach Rushing was standing over me.

"Calm down, Buster. You just got the wind knocked out of you. You ain't goin' to die. Relax." Coach said as he lifted me up and down by my belt in order to replenish my supply of oxygen.

Beadle's knee hit me flush in the chest and stomach. He got the best of this match but I later returned to the game. Nothing serious, everyone thought, but if you've ever had the wind knocked out of you, you do think you're going to die. Artesia's missed extra point near the end of the game allowed the game to end in a 12 to 12 tie. It was like kissing your sister but I got smacked pretty hard. It took three weeks to find out really how hard.

I kept getting sharp pains in my chest every time I made a hard tackle. I was getting gun shy — afraid to hit someone. Mom took me to the doctor for x-rays. They were negative. But, something was definitely wrong. Finally, Mom took me to Dr. Simon, an orthopedic specialist. He didn't even need to get an x-ray.

"My God son, you've got two broken ribs. I can tell by just feeling them. You've been playing three weeks like this?

Damn, you're lucky you didn't puncture a lung," the Dr. said emphatically.

Mom gasped at the doctor's verdict as she sat there on the edge of the chair biting her finger nails.

I missed the Las Cruces and El Paso games which we lost (my playing wouldn't have changed the outcome), and there was another two weeks before our Thanksgiving game against our hated rival, Highland High. The doctor said I should be able to play if my ribs "calcified" well. I discovered that I healed very rapidly, which would bode well for all the broken bones to follow in the future.

Highland was a heavy favorite. Earlier in the season they had beaten an El Paso team 93-0! Jack and I couldn't believe it as we sat reading the Saturday morning paper at his house. I think Tommy McDonald scored six touchdowns and set a State record for rushing yards. "How could we stop this guy?" we thought.

Over 9,000 fans flocked to Public Schools Stadium on Thanksgiving Day 1951 to watch what had become in just three years an intense rivalry. It was a warm, clear and beautiful fall day. My Dad captured most of the game on film. The left side of my chest was protected by an abnormally large rib pad concocted by Coach Tony Valdez, who was a master at protecting us from injury, both psychological and physical.

Bob Cummins, our star center and Co-Captain, who was one-eighth Choctaw Indian, vividly recalls the tense and quiet locker room just prior to the game.

Coach McDavid held up the morning paper (Albuquerque Journal) so we could all see the headlines naming Highland as heavy favorites. He read most of the article to us. No one said a single word even when we ran out to the field.

The game got off to an ominous start when, in the second quarter, Dave Mohar from HHS blocked Freddy Leyba's punt near our end zone and by virtue of a safety we went down 2-0. Rather than demoralizing us however, the shock of the blocked punt fired the team up.

Phil Harris intercepted Tom McDonald's pass on the Hornets' 46 yard line and the Bulldogs were not to be denied. Phil caught a short pass from Otero for eight yards and Fred ran for ten. Then, using one of our best plays, Davey hit Fred with a screen pass in the left flat and our speedy back outraced all the Hornets to the end zone. In one of my favorite pictures, Jack and I are shown together down field watching Fred rolling towards the end zone. It doesn't appear that the "Blond Bookends" were much help on the play but we didn't get in the way either. Sam Short made the conversion and we led 7-2. A few minutes before the first half ended, Donn Lindberg made several crafty runs, one for 16 yards, and then scored on a one yard plunge. Sam again made the kick and we led 14-2 at halftime. A monumental upset was in the making.

Then, according to Burl Humble (Class of `52), one of the most unusual calls ever made by a referee occurred. Taking a handoff from Davey, Fred plunged into the line, legs churning as he always did, for extra, precious yards. A flag was thrown:

"Personal foul—unnecessary roughness!" The referee barked. The man in the zebra shirt then pointed to his knee. He called the penalty on Fred for using his knee while running! Dudley DeGroot, the UNM football coach who was in the stands and witnessed the incident, reportedly said it the most outrageous call he had ever seen by an official in a game.

The Hornets closed the gap in the third quarter when Tom McDonald scored on an eleven yard run. AHS 14 — HHS 9. The Blue and Gold side of the stadium went nuts as the Highland hopeful sensed that their team was gaining momentum and started moving the ball on the ground. Then, in what Coach Hugh Hackett of HHS said, "was the turning point of the game," I helped our cause.

The Hornets, utilizing a single wing attack with McDonald at tailback, continued to sweep my end with three blockers leading the way. I had been waiting and holding my ground trying to take out one or two blockers leading interference. Tired of being pummeled by the blocking backs and pulling guards, I made a decision on my own. As soon as the ball was snapped I shot off my left end position, straight for McDonald. I was deep into the backfield before the blockers could react. I hit McDonald hard before he took two steps and ... he fumbled! We recovered the ball on the HHS 25 yard line. The Hornet's Stinger had been plucked. With Fred and Phil pounding the line we moved the ball to the Hornet one and Joe Orona, filling in for Donn, bulled over for the TD. AHS 20 — HHS 9. Later in the fourth period, Fred returned a Hornet punt 52 yards to our opponents 17 yard line and with Fred, Phil, and Joe alternating we moved the ball down to the one-half yard line where Donn took it in, obliterating any chance of a Hornet comeback. Final score, AHS 26 — HHS 9.

The "stats" were indicative of the score. We had 300 total yards offense as opposed to Highland's 194. More importantly, Freddy truly outshined the highly touted Tommy McDonald. Fred had 102 yards (6.4 average/carry) rushing to Tommy's 103 (4.7 average/carry). We finished the year 6 wins, 3 losses and 1 tie and first place in the Class A Conference, plus we were also City Champions.

Since my injury in the Artesia game James Beall and Buddy Jackson, as seniors, got well-deserved playing time. James who also played behind me with Buddy, wrote in my yearbook:

"To a better man than me. Keep it up. Your friend as always."

— James Beall

A real touch of class.

For Freddy Leyba, who was one of my AHS heros, it was a fitting end (except for track and field the next spring) to his sparkling AHS athletic career. To some, Fred was a belligerent bully when driven by the demons of drink, but to me, he went about his business on the field with quiet determination and he never harassed or belittled me as a sophomore. He helped me learn how to throw the javelin and encouraged me to take it seriously (which I did). Fred died much too soon. A victim of his weakness. Jimmie Stevens, who tracked all of us former Bulldogs tenaciously, called me in Phoenix and told me that Fred was dying. I couldn't speak to him but I wrote him a letter thanking him for being a great teammate and an inspiration for my success. Jimmie told me that during his last days he acknowledged my letter. He couldn't believe that I would have remembered him. How could I have forgotten?

———————

The rumor around the AHS gym was that our new basketball coach, Robert Heinsohn, was a former Pro. (He played one year for the St. Louis Brewers.) At 6'7" he was an imposing figure. 1951-52 was his first year at AHS. He last coached at Wagon Mound, New Mexico, a very small northeastern New Mexico school, and had a two year record of 30 wins and 14 losses. My basketball career at AHS was memorable for its lack of success. I'm sure that it had something to do with my lack of talent. It also had something to do with the fact that I had discovered another (conflicting) sport that aroused my competitive juices. Skiing. And it raised my coach's ire.

Directly to the east of Albuquerque rises the Sandia Mountains. At the crest of the 10,500' peak was La Madera (the wood in Spanish) which is now called Sandia Peak. Jack had introduced me to the area the winter prior and we looked forward to enjoying this challenging sport during the winter of 1952 until—until Coach Heinsohn said, "No damn skiing, you hear?"

Jack really screwed things up for both of us. He took a spill which left a nasty gash on his cheek one weekend and he made the mistake of telling the Coach that it happened while skiing. Jack toed the line since he had made the Varsity and vowed to quit the sport. I continued to pursue the exhilaration of the mountains as surely my ancestors in Sweden may have done centuries before. I played on the "B" Team coached by John Caton. Coach Caton, at least, thought I was a player with "po" — potential.

I got the urge to ski race. I had two things going for me. Good balance and no fear. A prescription for success and trouble. In downhill racing, whomever got to the bottom of the hill first won. It didn't matter how you looked and considerable footage of Dad's movie film tells the story. My form or technique was terrible. I learned to race before I really learned to ski. My priority was "bass-ackwards." There was also another attraction — "snow bunnies" — otherwise known as girls.

The ski club at AHS, founded in 1938, combined its trips with the club at Highland High. The club had planned a weekend up at La Madera and two "older women" (they were seniors) from Highland, Mary Ann Burns and Elsa Johnson, had taken me under their wing, so to speak. They drove down to the "Lazy Q," our name for our ranch-styled home, to pick me up. Mom came out ostensibly to see me off and I introduced her to the girls. Mary Ann and Elsa got their admonition:

"I want to remind you girls that Buster is only fifteen," she said to my chaperons.

"Yes. Yes, we know, Mrs. Quist," said Mary Ann with a perplexed look on her face.

As we were driving down the circular drive Mary Ann turned and looked towards me in the back seat and asked," What's with your Mom? Geez, (she used that expression, too) does she think we're going to take advantage of you or something?"

"Yep. That's what she thinks," I said matter of factly.

"You've got to be kidding, Buster," Mary Ann added.

"No actually, she's worried about me. She thinks I'm oversexed." (My Mom's term.)

With that both of the girls rolled their eyes and looked at each other. They must have thought, "what are we getting into?"

I didn't fall in love with either of my companions. I fell in love with the mountains. I discovered that I must have been a mountain man or maybe a mountain lion in my previous life. (If there is such a possibility.) Or, it was my heritage. I can vividly remember being out on the slope by myself late that Saturday night with the moon eerily reflecting off the freshly fallen snow. The quiet, save the wind softly whistling through the pines, was deafening and overpowering. The smoke from the fireplace inside the lodge gave off multifarious odors perfectly compatible with the environment surrounding me. I was hooked for life. My only regret was that Glo wasn't there to experience it with me. She never learned to ski.

A month later our combined ski teams went on a long trip to Flagstaff, Arizona, for a meet with Flagstaff High at the Snow Bowl. In addition to Mary Ann and Elsa, Sid Cutter, who played starting guard on our football team, and Jack Douglas and Patrick Hibben from Highland also made the trip along with several others. Tony Wilson, who had a long and illustrious career at AHS mentioned earlier, was our Coach and "Chaperon."

It was more difficult getting up the mountain than down. "Flag" only had a rope tow. A skier had to hold on to a fast moving rope in order to get to the top of the mountain and the start of the race course. The girls had a tough time. Mary Ann wore out a pair of gloves on the rope, which was like trying to hold onto a greased chrome pole. We finally got steel clamps to assist in our effort to make it to the top. The most memorable moments on the trip weren't on the mountain. It was in the Monte Vista Hotel.

Sid Cutter was a "wildman." He skied with reckless abandon. And, he was my skiing mentor. His lifestyle off the hill was a carbon copy of his strategy during the race. Go all out. Balls to the wall!

Sid and Jack Douglas got rip-roaring drunk the first night in Flag. There was a muffled knock on my door about 2:00 a.m.

"Youjh gotta help me. My roomie esh sick and I can't move `em," Sid pleaded to me, slobbering and wobbling in the hallway and finding it difficult to remain vertical.

We went across the hall to Sid's room. It was a sight that would make even the most experienced nurse in an AA drunk tank toss her cookies. There was Jack, nude as a new-born babe, sitting on the edge of the bath tub passed out with his head resting on the toilet seat. He had crapped all over the floor and the bath tub and most of his vomit had missed the intended target. The odor without the visual enhancement, was overpowering. I made a quick one-eighty to the hallway.

"Bushter...aren't sha goin' to help me?" Sid asked holding onto the bed post which must have been rocking as if it were in an 8.0 earthquake.

"Geez, not me, Sid. I'll throw up all over the place too," I said as I was out the door to my room.

An ice cold wind cleansed the smell from my mind as I

opened the door to my room. Strange. The window wasn't open when I left just ten minutes earlier. My "roomie" (Patrick Hibben) must have opened it. I stumbled into my roommate's bed as I groped for the bedpost in the dark.

"Who's there?" Pat shouted.

"It's me, Buster. Sid woke me up," I replied.

"Damn! You scared the s... out of me," he cried.

"Sorry...didn't mean to... Hey why did you open the window" It's zero out there," I asked.

"I didn't open the window," Pat replied anxiously.

"It's closed now...and locked," I said as I crawled into bed wondering why Pat was so noticeably edgy. Putting all the distractions behind me, I gathered the heavy quilts around me and fell asleep.

Sid and Jack, green as the Jolly Green Giant, made the bus in the morning heading up the hill. I was relieved that they were upright and breathing. That image of Jack sitting in his own excrement and vomit cast a long shadow on my psyche. If that's what happened when a person drank too much I sure didn't want any part of it. And, I never did. Tight, yes. But, a fall down, s...-faced drunk, never in my lifetime.

No one on our team made it through the race without falling the first day. Anxious to get out of my ski clothes and take a shower, I headed for my room. As soon as we returned to the Monte Vista Hotel, Pat didn't get off on the second floor. Opening the door I discovered why. His bags and all his stuff were gone. My roomie had moved out.

What did I do to piss him off? Was he mad because I woke him up in the middle of the night? And, he said I "scared the s... out of him." Was I snoring? Was it because I was a Bulldog and he was a Hornet? It didn't take long to find out. At dinner I asked Pat, "what's the reason for moving out?"

"Read that magazine in the room. The story is on page 10." He said.

Right after dinner I went to the room and got the tourist guide which all hotels have to inform visitors of all the town's highlights. I got the "lowlights."

The Monte Vista was a four-story red brick building located in the heart of town, just off the famous Highway 66. It was built in 1926 and opened on January 1, 1927. It hosted such movie stars as Gary Cooper, Jane Russell, Spencer Tracy, and numerous other Hollywood names as more than one hundred films were made amongst the red rocks of Sedona and Oak Creek Canyon. It was page 10, however, that got my attention.

In the early 1940s two prostitutes were stabbed to death and thrown out of a second story window—presumably by a disgruntled customer—at the Monte Vista. Ghosts of the two girls have (reportedly) continually haunted the halls of the hotel since then. Maids, bellhops and guests have reported strange odors in the room where the dastardly deed was done. Furniture, mysteriously moved on its own. The room? 216 of course. My room.

It made me wonder. Were the ghosts of the two girls trying to re-enter our room through the window? At fifteen I had fantasied spending a night with a girl but this Saturday night in Flagstaff was a little weird. I could have slept with a ghost and didn't even know it.

Even John Wayne reported that he had encountered a ghost in this room at the Monte Vista in the Fifties. Big, honest, fearless John said the ghost was "friendly." Ghost or not who would try to mess around with John Wayne?

I shared the story with Mary Ann and the entire gang on the long trip home. It was easy for them to say it was all a bunch of "hooey." They didn't have to spend the night alone in room 216.

Several tragic incidents occurred years later in the lives of Pat and Mary Ann that further illuminates and preserves this memorable trip in my mind.

While at Highland High School, Mary Ann met and fell in love with John Michael (Mickey) Craig, a tall, handsome and athletic teenager one year her senior. They married in 1954 and began raising a family which grew to seven children (They lost one child at nineteen months of age.) The Craig family moved to Durango, Colorado, where Mickey and Mary Ann owned and operated a dude ranch and later were involved in real estate development. My family and I remained in close touch with the Craigs, spending a holiday at their ranch, and I worked with them on various insurance programs.

All seemed to be going well for the family until 1975. A recession, caused by the oil embargo and Watergate, slowed the real estate market in the then popular tourist town, but it was a visit from another Albuquerque High friend, Dale Mackey, that inalterably changed the Craig's and their children's lives forever.

Mickey was mesmerized by Mackey's story of everlasting life through Human Individual Metamorphosis (HIM). Spellbound, Mickey announced to Mary Ann that he was joining this mind-controlling cult and within a matter of days he abandoned his bewildered wife and six children for the unknown.

Sitting in my insurance office in Phoenix in 1977, I received a telephone call from Mary Ann.

"Buster? How long does a person have to wait before they can file an insurance death claim on a missing person?"

"Seven years. Why do you ask?" I replied perplexed.

"Mickey has disappeared. He's been gone a couple of years. I don't know whether he's dead or alive."

This incredible saga continued for over twenty-five years. At times Mickey would attempt to contact the children so the family knew he was alive. In the mid-Eighties I ran into a gaunt, chalky complexioned, snow white-haired Mickey in a bank in Scottsdale, Arizona. He wouldn't acknowledge that he knew who I was and hurried to exit the bank.

The HIM spent all these years preparing to travel to the great beyond where they would find perpetual life in a perfect world. The passing of the Hale-Bopp Comet was their sign to leave. John Michael Craig and many other followers all poisoned themselves on that fateful day. (Dale Mackey, '52, was no loner among them.)

Mickey's story is as bizarre as it is tragic. The redemption is the courage and determination that Mary Ann exhibited to deal with the business complexities that Mickey fled, and the challenge of raising six children on her own. Mary Ann credits her community of Durango which supported her in her darkest hour. True, but I think it was the same steely determination that my friend demonstrated in order to reach the top of the ski run in Flagstaff in 1952 that enabled her to climb her own mountain and meet her greatest challenge. If there are medals for the greatest mothers, Mary Ann's would surely be golden.

Patrick Hibben and I remained ski buds. We both got Friday afternoons off school for ski practice. I would pick Pat up at his house at noon and by 1:30 we were skiing at La Madera. Pat's father was the nationally known archeologist Frank Hibben, who was a professor at the University of New Mexico. Not too many years later, Pat along with Ellis Hall (principal shareholders of the Bank of New Mexico) and his wife and daughter were killed in a plane crash, returning to Albuquerque after a trip to Alaska. This tragedy haunted me for years. I've often wondered if the images that disturbed Pat that night in Flagstaff were premonitions of the future.

The loss of the Ellis Family was reminiscent of another Albuquerque icon. The loss of Dr. Lovelace and his wife were also killed in a plane crash near Aspen, Colorado. This prominent family was tragically marked. Their twin sons died a few years earlier after they contracted polio. Chris, their daughter, a striking and gracious blonde who dated my friend Jack in the mid-Fifties, just passed away as I was writing this memoir. I will never forget the day at the Albuquerque Country Club when she drove up in her new gull-wing Mercedes and wowed us all. She was a sweet, classy lady.

There were happy endings too. It's only fitting that the daredevil in Sid Cutter would allow him the opportunity to ascend to heights only reserved to a courageous few. Sid, who learned to fly an airplane at the age of ten, co-founded hot air ballooning in Albuquerque in 1973, when the World Championships drew 132 balloons from 14 countries to the Duke city. The Albuquerque International Balloon Fiesta is now the largest event of its kind in the world. Sid, who has twice been US National Balloon Champion, has received the prestigious Diploma Montgolfier from the Federation Aeronautic Internationale. Not bad for the former Bulldog who took off on his first flight without any instruction on how to fly the balloon. That would surprise most people, but not his classmates and teammates that know him well.

The 1952 *La Reata* records that "Albuquerque High put upon the basketball court this year, a group of players, small in stature, but big in heart and full of spirit. To Coach Heinsohn, who stands approximately six feet six inches, this squad looked small indeed." Actually, this team wasn't as small as portrayed.

Mike Padilla and Jack, both sophomores who were the backbone of our team at Washington Junior High, were 6'2". Tom Curley and Dick Trott, juniors, were also 6'2" and were muscular. And Tom Isaacson, a senior, was 6'3" and a smooth, savvy veteran of the hardwood.

"You're going to learn how to play the game like the big boys play it," Coach Heinsohn announced to the team when the squad began the season. "After practice we're going to review films of the top college teams in the country so you can see how to run a disciplined offense. Basketball isn't a game of helter-skelter. It's a game of precise plays and working the ball inside for the high percentage shot."

The hard conditioning program and disciplined play seemed to be working as the team won its first four games in a row, including a 43-40 win over Highland. Jack made the varsity and I can vividly recall watching his first game against HHS from the "A" Club room above the basketball floor with butterflies in my stomach hoping that my best friend would "do good." He did. He played consistently and he lettered. So did Mike.

The Bulldogs were 12 and 6 going into the last month of their schedule. Coach Heinsohn, a tough disciplinarian, suspended star guard Julian Montoya for a month after a one point win at Raton, and the team then lost seven of its last eight games and never got past the District Tournament. An eerie prognostication of what was to reoccur in the future.

Lloyd Wayne, the outstanding wrestler from the class of 1950 revisited his *alma mater* and assisted Coach Rushing with the Wrestling Team. The outstanding performers from this team were Pantaleon Tafoya, John Carpenter, Paul Lambert and Burl Humble. Burl recalls one of Coach Rushing's unusual teaching techniques:

Coach believed that bridging (the ability to arch your

back while lying on the mat which put most of the wrestler's weight on his shoulders and neck) was a critical maneuver to avoid being pinned. To test our ability to bridge, Coach and all 250 pounds of him, would sit on our stomachs as we tried to bridge. It was darn near impossible.

Sam Short, a pretty hefty guy himself, had no one to wrestle in his weight class. Coach Rushing took up the challenge. Sam decided that finding an after-school job would be more productive. Jimmie Stevens, with no prior experience and only two weeks of coaching, won his first match that featured more takedowns, escapes and reversals than ever witnessed by his team. Coach Rushing was laughing while Jim was expending every ounce of energy he had. Paul Lambert turned his focus to wrestling because boxing, where he excelled, had been discontinued as a sport at AHS.

It is difficult to imagine how one coach could be responsible for four teams that were competing at the same or overlapping time of the year, but somehow, Tony Valdez saw to it that the Pentathlon, Swimming, Tennis and Golf Teams had a coach to guide them. Tony was like Spiderman. He was everywhere doing good deeds.

The Swim Team had less coaching than the other teams since Jimmie Stevens, Walter Myers, Mahlon Love, Gordy Modrall and Mike Schlick competed the previous summer in AAU meets around the state. Mike's father, Carl, owned the Acapulco Swim Club located near the airport, which served as a hangout for the swimmers and their admirers. Rumors were constantly swirling around the AHS campus that nocturnal meets included skinny-dipping so coaching wasn't encouraged.

The golfers who practiced at the UNM course were led by Herman Kraul and Le Roy Weller, who were close to "scratch" (even par) shooters. Bob Matteucci played to a three or four handicap and Doug Balcomb and Richard Byran completed the four man team that competed for the State Companionship. Schools particularly in the southern part of the state were, by 1952, producing competitive teams but the Bulldogs finished second to Highland in the State Tournament. HHS was led by Earl Puckett who went on to become an accomplished professional.

Bob Matteucci recalls Coach Valdez' constant admonition as the team practiced in January and February. "I don't care how bad the weather is guys. Go out and play. You never know when it will be like this in a tournament." Tony, aside from all else, knew New Mexico weather.

Bob was selected by the *Albuquerque Journal* to become a trainee in the newspaper's sports department. Bob was tutored by J. D. Kailer, one of Albuquerque's most prolific sportswriters covering the past fifty-plus years. Part of Bob's account of the AHS-HHS football game appears in the next chapter.

Coach Valdez' Tennis Team won its first three matches of the year including a 14 to 1 thrashing of the Hornets. The Bulldogs were led by Chuck Vidal, Don Smiley, Richard Vigil, Tony Ball and Robert Sanchez.

1952 was the last hurrah for hockey at AHS. According to Norm Mugleston the toughest task was practice:

We had to be at practice at the ice rink up on Truman by 6:00 a.m. George Snelson was the star player at Highland. His dad owned the ice rink so we had to share practice time with HHS. We just couldn't beat those guys. They were darn good.

Robert Des Jardin, who played center, was the Bulldogs' outstanding player. Other first team players were Rob Myers, Bruce Briner, Ray Wheeler and his brother Leon. In addition to Norm, whom we all referred to as "Mugs," other players who got time on the ice were Dale LaMaster, Ron Cervantes, Bobby Abbott, Maklon Love, Fred Zichert, Eugene Holly, Erwin Betts, Dick Murphy, and Ray Dunaway. The team finished the last season with a won 4 lost 4 record under Coach George Foehr.

Jack and I looked forward to track and field coached by Pete McDavid. During one of the first days of practice at Public School Stadium, Coach came up to me.

"Buster, 'Doc' Ledbetter says you've got an incredibly strong arm. He says you can throw a baseball 300'. I want you to try the javelin."

"Okay, coach. Show me how to throw it," I said, eager to try.

The javelin weighs less than two pounds, but it is over eight feet long. After a few tips I took a few steps and attempted to throw it.

"Damm! It hit me in the back of my head, coach," as I smarted from the sting of the tail of the javelin clipping my ear.

"It's really a pull, Buster. You can't throw it like a baseball," Coach McDavid said as he demonstrated the correct arm motion.

The next toss was more successful. Thus began a twelve-year love affair with the spear that would take me halfway around the world and be a major part of my life until I was twenty-eight years old.

The real star of our track team was the National Five Star Champion, Bob Campbell. Bob was a senior and older brother of Joyce who was one of our original gang from La Wash. The five star event was tailor made for Bob. It was like the penthalon (five events) but the five different tests were the 100 yard dash, the broad jump (now called the long jump), the high jump, the shot put and the 880 yard run. Bob was the State Champion in the broad jump (22 feet) and second in the State in the high hurdles so he had the speed for the 100 yard sprint, and obviously he could jump. Out of the thousands of competitors around the country, Bob had the highest cumulative score for all five events. A heck of an honor plus he was (and still is) one of the greatest guys you would even want to meet. Bob was also Senior Class President.

As a testament to how close Jack and I were athletically in these events, we finished thirty-two and thirty-three in the nation. I can't remember which of us won out over the other. Fortunately for Jack, the javelin throw was not one of the events. H.B. finished seventeenth.

Freddy Leyba, who mentored me all that spring, finished second in the javelin at the State meet and I finished fourth. Jack finished in a five-way tie for fifth place in the high jump. Not bad for a couple of skinny sophomores. The winner in the javelin was Benny Garcia from Alamogordo, New Mexico, who, just four years later, would make the U.S. Olympic team beating out Bud Held, the world record holder, for the third spot on the team by one-half an inch. The closest margin ever. I would meet up with Benny and Bud a few years later.

Unexpectedly, the 1952 Baseball Team proved to be a diamond in the rough. A writer for *La Reata* called this the "Canine Nine." Tom Isaacson, who had been recently named to the North All-Star Team for his outstanding basketball season, recalled a humorous moment as baseball always seemed to foster them.

Guys on the team watched the Dukes and Pros on TV chewing tobacco and some of them tried it. Tom Curley, Dick Trott and I were walking up to the practice field when Coach Rushing stopped and offered us a ride. Tom and Dick had just stuffed a plug of tobacco in their mouth and they sure didn't want Coach to see them chewing. By the time we got to the field they had to spit so bad they must have swallowed some of the juice. Rushing knew all along what was happening and he just let 'em stew in their own juice.

Curley was one heck of a ball player and went on to become a pro. Royce Ankeney had an unhittable curve ball and he would later play for the Albuquerque Dukes. Outstanding players on this club were Jack Brown, Don Miller, Mel Sedillo, Dave Otero, Ruben Rubio, Jim (Punkin) Elizando, Louis Neal and Eddie Akers. The Bulldogs won every game in the regular season and won the District Tournament, but lost to Las Cruces in the finals at State. A disappointing end to a great season. This writer was not a member of this team but within a few weeks I would join the "boys of summer."

"Why are you wearing that "I Like Ike" button?" Jack asked as we sat down in the patio between classes one day.

"Oh, Dad was passing them out to all his employees and he gave me one," I replied as the country was getting election fever. "Who does your Mom and Dad support?"

"There's a split ticket at our house," Jack informed me. "Dad's a Republican, of course, but Mom is a liberal."

"A what?" I asked, really not knowing what the term meant.

"They're the people who champion the underclass. She

177

voted for Henry Wallace in 1948. He was FDR's VP for four years until 1945. Dad is always embarrassed when she talks about politics around their friends," Jack said, volunteering on a subject I knew so little about at the time. It really piqued my interest.

"I thought you were either a Republican or a Democrat or a Communist. Dad's company is headquartered in Kansas City and they didn't like Harry Truman so Dad didn't like Harry either," I added.

"Mom's father was the first Anglo born in Trinidad, Colorado, and his father was a Methodist Minister. When Mom was young in 1913 there was a big strike at the Colorado Fuel & Iron mine in Ludlow near Trinidad that was owned by the Rockefellers in New York. Young John Rockefeller got the State to send in the militia to quell the riots at the mine and they killed twenty-four people, including several women and children. It was horrible. She never forgot that and blamed it on capitalist greed, you see?" Jack informed me.

"Ah geez. I'll ask Mr. Werstler, my history teacher, about it. I'd like to learn more," I added as the bell rung for our next class. I had just had a political science class with Jack as my instructor. As I have said previously, Jack was a pretty smart guy. In fact, the smartest guy in our class. That's one reason he was our President. And, he was popular.

At this time, TV was just beginning to impact America even though only a small percentage of homes in the U.S. had sets. As affluent as the Strombergs were, they didn't have a TV. Nor did Glo or most of my friends. Our family gathering around the radio had been replaced by a visual medium. We were fascinated by it.

We had our first insight into our new enemies, real and imagined, when we watched Senator McCarthy and his committee investigate Communists within our own government and the movie industry. McCarthy was a demagogue but given what we know today about Harry Hopkins, Alger Hiss and others, there <u>were</u> "Pinkos" in our government. We watched with trepidation as the Rosenberg's were found guilty of treason and sentenced to death.

The Rosenberg story touched all New Mexicans. David

Greenglass, Ethel Rosenberg's brother, worked at Los Alamos on the Manhattan Project. Greenglass, despite being employed as a low level machinist, was able to steal vital secrets to the atomic and plutonium bombs. He delivered them to a Soviet agent at a meeting in the Franciscan Hotel in Albuquerque in 1945. It was Greenglass' testimony that ultimately led to his sister's conviction and her and her husband's execution. Los Alamos, fifty-five years later, unfortunately, still remains a controversial place unable to contain its secrets.

Lipsky makes a valid point when he says:
> The separation of sports and politics has had ethical overtones as well. Sports, in contrast to politics, has been seen as a moral realm where character is built and virtue pursued. The traditional lionizing of the sports hero clashes with the negative perception of politicians.[16]

In contrast to the dire machinations of the cold war, our spirits were lifted and carried away by a new vehicle called the "sitcom" or situation comedy. A new phenomenon, "I Love Lucy," made us all feel better about ourselves. Dad thought Bob Hope was the funniest man alive until he saw the crazy antics of Lucille Ball. Lucy and Desi gave us one of our rare moments to see our parents laughing together. Adlai Stevenson's biggest faux pax during the 1952 Presidential campaign was to deliver one of his major speeches opposite "I Love Lucy." America tuned him out to watch Lucy and he lost the election — A result that didn't go unnoticed by the "image makers" of the future.

AHS had three school publications: *The Record, La Reata* and the *Yucca.*

La Reata (The Lariat in Spanish) is the yearbook or annual which is published at the end of each school year. It first appeared in 1909.

---

[16] Lipsky, IBID, Page 5-6.

My three memorable years, the faces of my classmates and their salutations are preserved forever as a part of this memoir.

The Record was our newspaper of which only a few pages have survived amongst my collection of memorabilia. Numerous monthly editions of the *Yucca*, however, have survived and the poems, short stories, editorials and reviews are remarkable in their creativity, style and content. One of the *Yucca*'s most prolific writers in 1951-52 was my good friend Jimmie Stevens, aka, "Fish" for his swimming prowess.

Jimmie must have had an affinity or at least a curious interest in insects. In "Flight of the Mosquito" Jimmie ends with his creature's creative soliloquy:

"I draw my little dagger,
I cock my little eye.
And make the merest Christian
Hate God, and wish to die!"

Jimmie also finds poetry in the preservation of another pesky insect in *The Sand Fly*, and reveals the depth of his religious convictions when he opines, "The more man denies himself, the more he shall obtain from God." Jimmie was equally devoted to the perpetual memory of his school and his friends. No history of AHS in the early 1950s is complete without a tribute to this remarkable young man who epitomized, "Bulldogs Forever." Jimmie's heart, which he had freely dedicated to so many worthwhile causes, gave out before he could collaborate on this memoir.

—————

"Buster, what are you doing this summer?" Coach Rushing asked as my Sophomore year at AHS was about to end.

"Ah geez, I don't know Coach. My sister's boyfriend wants me to work for him part-time. Why?" I asked.

"I coach the Bulldogs in the American Legion summer league. The way you throw the javelin, you ought to make a heck-of-a pitcher," Coach said as I entered the gym to clean out my locker.

"Hey, that would be neato, Coach. I love baseball. I didn't pitch last summer but I really had fun the year before. What time do you practice? Byron wants me to work from about noon to 7:00 or 8:00 p.m.," I responded.

"We practice early in the morning and our games are at night a couple times a week," Coach replied. "We start on Monday morning."

"That's terrif, Coach. I'm sure that will be okay with Byron. I'm driving a scooter selling ice cream and snow cones. I'm a 'good humor' man," I said as I laughed.

Joannie's boyfriend, Byron, and his close friend from Carlsbad, Cecil Brininstool, had bought several used Cushman scooters that had been rigged up with a large freezer in front of the handlebars in order to sell ice cream, popsicles and snow cones to kids during the summer. We would load up every morning at Darrows Ice Cream Factory. They gave me a route in the northeast heights including Hoffmantown, a new subdivision, to work every day, and I had time in the mornings to practice baseball.

The Bulldogs were an experienced team. Although the team had also lost in the State American Legion finals to Las Cruces the year before, we now had Royce Ankney and Mel Sedillo, veteran pitchers, returning. After our first two wins, I got my initial start against Galles Motors. I had never been as nervous in any kind of a game as I was when I took the mound against Galles. I walked the first three batters I faced. Coach Rushing came stomping out of the dugout, hands in his back pockets, with a scowl on his face. I was sure that he was going to tell me I couldn't "scatter s... with a rake" and take me out.

"Hod damn, Buster, you can't strike out the whole damn team. Just throw the damn ball over the damn plate!" he demanded in no uncertain terms. Before I could manage a meek reply, he returned to the dugout.

"Calm down, Buster," Jack Brown, my catcher said. "You're throwing too hard. Ease up. They can't hit you. They're scared out of their shoes of your fastball. Hit my glove, okay?" Jack said as he tried to settle me down.

He did. I struck out the next three batters and Galles didn't score. Jack ran to meet me and slapped me on the back as I crossed the third base line. He was ecstatic. My teammates were cheering my successful debut under fire as I sat down in the dugout. Coach Rushing glared at me and didn't say a word. I guess he thought that I ignored his order. He was a tough taskmaster but he sure got the results.

According to an article in the *Albuquerque Journal,* we won the game 4 to 1. I pitched a two hitter but walked 11 batters in a seven inning game but also struck out 11 out of 21. Obviously, I could deliver the "heat" but I would have to learn how to control my fastball. I would also have to develop a second pitch. I did. A "change up."

Our team was undefeated for the first half of the season. Our rival, Highland, won the second half. We faced the "Hornets" for the City title and the right to go to the State Tournament. Apparently I had solidified my relationship with Coach Rushing. He picked me to pitch the big game. I was undefeated.

I pitched a one-hit shutout through five innings but Highland's three hits and our three errors led to four runs for Highland in the sixth and a 4 to 1 loss. Mike Hoeck pitched a brilliant one hitter for the Hornets who went on to win the State Tournament. It was my only loss for my first year. A bitter defeat but it whetted an appetite that would feed on success the next summer. I relished my role. It was like playing "king of the hill." My teammates relied on me. Jimmy (Punkin) Elizando nicknamed me "Zzit". I didn't know if it was for my fastball or the "zits" on my face. Some of my teammates that were upperclassmen were Davey Otero, Don Miller, Tom Curley, Richard Trott and Eddie Akers. Mike Saul, Bill Easley, Bob Fink, Bob Stover and I would form the nucleus of next year's surprise team.

Thanks to meticulous chronicling by my Mother, all of my past involvement from grade school to the YMCA through Junior High, High School and College is evidenced in numerous scrapbooks. Without them I could not have effectively written this memoir. There was, however, a gap in the record during the summer and fall of 1952. A major crisis occurred.

"I need to talk to you kids," Mom said to Terry and I as we were swimming in our backyard pool. "Come on in the house," she directed us.

I sensed that there was something seriously wrong. Mom had something on her mind. Terry and I had recently avoided any problems and Joannie (my sister) was a saint so

I didn't know what it was all about. We went into the den, which seemed to be the area of the house reserved for these types of conferences. Mom's face had deep furrows across her forehead. She wrung her hands nervously. Her eyes were glistening but unable to tear. I was worried.

"Kids...your Mom has cancer," she said somewhat relieved that she had the courage to say it.

"What's cancer?" Terry asked, as I felt a tightness in my throat. I knew what cancer was.

"It's a very bad disease kids. Your Mom has to have surgery. I could be sick for a long time," she added. "I've told Joannie already."

My immediate reaction was, "My God, is Mom going to die?" But, you can only think that. You don't want to ask your Mom if she's going to die. Terry, who was just about to turn fourteen, looked deeply concerned and puzzled. He didn't know what to say either.

"What's going to happen?" I finally asked as the tension engulfed us. "Where is Dad?" I thought. He should be here at a time like this.

"I'm going to be out of commission for quite awhile," Mom advised us, though I didn't quite know what she meant. "I'm going to have surgery in Clovis as soon as possible. Dad says that Dr. Conway is the best cancer surgeon in the state and he'll operate on me. Gramma Anderson is coming to Albuquerque this week to take care of you kids and the house while I'm gone. You'll like that, won't you?" Mom stated as she fidgeted anxiously sitting on the edge of the wrap-around bamboo couch which was the centerpiece of our den.

"Of course," we both responded because we both were so close to Gramma.

"Please promise me that you'll be good kids and that you'll come to see me after my surgery, okay?" Mom asked even though she didn't need to.

"Geez Mom, of course, we will. How long will it be before you're home?" I asked, still not having any idea what this whole situation entailed.

"We don't know yet. There are a lot of ifs. I won't be able to do much around the house when I get home. You kids are really going to have to pitch in and help out, okay?" Mom pleaded in earnest.

Not knowing what to ask Mom and also feeling reluctant to probe into the mysteries of cancer, I later asked Joannie to explain to me how bad the situation was.

Byron, who was in pre-med, had the best insight into Mom's cancer. She had a tumor in one of her breasts. She was going to have a radical mastectomy. Radical was an appropriate and defining word. It was impossible for me to imagine. I was repulsed by the thought of my Mom losing a breast but I wanted her to survive. The doctors certainly knew what was best, I thought. Mom was a strong believer in God. Certainly God wouldn't let Mom die. She was only forty-six years old.

To Mom, her three kids were the most important reason for living. It must have been devastating for her because she would be so far away. It was 200 miles to Clovis, New Mexico, which was on the Texas and New Mexico line and we couldn't be there for her. She spent most of her time in the hospital alone. Dad was there periodically but felt he had to manage his business, which required him to visit his offices all around the State. I can only remember the three of us being with Mom once while she was confined to the hospital for about a month. Finally, she came home. Words can't describe how happy she was to be at the "Lazy Q." She was strong. She was resolute. Certainly, she would win this battle. But, within a year, fear hit us hard again. Another tumor in her other breast. We were devastated. A second radical mastectomy. It seemed that the nightmare that our family had just experienced was replicating like the disease itself. Certainly it must just be a dream, we thought, that never reaches resolution and plays over and over again. But, it wasn't a dream. It was real. Mom's battle to survive seemed now to be doubly difficult.

During her second convalescence, Mom was a different person. Coming face to face with your own mortality has a profound impact on all of us, and in many respects, it was her finest moment. In the past she had difficulty coping with everyday problems. It was the small stuff that got under her skin as she made mountains out of molehills. But now, faced with a battle against the big "C" and the greatest crisis in her life, she was a rock and she appeared to be at one with herself. Maybe her steely determination and fortitude to beat the odds was inherent in her Scandinavian heritage. Maybe it was her arduous childhood that gave her the strength to survive. I don't know. But, she did. She lived to see her kids grow up. She lived to love all her grandchildren. Her major health crisis temporarily was over but within seven years there would be another horrible hill to climb.

Much is now known about assessing the potential risks for various diseases based upon a personality profile. Doctors have, for quite sometime, labeled a person who has an "A" profile as a candidate for a heart attack. Typically, anyone who is overweight, a heavy smoker, an aggressive hard charger and a workaholic, is a perfect candidate for a heart attack. Based upon current knowledge, not known forty-five years ago, Mom had a profile for cancer.

She was uptight. Even in a relaxed atmosphere like at our cottage in Sand Bay or Fish Creek in Wisconsin, there was always a room that wasn't clean (enough), clothes that had to be pressed (clean wasn't enough), or a meal that didn't "come out right." But, if she did get it all done, no one really appreciated what she had done for them. She was the epitome of the "pity poor me" syndrome. This may seem to be harsh but that was her tape. We all get tapes from our parents. And it replays over and over during our entire life. The three of us wish we could go back to the 40s and 50s and appreciate her more or maybe even help her change her outlook on the world, but we can't. All that we can do is remember her as she was, first and foremost, a wonderful Mother who devoted her life to her kids. She did so much for us. We just wish she had done more for herself.

CHAPTER SEVEN: "CHAMPS" 1952-1953

JACK AND I LOOKED FORWARD to our Junior year as football practice began. We had an experienced backfield led by Davey Otero, our smooth-operating quarterback. Phil Harris, Jimmy's big brother who now weighed 178 pounds, was a hard-hitting, bruising fullback who complimented H.B. and Jack Brown, who were shifty halfbacks. Our line averaged only 169 pounds but we had two small, scrappy guards, Mariano Marcelli and Anthony Simon, who compensated for their lack of size with quickness. We had 87 players report for practice and Coach McDavid thought we had a potential for a good team. AHS also added George Foehr, the ex-Hockey Coach, to the staff.

We edged Gallup 19-13 in our first game even though, statistically, the margin was much greater. Coach gave me an additional responsibility, kicking extra points. I missed two out of three but we won.

At Monday's practice, Coach McDavid pulled me aside and asked that I also learn how to play quarterback. Our backup QB, Jim (Punkin) Elizando, had been ruled ineligible and since I had the experience at Washington, I was the logical candidate. What I didn't expect, was to be called upon to perform at the very next game.

I don't know what Coach McDavid had in mind when he asked me to switch from left end to quarterback in the first quarter. If he was testing my adaptability and courage, he really raised the ante. El Paso High School was a tough team. They were two touchdown favorites. I was nervous as hell as I called the first play in the huddle and lined up under center. Only problem, it wasn't the center! I had my hands under Tony Simon's butt. Mike Schlick, our center, not feeling my hands, stood up and called time out. He probably saved a fumble on our 20 yard line. Not an auspicious start at quarterback.

The team rallied behind me. I was as green at quarterback as my Bulldog uniform. We methodically drove the ball down the field to the El Paso 17 yard line. Coach McDavid sent Davey back in at quarterback. I switched to end. On the first play, Davey threw me a pass on a corner route which I caught for a touchdown. A pretty unusual juxtaposition of players even for high school. Unfortunately, I missed the conversion.

Down 13 to 6 with time running out, Phil Harris made a nifty run to the one yard line and then bulled over for the TD to make the score 13 to 12 in favor of El Paso.

Howard Peterson, the sportswriter for the *Albuquerque Journal*, wrote:

"Quist, who scored the Bulldog's first TD, was rushed by a swarm of Tiger tacklers and his place kick went wide of the goal posts."

Howard sugar-coated my miss. The truth, evidenced by a revealing photograph, shows that it was simply a bad kick. Sportwriters in the Fifties were empathetic. Today they are brutal. My two missed conversions cost us a big upset, but my other "conversion" (to QB) was somewhat of a success.

Jack, H.B., Jimmy and I were having lunch in the patio on Monday after the game. Smitty's "Tamale Cart" was our second preference to the Chili Bowl which was a block away on Broadway.

"I think you've got a club foot, Buster," H.B. concluded as the discussion focused on my two missed extra points.

"Geez, you guys. I'm sorry, okay? Hell, if I had a square toe on my shoe, like Lou Groza has, I could make 'em. With the rounded toe, I've got to hit it square in the middle of the ball, otherwise it goes right or left," I responded, which caught the guys by surprise. "Besides, I'm a punter. Punters don't kick extra points. It's completely different."

"Whatyamean a square toe?" Jimmy asked.

"I watched the Browns game on TV Sunday. It looks like Groza has a special shoe with a square toe. He never misses, you know," I added.

"Gotta hand it to you Buz. That's a pretty creative excuse," Jack reasoned as our focus turned to a "gang" of girls approaching us. They sounded like a gaggle of geese as they all seemed to be all talking at the same time. The "gang" was Glo, Riette Lewinson, Carol Jones, Joyce Campbell, Mary Kay Hicks and Arlene Garcia. They were all carrying their books with both arms pressed against their chests. Still no backpacks.

"Sorry you guys lost," Riette said with a sincere look of sympathy on her face. Riette was always sincere.

"Yeah, if it weren't for Buster's club foot, we would've won," H.B. continued using his reasoning for my failure.

"A what?" Glo asked quizzically. "It's size eleven but it's not a club foot," she added laughing.

"Riette," Jimmy interjected addressing the diminutive doll that we all loved to tease, "We've heard that you're suing the City."

"What? Suing the City? For what?" Riette questioned, cocking her head at an angle, with a perplexed look on her face.

"For building the sidewalk too close to your butt," Jimmy responded quickly, unable to contain his laughter in the middle of his quip.

"Oh Jimmy! Jimmy Harris. You're always making fun of me. Gee whiz, guys," Riette said as she paused. Then her girlfriends also laughed. Riette, first embarrassed and then seeing that everyone got a kick out of Jimmy's remark, also joined in the levity of the moment.

As the six girls moved away from us all our eyes were naturally fixed on their posteriors. What struck me, in addition to the obvious, was their uniformity of dress and manner. All of them had calf-length skirts of similar material and a solid color. All their blouses and sweaters were somewhat the same. And, of course, they carried their books the same way. They all wore the era's most notable dress item — bobbysox.

I was about to make this observation known to my "buds" when I looked at our attire. We all had on Levis. Not Lees or Wranglers or Ralph Lauren. Levis. Jack, Jimmy and I had on white T-shirts. Plain white T-shirts. No lettering. No logos. No distinctive markings. We had our choice. White or white, when it came to T-shirts. H.B. had on a blue and white stripe cowboy shirt, one that had the snap-on buttons and the tell-tale angular stitching below the shoulders and on the pockets. He was wearing cowboy boots, and so was I. H.B. and I were dressed somewhat like the "Stompers" but we were definitely, the "Rah-Rahs."

The "Stompers" were the cowboys, as defined earlier. The real ones and the drugstore variety. They were also called "s... kickers" because they (supposedly) came to school with horse manure on their boots. The toes of their boots were pointed (so the myth went), in order to smash cockroaches in the corners, but that's probably taking the image a little bit too far. After all, I had to clean out the corral too at the "Lazy Q."

The "Rah-Rahs" (like the cheerleaders chant, rah-rah sis boom bah) were the jocks and those who were considered the class leaders. Some of us, like H.B. and myself, straddled both social labels. But you were identified by membership in one group or the other and you wanted it that way. Uniformity and conformity of dress, activity and association were standards. Many people looking back to this era believe we were almost as colorless as our clothes. But that was all about to change. Like Teresa Brewer's number one hit recording, *Music, Music, Music*, new sounds immeasurably would soon begin to change our lives and all of America. And, a new magazine *Playboy*, taunted our male fantasies as Hugh Heffner challenged America's puritanical attitudes on sex. That one unforgettable picture of Marilyn Monroe...OOH, LA, LA!

I was partly responsible for a trendy new "look." I began having my hair "styled" in a crew cut at "La Wash." It must have caught on. A picture of Tom Curley, Billy Gore and Bob Sanchez in the *La Reata* depicts the new fad.

In the mid-nineties, while meeting privately in Scottsdale with Michael Jordan and Charles Barkley, who were then at the top of their game, I suggested to them that it was this writer that started the "Bald is Beautiful" look. Actually that was a lie. Yul Brynner was the trend-setter. The two famous "boys of winter" thought I was "cool."

189

Jack and Arlene repeated as President and Vice President of our class, reinforcing both their popularity and recognition as leaders. Rosie Chavez was elected Secretary-Treasurer. Mary Kay, Carol and Joyce also repeated as our Majorettes along with senior JoAnne Ticknor again the head of the group. Jumping up and down and furthering the tradition of male hero-worship (according to Jack's sister who was now removed from these banal traditions) was Connie Abbott, Connie Chavez, Pat Looney, Jean Cornell, Sally Crook and head cheerleader Emily Lanigan. Glo continued her participation on the Drill Squad despite the fact that it often conflicted with her job at Korbers. She also was a Counselor's Aide with Arlene, Riette and Gwen Crowe, another La Wash grad.

Phil Harris, who was probably the most handsome guy in his class, did a "three-peat." He was elected Class President for the third straight year. Johnny Archuleta, Vice-President and Marilyn Bebber, Secretary-Treasurer, were elected for the first time.

The new incoming class of sophomores elected Donnell Montoya as their President, Nisa Elkins as Vice-President and Terri Gallegos as Secretary-Treasurer.

Another integral part of the student body infrastructure was the Student Council. Larry Walker was elected President, Sam Short our Vice-President (both Seniors) and Virginia Shaver, a classmate from Washington Junior High, was Secretary-Treasurer.

In the Fifties, as Kathleen Parker lamented, "We knew who the geniuses were, but who cared." Certainly sports were center stage during this period but to say no one cared is a little over the top. This writer certainly knew who the "brains" were and readily acknowledged their achievements and value to our school as did many of the "jocks." Larry Bonaguidi was selected as President of the Honor Society, Carol Bambrook, Vice-President and Mary Van Atta, was Secretary-Treasurer. Thirty-six out of the 43 Honor Society members were girls so it was a distinction where the girls could compete and excel, and they did.

Bulldog Day (Homecoming) was a big deal at AHS. Most of the homerooms built a float and we had our own parade down Central Avenue. Creating a catchy theme and stuffing all that wire mesh with crepe paper was a monumental task. Fortunately, the team had to focus on the game and we were relieved of the late night efforts to get the floats ready. Our Bulldog Day Queen was Barbara Sloan, who won our hearts despite her disability (She passed away shortly after her Senior year). Jackie Barnes, who was selected as "Miss Teen America" in a national contest during her Junior year, was one attendant and Rachel Sena was the other. We might as well have spent the night before helping our classmates. We played like dogs — not Bulldogs. We lost 14 to zip to Artesia who were also Bulldogs. A different breed—Pit Bulldogs. We played our worst game of the year.

We took a 4 win 2 loss record into the toughest part of our schedule. We had to play Carlsbad, Las Cruces and Roswell, three weekends in a row. Jack remembers coming into Carlsbad on the team bus noting the large sign north of town proclaiming, "The Carlsbad Cavemen—Home of the State Champs." Jack said, "Football must be a big deal in Carlsbad." He was right. Football was a big deal in not only Carlsbad, but in all southeastern New Mexico. Being there was like being in west Texas where football wasn't just a game. There, the American tradition was taken to a new level. Most of the folks in Carlsbad spoke a different language too—Tex-Mex. A definite "twang" which you would experience in Midland-Odessa or Lubbock. We were in unrecognizable and hostile country. But it was an area, unknown to me then, that would become my second home. There was even a more telling and distinguishable characteristic that separated the north from the south. Blacks, Negroes then, didn't attend Carlsbad High School or play football. That is, until this year, 1952. A major societal change had occurred. The racial barrier was finally breached in this previously segregated section of New Mexico.

Ralph Bowyer, the head coach at Carlsbad High, was a great athlete at the University of New Mexico and his coaching record was almost without equal, as noted earlier. What is not well known about Coach Bowyer was his courage. Risking his job he confronted the Carlsbad Board of Education and the townspeople over the race issue. He succeeded.

John Wooten, a hulk of a kid who played tackle, was the first Black to play at CHS. I remember him well. He played just off my right shoulder the entire game. Despite the fact that we had four Blacks on our team John was a man on a mission. He and his teammates played inspired football. We lost 20 to 13.

In a recent interview with Ralph, he recalled the vitriolic attacks that he took from other southeastern New Mexico coaches and fans for breaking the color line.

Two weeks later, we played Roswell, which is only 80 miles to the north of Carlsbad but still in southern New Mexico. It was our first game against the Coyotes since 1947, the year that Roswell had refused to play AHS because we had Blacks on our team, as noted in Chapter Five. That also changed in 1952. Poetic justice was served when a desperate end-of-the-game pass deflected off my outstretched fingertips into the waiting arms of Velma Corley (our Black right end substituting for Jack) who took it into the end zone for an 8 to 6 victory. Of our five losses in 1952, four were to teams from the south. This wasn't the case in the Thirties and Forties as evidenced earlier.

In the three years of football at AHS playing 31 games our record was 18 wins, 12 losses and 1 tie. Of the 12 losses, eleven were to teams from the south. I've speculated on the reason for this imbalance earlier but only one thing was certain. It was rare that one state could be split on the issue of race. One of the most positive aspects, of course, is that our era saw and experienced the resolution of the race issue in New Mexico when we were in high school. Times were "a-changin."

We had three weeks to get ready for THE game of the year against Highland on Thanksgiving Day. Anticipating a huge crowd of 12,000, the game was moved to Zimmerman Field the UNM stadium. Our cheerleaders led a "heated" rally at the bonfire the night before the game. All the talk was focused on how to stop Tom (TommyGun) McDonald. He had already scored twenty-two TDs in nine games and with two touchdowns he would break Chuck Hill's state record of 144 points in one season.

Mike Sutin, a student at HHS, writing for the Albuquerque Journal, said,

On the basis of their 7-2 won-loss slate the Hornets again loom as statistical favorites in the contest but in past years the Bulldogs have shown a great tendency to improve as the season progresses, win with startling comeback spirit and have displayed quite a flair for beating the Hornets regardless of who was favored.

Our record of 5 wins and 4 losses didn't stack up against HHS, but they had wins against Raton, Tucumcari and Los Alamos—two of three schools that were lightly regarded in Class B. All the "stats" were meaningless, however, in this rivalry, but Tom McDonald supported by backs Rusty Shaffer, Billy Wagner, Jim Curd and Dave Mohar and standout linemen Teddy Rhodes and John McCormack were, no question about it, a formidable team.

Our Bulldog eleven jumped out in front quickly. Davey Otero, our slick ball-handler, "baffled the Highland defense," according to the *Journal* and we went 54 yards in 11 plays with H.B. taking it in from the one. Fortunately, I made the extra point, round toe shoe and all.

Still in the first quarter, Foy Graves, playing linebacker, picked off a McDonald pass and we had possession on Highland's 37 yard line. McDonald, playing tailback, wasn't considered a serious threat (by some) as a passer. He would lay the ball in the palm of his hand seemingly not gripping the pigskin and throw in a sidearm motion. Davey hit Jack (Rabbit) Brown with an 18 yard pass and we worked it down inside the Hornet 20. Then, on a strange play described by Howard Peterson, the *Journal* sportswriter:

However as Harris drove for the score, the ball squirted out of his hands on the seven. But Quist, who was one of the stars of the contest, picked up the pigskin and rambled into the end zone.

I missed the conversion but we were up on the heavy favorites, 13-0. A few minutes later I knocked the ball out of McDonald's hands while he was attempting to pass but I couldn't take it in for a TD. Later, Tommy did complete two passes for 46 yards. And Wagner, on a double reverse, scored late in the first quarter. AHS 13 — Highland 6.

In the second quarter our offense revved up again. With

193

Phil gaining 26 yards on one carry, he and Jack Brown consistently ate up turf down to the two where Phil carried it to pay dirt. My conversion was good and we had a surprising 20-6 lead. Mike Sutin's forecast was coming true.

Up to this point in the game we had held the vaunted Tommy Gun in check. Just before the half he broke loose on a 47 yard burst off tackle, but our secondary caught the speedster from behind. We couldn't hold, however, and Tommy scored two plays later. Halftime: Bulldogs 20 — Hornets 13. And Tommy had exceeded Chuck Hill's record.

According to Bob Matteucci, a close friend and a senior at AHS who was writing for the *Albuquerque Journal*: "Phil Harris, the great Bulldog fullback, gave a spirited speech at halftime. Players said he almost fainted from loss of breadth when he finished." We must have gotten so jacked up during the intermission that we came out flat in the third quarter. The Hornets dominated the period and took a 26-20 lead into the fourth. It was Bulldog time. Matteucci said:

> The Bulldog bench was a madhouse of excitement in the last five minutes of the Thanksgiving Day fracas as players, band, coaches and over 500 Bulldog fans were all clustered around the sidelines for the rally that never came.

The "underdogs" had run out of gas. We couldn't muster a rally that almost everyone including our rivals, had expected. HHS scored again with only seconds remaining for a 33 - 20 victory. We were the first Bulldog team to lose to our rivals and the Bronze Shoe left our trophy case for the first time.

For Fred Allen, Jack Brown, Clemente Chavez, Thestal Findley, Foy Graves, Phil Harris, Marciano Marcelli, Norman Muggleston, Davey Otero, Johnny Romero, Mike Schlick, Anthony Simon, Phil Casias, Eddie Akers and Bob Cross this was their last football game dressed in the Green and White. All seniors want to make their last game, particularly this one, a winning experience but not everyone can. Coach McDavid said, "You all played a good game boys, that was about all we could do," which probably meant, it's not whether you win or lose, it's how you played the game that counts.

There was some consolation to a football season recalled for its disappointment. Eight of us were selected to the All-City team (offense and defense). Jack and I as ends, Bob Cross, Marciano Marcelli and Mike Schlick as interior lineman, and Davey Otero, Jack Brown and Phil Harris as backs. Davey, Phil, Mike and Bob made the All-Star North squad. Jack and I were the only All-City Juniors as ends and we both garnered 60 points out of a possible 70. Twice as many as the second team selections.

Tom McDonald, despite being the epitome of an enemy, was truly the real deal. He not only broke Chuck Hill's scoring record with 151 points, he starred on Highland's basketball and track teams. Highly recruited by numerous schools Tommy enrolled at the University of Oklahoma and, playing under Bud Wilkinson, was a standout member of the teams that never lost a game in his three years while winning an incredible 47 straight and two national championships. The HHS hero was second to Paul Hornung in the Heisman Trophy balloting and went on to become an outstanding receiver for the Philadelphia Eagles in the National Football League. Deservedly, he was recently inducted into the NFL Hall of Fame.

On one occasion in this 1953 game I made a good, hard tackle on the future All-American. He quickly bounced up seemingly unfazed and patting me on the top of my helmet, he said, "Nice tackle."

Tommy was a class act. Too bad he wasn't a Bulldog.

"A" Club was for all lettermen. In order for football players to be eligible for the club, a player had to play a specific number of quarters during the previous season. There were about twenty new members from the 1952 team that had to be "initiated" into the club. Jack and I made the club as "Sophs." The ritualistic ceremony included shaved heads with green "A"s on some of the bald pates or faces. As ridiculous as it looked, it was truly a badge of honor. Not everyone agreed. Certainly not Gretchen, Jack's sister, who was one year out of AHS.

"The whole damn thing is ridiculous," Gretchen said as Jack, Jim and I were working out with weights at the Stromberg's new addition located directly behind their old house. It was our hangout.

195

"What's ridiculous, Gretchen?" Jack shot back at his sister, already knowing her view on the subject but provoking a response for our benefit.

"It's the whole male hero worship thing. The football games, the "A" club, the letter sweaters with all the stripes and do-dads on the arm. Even the Band and the Drill Squad. All to glorify you guys as heroes. It's all a dumb, male ritual. What do we get to do? Jump up and down and cheer to pump up your egos," Gretchen elaborated profoundly.

"Damn. Why don't you tell us what you really think?" Jimmy said as we witnessed possibly one of the first feminist protests since the woman's suffrage movement.

(Title IX in the 80s changed the way things were. Gretchen had to be pleased. Geez, women are now not only playing tackle football they are venting all that pent up anger boxing in the ring. It's a thing of beauty to watch.)

After Gretchen left, Jack made a timely and astute observation about being a star and hero worship.

"I went into Chuck Hill's Sporting Goods store the other day. Chuck Hill, boy, now there was a real star. A real Albuquerque hero. Here he was just out of UNM and he had his own store up near the "Triangle" on Monte Vista. He was probably the best football player at AHS and UNM. He was a god. And now he was waiting on me at his store. He looked, to me, like he was trapped. He acted like he wanted to be somewhere else and he..."

"Playing pro football," I interjected.

"Precisely. Yeah. You've got it, Buster. Yeah. I'd say that being a star is a curse. There wasn't any more cheering. What could he do now to hear the cheering? Be a politician?" Jack asked all of us.

"Gee whiz, Jack. What are we lifting these weights for? What are we going to Vic `Tummys' for?" (Actually Vic Tammy's Gym) H.B. inquired. "We don't want to be stars if it's a curse, do we?"

"Hell, we're not going to be stars, anyways, are we?" I asked

"Of course not," Jack agreed.

Jack was right. Chuck was trapped. Possibly a victim of his own success. Fame and fortune are often rivals, not teammates. Success on one field doesn't guarantee success on another. (Another example of the intransigence of Parker's theory.) Impatient and in a hurry possibly to regain recognition and respect, Chuck made some bad investments. Some involved close friends. When they failed he must have felt that the cheers had turned to jeers. He left Albuquerque and shortly thereafter he was found dead in his car parked in his garage. Some said that it was suicide. The Coroner's report said it was an accident. One thing was certain. It was devastating and it left those of us who knew him well and his family, wondering why. He was a true AHS hero. An Icon. He was my hero, too.

Lipsky validates this tragedy when he says:

> The power of the audience, the Greek Chorus, gives the contest its dramatic and social reality. The athlete is like an actor enmeshed in a performance, fueled by the collective approval of the crowds...He (the athlete) fears the end of his career because it will mean the termination of his crowd-induced high.

Our Cheerleaders for the 1952-53 school year were: Connie Abbott, Connie Chavez, Pat Looney, Jean Cornell, Sally Crook and Emily Lanigan. Connie Abbott, Connie Chavez and Jean Cornell attended the 50th Reunion of the 1953 Class. I asked each one of them what it meant to them to be selected by their classmates.

> Connie Abbott: "It was one of the most fun things I've ever done in my life. I felt that I had really achieved something."
> Connie Chavez: "It was a great honor to represent my school and to be chosen by my classmates."
> Jean Cornell: "I felt that we were not only supporting our team we wanted recognition for ourselves. And, you know, all of us in our group have been successful in life. Being a cheerleader, I believe, had something to do with that."

In short, what this writer learned from this still gorgeous group was that all their jumping up and down brought "a spring in their step." And, quite possibly, their's was a majority view.

"Mom, my back is killing me," I divulged to my mother during breakfast.

"Did you get hurt during the Highland game?" she asked.

"No. Before that. The last month or so. It was so bad this morning I couldn't tie my shoelaces," I continued.

"Tell you what, Buster. I've got a checkup this week up at Medical Arts Square. Why don't I get you an appointment to see a doctor at the same time?"

"That's great. The way that it is now, I can't start basketball or ski or do anything," I concluded.

I saw Dr. Parnell, an orthopedic surgeon. He took x-rays and Mom and I waited for what seemed an eternity in one of the examining rooms. I had just discovered why doctors clients are called "patients." Without patience a person wouldn't ever get treatment.

"Your son has spondylolysis, Mrs. Quist," Dr. Parnell said as we both anxiously awaited the verdict. The medical term meant nothing to either of us, of course.

"Spondylo..., what?" I asked fearing what the answer might be. Mom, still recovering from her medical trauma had a familiar anxious look on her face.

Dr. Parnell had a detailed anatomical picture of a skeleton on the wall of the examining room.

"This is lumbar number three and here's number five. Buster's pain and stiffness is caused when one or both of these bones in his spine move forward and get out of alignment. There is also a narrowing of the L3-4 disc interspace and spondylolysis at L5-S1," Dr. Parnell added.

"How did that happen?" Mom asked as she looked closely at the skeleton where the doctor was pointing.

"It's congenital, Mrs. Quist. Buster was born with the condition. Probably you or Mr. Quist has the same thing," the doctor added.

"What can I do for it?" I asked anxiously.

"Surgery is the best cure," the doctor stated matter-of-factly.

"Surgery?" Mom and I asked in unison.

"Yep. We fuse the spine so the lumbar joints don't move out of alignment," he added, as he pointed again to the bony figure on the wall.

Mom, recoiling at the mention of the word surgery, asked, "But wouldn't that make Buster's back real stiff? Would he be able to play sports? He participates in everything, you know."

"Yes, I know Mrs. Quist. I read the sports section. Buster won't play football or track with a spinal fusion. Sorry," Dr. Parnell said reluctantly.

"Geez, Mom. I can't do that. I can't have a back operation that will prevent me from playing sports. I'm just starting to get good at sports," I pleaded, visualizing, as I looked out the window, what I would look like with my spine welded like that chain link fence in the distance.

"Will it get worse if Buster continues to play, doctor?" Mom asked.

"Most "spondylos" get progressively worse, Mrs. Quist."

"Isn't there something else Buster can do?" Mom persisted.

"Well, that's not in my area of expertise but you could see a chiropractor. I don't agree with their methods, but you might give it a try," Dr. Parnell said as he quickly picked up the x-rays and left us in the examining room.

Mom, probably aided by her own recent experience, agreed with me 100%. Surgery would only be a last resort. A major, life changing decision was made that day. Some damn painful days were ahead but intuitively, one thing seemed certain. There couldn't be a "spring in my step" if there was a fusion in my back.

———————

"How would you like to go to the Rose Bowl, Buster?" Dad said just after Thanksgiving.

"How come?" I asked.

"The UNM Booster's Club is helping to send the Lobo football team to the Rose Bowl since they had such a good season," Dad added, "Wisconsin won the Big Ten. They're going to play Southern Cal. The Boosters have chartered a rail car and they have some extra seats."

"Geez, I wonder if Jack would like to go?" I asked. "I'll call him."

"Buster, you'll need some money. I'll pay for your train

ticket but you'll have to earn your own spending money," Dad insisted.

Jack thought the trip would be "neato." Just as I secured a delivery job at a flower shop on the "Triangle" near UNM, I thought of Karen, my first love.

(Karen was Karen Markwardt whom I had met at Sand Bay in Door County, Wisconsin, where my parents built a fabulous summer house in the late Forties. When we met on the beach in the summer of `49 I was 13 and going to be an eighth-grader and she was 15 and going to be a sophomore in high school in Manitowoc, Wisconsin. Now she was a freshman at the University of Wisconsin.)

I called Karen's dad in Manitowoc and secured her phone number at her dorm. Would she be going to the game? Would she even have any interest in seeing me? A high school kid?

"Karen? It's Buster. How are you?" I said as I nervously broke the ice.

"Oh, gosh," Karen responded quite surprised to hear from me even though we had several dates during the summer of 1951 when Jack and I worked in Door County.

"Karen? I'm going to the Rose Bowl Game. Is there any chance that you'll be going?"

"Yes—yes, I'm going with a bunch of guys from UW," Karen replied enthusiastically.

"Guys?" I inquired.

"Oh, friends, you know," she clarified which quieted ny anxiety.

"I'd sure like to see you. How about New Year's Eve?" I asked boldly, not expecting a favorable response.

"Oh geez, that would be 'cool'," Karen replied using a term that I wasn't familiar with but I assumed that "cool" was good. Probably college talk.

Pleased as all punch, I had a date with the most gorgeous girl I had ever met. I couldn't let Mom know. She feared that this "older woman" might take advantage of me—whatever that meant.

Jack and I were the only "kids" on the trip. The Lobo team members were incredibly gracious. They had just finished their season 7-2 and were the best defensive team in the nation. I got to talk at length to guys like Chuck Koskovich, Mike Prokopiak, Ralph Matteucci, Dave Matthews, Bob Lee, Larry White and others, who would become good friends years later.

We got off at Pasadena and stayed at Occidental College. Karen was in downtown L.A. at the Roslyn Hotel. New Year's Eve had arrived. I took the trolley downtown which was a long start and stop trip. My mind was racing wildly while the trolley rolled rhythmically. Here I was, age 16, going out with a college girl. She was the age of some of the Lobos on the train. I looked so scrawny compared to the Lobos. Would I be embarrassed looking so young? Would she change her mind once she saw me? I had just about beat myself to death by the time I got downtown. But, I had "morphed" myself. With a suit and tie, top coat and hat I sure looked older. Karen had never seen me "dressed up." I knocked on her door and held my breath.

"Buster!" she screamed enthusiastically. A different reception than I got the summer before in Fish Creek. "Wow, you never cease to amaze me. Geez, you look great, you're so tall" she added.

So far I had passed muster. Karen introduced me to five or six friends of hers in the room and after removing my hat and coat, we sat down on the bed and had drinks. Some of the guys were pretty smashed already and it was only dinner time.

Karen was totally different than she was the summer of 1951. She held my hand and looked directly into my eyes as we sat on the bed. She let me know that I was her "beau." Incredible as it was, the two and one-half year difference in our ages, monumental at this point in time, seemed irrelevant. I relaxed and laughed as we recalled our first meeting in 1949. I told her that she was my very first love. I didn't tell her I was going "steady." That was high school stuff. This was a "mature" relationship. A lot more mature than I could handle as I soon would experience.

We had dinner in the dining room at the hotel. We were surrounded by noisy Badgers from the University of Wisconsin but we were alone in their midst. The waitress didn't

201

even ask me for an I.D. We danced, both recalling that day at her cabin when she taught me how to foxtrot. I had now mastered the Texas Two Step, but our differences in technique was of no consequence. As long as we were close nothing else mattered. The New Year, 1953, arrived and everyone went bonkers. Karen kissed me passionately. We adjourned to her room.

Karen's roommate and her date were already in the room. They didn't want the lights on and we groped through the dark trying to fix ourselves another drink. It was the first time I really had a cocktail. Karen suggested that I take off my shoes, suit coat, and tie and that we sit on the bed. All my fantasies about Karen were becoming reality. She was as warm, affectionate and passionate as she was gorgeous. Awkwardly, we began removing our clothes and slid beneath the sheets. We were approaching that critical moment of decision when it became too apparent to ignore that Karen's roommate and her boyfriend had already passed that point. I had forgotten that they were in the bed beside us until the rocking and rolling of the bed and moans of passion overwhelmed our intimacy. We couldn't help but be distracted. Karen whispered:

"Buz" I'm afraid that if we start we'll never be able to stop."

"Whataya mean?" I asked not really wanting to acknowledge the full impact of her concern.

"One of my girlfriends at Madison who just got pregnant told me that. I'm afraid that I'll get pregnant," Karen murmured softly, quivering with emotion and trepidation as we professed our love for each other.

The pause allowed all of Aphrodite's detractors to draw a cold blanket between us. My promise to my Mother with my hand on the Bible not to have sex. The constant admonition from my parents that this act, if I let it happen, would ruin my life. Was it right or was it wrong? Is this the girl I wanted to marry? How could I? I was only 16. And, what about Glo?

I desperately had to go to the bathroom. I wrestled with my conscience as I relieved myself and the pause tempered the heat of the moment. My conscience won. I couldn't do "IT." Unbelievable as it may seem to the "boys" (and many readers), reason conquered passion.

We were both frustrated. It was now about 4:00 a.m. The team was leaving at 7:00 a.m. for the Rose Bowl parade and the game. If I missed the bus I would lose my group for the entire day. I had a long trek back to Pasadena. Karen was noticeably angry. Was she mad at me or herself? I was almost certain that I would never see her again. It was truly an "un-defining moment." A moment that would haunt me for exactly 50 years—almost to the day.

What if Karen and I had made love? Given our similar midwestern roots and value systems, hatched from the same Christian mold, Karen and I would have been totally committed to each other. As I reflect back to that day a half-century ago, there is little doubt that I would have returned to the Green Bay area in the summer of 1953 to work and be close to my "first love of 1949." I, unfortunately, would not have been a member of the Bulldog American Legion Baseball team that won the State Championship that summer and, assuming that our romance would have flourished, I may have enrolled at the University of Wisconsin in the fall of 1954. There are defining moments in everyone's life. New Year's Eve 1952 was one that could have changed my life but nevertheless, I would have remained a Bulldog forever.

The trolley ride back to Pasadena was painful. I wasn't thinking or was too absorbed with the events earlier and I got off the trolley at the wrong stop. Within ten or fifteen minutes I realized that I was hopelessly lost in a residential section of Pasadena. I saw a light on a house on the darkened and foreboding street. I approached the house and knocked at the door.

"Who is it?" A voice shouted.

"I'm lost. I need directions to Occidental College," I asked.

"Get the hell away from here," the angry voice bellowed. "Honey, go get my shotgun. There's a drunken kid out here on the porch," the man said in a threatening voice.

I wanted to explain. I could see the man in the window. Damn! He did have a gun! I took off running across the lawn unable to see anything in the dark compounded by a misty fog enveloping the area. I tripped over a small fence and landed face first on a dew-ladened lawn. I didn't look back to see if my protagonist was chasing me. I hit the pavement running.

If I had an idea where I was prior to this incident, I sure as hell didn't know now. I walked for a half an hour. The sun was coming up. Finally a man was getting in his car going to work. He sensed my plight, given the fact that my coat was splashed with mud and I lost my hat. I was only a couple blocks away from Occidental and the good samaritan took me to my dorm.

Jack and the Lobos were already in the shower and the older guys were shaving when I made my entrance. I didn't even shave yet.

"Lookee who is here," Mike Prokopiak yelled to his team-mates.

"Been out all night, Buster?" Chuck asked.

"Here we've been out all night chasing pussy and the only guy that gets laid is the 16-year old kid," Mike said laughing as many of the guys joined in.

"And, you ought to see who he was with," Jack added. "She's a fox. And, a freshman."

I couldn't tell them the real story. They wouldn't have believed it anyway. I took a hot shower (when a cold one would have been more suitable), changed clothes and boarded the bus. I was confused and disconsolate.

After a couple of hours of looking at floats and scantily-dressed girls we went to the game. The Trojans won despite Alan (The Horse) Ameche grinding out the yards, but my thoughts were on the main event of the evening past. There weren't any winners or losers in that game. Only memories of what might have been. It might have been the right person and the right place but the right time in my life it wasn't. I was, in reality, only a kid and like Don Quixote, in quest of an impossible dream.

I had bought myself the new suit (at the Stromberg's store of course) that I wore at the New Year's Eve party in L.A. for $30. I had also intended to wear it to the Green and

White Ball, which was a semi-formal dance to be held at school the next weekend. Glo had been looking forward to the occasion. I felt that I had to be honest with her. I felt compelled to tell her about Karen. We had lunch in the cafeteria because it was too cold to eat out on the patio.

"I've got something to tell you Glo that's not pleasant," I said as I broke the ice. She had her eyes on me since the moment we sat down at the table. She must have had an inkling of what I was going to say. Maybe Jack had said something about our trip. I didn't know.

"I met Karen in Los Angeles," I confessed. I had mentioned Karen before so Glo knew who she was.

"And..." Glo countered as she waited for the second shoe to drop.

"We spent the night together but..."

"You what?" She shouted, as she cut me off. "Buster, how could you do that to me?" Glo said so loudly that it pricked the ears of everyone sitting near us.

"Geez, Glo, not so loud," I pleaded. "We didn't make love, I assure you."

"We were going steady, Buz. But not anymore," Glo said angrily as she pushed her tray away in a huff and left me sitting by myself. I was embarrassed as a few of the girls next to me giggled. Lunch was hard to swallow. We both missed the Green and White Ball.

In retrospect, telling Glo was a pretty dumb thing to do. I already knew that I had a very slim chance for a relationship with Karen in the future and it hurt Glo a lot. The toughest class in any high school is interpersonal relationships. It is truly the school of hard knocks. Fortunately, Glo and I were both stag at the Sen-Sims Tri-Hi-Y dance a couple of weeks later and we made up. It was exciting to make up. We would experience that a number of times over the next two and one-half years, as we had done since our days at "La Wash." But, Karen was always present in the recesses of my mind.

After a series of chiropractic treatments and therapy, following my not-so-rosy bowl trip, I joined the basketball team. Coach Heinsohn and I had an informal "don't ask, don't tell" policy. I didn't tell him I was skiing and he didn't ask. I got plenty of playing time—on the "B" team. At home games I would play about twenty-five or thirty minutes in the preliminary game and then suit up again for the varsity game. Why? I don't know. When I did play I was tired and rigor mortis had set into my muscles. I couldn't bring much energy to the team.

I made the traveling squad and we had 5 wins and 6 losses going into the Tuccumcari game in the middle of January. We eked out a two point win at the Rattler gym on Friday. Three of us must have been in a celebrating mood. What action we hoped to discover in this sleepy ranching community that rolled up the sidewalks after 10:00 p.m. defied logic, but imagination can be the root of evil in the mind of a teenager. We discovered trouble. And trouble with a capital "T" was in the form of a 6'7" angry, hulk of a man waiting to pounce on us like a rebound as we attempted to sneak back into the hotel after curfew. Coach Heinsohn caught us red-handed. Jack, who was my roommate on trips, accurately assessed the risk (as he always did) and didn't participate in our nocturnal adventure.

Tom Curley, Dick Trott and I (the miscreants) were the three biggest guys on the team. We didn't play the next night at Forrest High but that was hardly the extent of our punishment. Since I was relegated to the role of observer, I made some opportune observations as David was about to smite Goliath.

Forrest, which had to be the town founder's name because there were very few trees in sight, is a peanut-sized farming community on the plains of northeastern New Mexico homesteaded by hard-working farmers at the turn of the century. Our big city bus driver had difficulty finding it on the map, and drove through the town several times before he realized that the city limit signs were back to back. The town had less than one thousand residents. The Forrest Public School had less than one hundred students and only one half of that number was in high school. There were, as I remember, only seven players on the Forrest team and one of them was probably an eighth or ninth grader. He was dwarfed by the cheerleaders.

In the movie "Hoosiers," a hard-nosed coach with a check-

ered past, played by Gene Hackman, is hired to coach in a small Indiana farming community that is as dedicated to the nurturing of its high school basketball program as its life-giving corn crop. Based upon a true story chronicled in 1952, "Hoosiers" is regarded as one of the foremost, inspirational and motivating sports stories of all time, when the small town "hicks" beat the biggest school in the state for the championship. Drawing an analogy between Forrest, New Mexico, and Old Hickory, Indiana, begged comparison. Forrest was "Hoosierville."

It was a bitterly cold January day with the unabated wind and dust blowing in our faces as we stepped off of our chartered bus dressed in sports suits and ties. Coach Heinsohn's dress code was mandatory no matter the environment. Our attire was as out of place in Forrest as tuxedos at a "stomp" (western) dance. We quickly made our way into the cracker box-sized gym which would be the platform for our performance in a matter of hours. With the bleachers encroaching onto the gym floor and one of the baskets protruding from a stage more accustomed to student assemblies and amateur drama than an athletic contest, we appeared to be standing on a volleyball court.

"I think we're playing the Lilliputians tonight," HB said as he laughed. "You couldn't get two regular-sized teams onto this floor at one time," he added.

Jack and I looked at Coach Heinsohn. He thought he had reached the outer limits of the boondocks when he coached at Wagon Mound. Now this. Not a highlight on his coaching resume. He must have sensed that Waterloo awaited his army as he shook his head in disbelief while at the same time, jabbing his toe on the floor to see if it was hardwood.

"Spider," coach called out to Jack, addressing him by the nickname that he thought appropriate, given Jack's lanky build. "Go with Ted (the team manager) and see if there's a dressing room for us. I wouldn't be surprised if we had to dress on the bus."

What I observed and the team experienced over the game's thirty-two minutes was unforgettable. The hustle and scrambling for rebounds and loose balls by our opponents was awesome. Their passing and teamwork had been honed to perfection through years of playing together since grade school. Their team chemistry was as compatible as oxygen and water. They were determined to beat the city slickers and they did, 54 to 52. And, most importantly, they had fun. Win or lose they would have had fun. That's the way they played the game. I admired our adversaries.

Mighty Goliath was felled by diminutive David. We were disconsolate and embarrassed. We barely spoke to each other on our three hour, showerless bus ride home. We should have gained a valuable experience that night, but neither our Coach nor any of us accurately articulated it. Forrest had all the intangibles that are necessary to win. Intangibles that we were in wont of. Coach Heinsohn said we were "hometowned." He said they didn't heat the gym deliberately to keep our hands cold. We couldn't run our complex picks and screens effectively because there wasn't sufficient spacing. Coach not only missed the message that night he, in fact, never got it.

Monday, Coach Heinsohn made the three of us curfew violators pay for our crime. Tom, Dick and I were forced to run laps around the gym continuously during the entire two hour practice. None of us could meet the rigorous requirement. We dropped off one by one like heart patients on a treadmill. We were history but we did open up three spots on the Varsity for "B" team players. The team really didn't miss me but they did miss Tom and Dick who were our muscle under the basket. Dissension began to fester as the losses mounted.

In order to tell this story I have to turn the clock back two years. Jack, Mike Padilla, Ralph Boan and I were the nucleus of the basketball team at Washington Junior High School in 1950-51 under the competent and motivating tutelage of our coach, Chester (Doc) Ledbetter. We amassed an incredible record of 22 straight wins, including two over the AHS sophomores in winning the Albuquerque City Championship. Mike Padilla, our center at 6'2" in the ninth grade, was our star. My principal objective as a guard (I was also 6'2"), was to get the ball to Mike and let him score which he did gloriously. Our team had both great chemistry as well as diversity as we had nine Hispanics and two Native Americas on our squad. We hoped to duplicate this success at AHS.

Larry (Junior) Walker, a senior guard on this 1953 team, was a school leader and in the context of the day, popular. He was Student Council President, Governor of Boy's State, and was in Jack's words "charismatic." Junior, possibly due to the fact that Tom Curley and Dick Trott along with myself who were the big men in the middle, were no longer with the team, seemed to take it upon himself to be the team offense. Shooting bombs from outside and not feeding the ball inside to Jack, Mike, LeRoy Weller and others, Junior rapidly gained the reputation as a ball hog. A 33 point loss to Highland opened an ugly sore that had been festering. Mike and the majority of the team who were Hispanic, vented their displeasure by ignoring Junior and freezing him out of off-court contact, which, of course, diluted the chemistry of the team. Coach Heinsohn wasn't pro-active and ignored the obvious, thereby assuring a losing season of 11 wins and 14 losses. In the three years of my high school experience this situation would be the only one that could be termed a race-related incident at AHS. In reality, however, the lack of teamwork on Junior's part could have occurred amongst any individuals regardless of race, given the circumstance.

A couple weeks and four losses later Jack, H.B. and I were having lunch at the Chili Bowl.

"How's BB (basketball) goin', guys?" I asked. "Sorry I haven't seen the games. Been skiing, you know."

"Yeah. You lucky dog. I wish I were up there too. Basketball just isn't any fun anymore. Coach makes the game too complicated running all those plays. I hate it," Jack, in a disgusted tone, revealed for the first time.

"That's no s...," H.B. added. H.B. had a way of putting an explanation point on everything.

"Geez, why don't you quit, Jack? You could probably make the ski team. I've got a good shot at it," I inquired. "Man, you do everything Coach asks of you. And, calling you 'Spider.' That's bush league."

"Yeah, I'm just a kiss-ass, I guess. I don't have the guts to quit. Mom wanted me to quit after Coach made us practice on Christmas day. I should have done it then. Boy, was

Mom mad. We beat Durango just before Christmas. Why did we have to practice on that day of all days?" Jack, talking more to himself than us, continued.

If we thought that things were bad at this point in time, as far as BB was concerned all we had to do was wait for next year.

The 1953 wrestling team again coached by Jack Rushing, got off to an inauspicious start. The Bulldogs lost their first five meets by lopsided scores. Losing two meets to the New Mexico School for the Blind was no embarrassment however. Led by Paul Tapia, who would star as one of the best wrestlers ever at UNM, these blind athletes were well-coached, incredibly focused and had developed an extraordinary sense of feel and quickness to compensate for their loss of eyesight. Led by Team Captain Clarence Black the "Dawgs" won their last 3 meets including a 25 to 11 victory over Highland. Some of the other team stars were Gordy Modrall, Phil Harris and Panteleon Tafoya.

Although not featured in this year's *La Reata*, Gordy won the New Mexico State High School Penthathelon Championship and set a new record. The all-around demanding test included a 300 yard run, pushups, vertical leap, pullups and bar vault. Gordy excelled at swimming and wrestling also. "Gordo" was not only a great athlete he was a terrific guy and really popular.

"I won't be able to meet you at the "Y" tonight for the dance," I said to Glo as we met in the patio before class.

"Why, Buz? We always go out on Friday," Glo responded with a look of disappointment on her face.

"I'm going to Santa Fe this aft' to ski with the team at the Basin," I further explained.

"Who are you going with? Is Lois going?"

"Lois? Lois who?" I asked.

"Isn't Lois Reidy on the ski team at Highland?" Glo pressed further, revealing a light shade of green.

"Oh heck no, Glo, I don't have any interest in her. Besides, this is serious skiing—racing. I want to make the N.M. Junior Ski Team and go to Sun Valley in March. I'm going to stay at John Dendahl's house Friday and Saturday and be home Sunday evening," I elaborated.

"Gee, Buz. That doesn't leave any time for us. I'm going steady with someone I never see. First it was the football games, out of town, then basketball, now skiing. Looks like I'm just `second team'," Glo added with a wry smile that was revealing.

"I'm sorry Glo. I wish that you would ski. It sure would be neato. I'll teach you anytime. John is going to come and ski at La Madera next week and we can go out Saturday, okay?" I asked, trying to appease my girlfriend.

John Dendahl was two-and-one-half years younger than I was but was the best junior skier in the State. If skiing competition was graded on style points John would always have won, hands down. The only advantage I had on him was that I had no fear and skied with reckless abandon. I also outweighed him by forty or fifty pounds—a decided advantage on the flat sections of a race course.

The Santa Fe Basin had the best snow and a double chair lift, but the trails and open slope from the top of the mountain to the lift were too short. We would ski down in less than a minute and have to wait in line to get to the top of the mountain. We were usually the first ones on the lift in the morning and the last ones off the mountain at 4:00 p.m. We were veritable terrors on the slopes. Grownups hated to see us barreling down the run. Kind of like snowboarders today.

La Madera was directly east of Albuquerque and it took us (if we didn't get stuck in the snow or stop and put chains on the tires) only forty-five minutes to get up to the ski run. The only major tow was a T-bar, but the trail was over a mile from the top at 10,500' to the bottom. It was basically an intermediate (blue diamond) area, but several slopes like "suicide" had a grade over 40° (black diamond). One weekend, I clocked a (then) record time of 1:25.5 in the mile downhill run according to an *Albuquerque Journal* article. A mile in a minute would equal sixty miles per hour so my average speed was somewhere near 45 to 50 mph. John posted a 1:32.6 for third place.

I remember the day as if it were yesterday. There was a heavy fog at the top of the bowl where the hill was the steepest and the fastest. No one in their right mind would blast off blind, unable to see twenty feet ahead of them, but "s... for brains" (as my competitors called me) did it. Bob Nordhaus, Sr., who later was one of the principals in Sandia Peak Ski & Tram Co. and our next door neighbor, was packing a sitz mark on the trail near tower five and he never saw me coming out of the fog.

"Track!" I yelled. Mr. Nordhaus dove to get out of my way. I yelled an obscenity at him as I continued downhill on my record run.

After the race, Mr. Nordhaus presented me with a gold arrow to commemorate my feat.

"Congratulations, Buster. That was a courageous run in the fog but I don't think you should call your next door neighbor a dumb s...' for repairing a sitz mark. It was huge. You could have buried a tip in it," he admonished me.

"Geez, Mr. Nordhaus. I didn't know it was you," I said, embarrassed at my own cockiness and disrespect for an adult. The Nordhauses were great neighbors and I skied with both sons, Dickie and Bob Jr., often.

There weren't many skiing venues in N.M. in the middle 50s. Prior to the world famous Taos Ski Valley there was Tres Ritos (Three Little Rivers in Spanish). Our junior ski meet there wasn't as memorable on the slope as it was off. John had a time of 82.9 in the event that could be best described as a giant slalom with Aspen trees as our gates. I placed second with a time of 83.5. John always beat me in the slalom but often I had enough margin in winning the downhill that my combined time for the two events was better.

Our chaperon, baby sitter and coach was Giuseppe Olmi, who hadn't been in the U.S. (from Italy) for too many years. He was an excellent skier and coach when you could understand his instructions, but he, unfortunately, wasn't up to the task of monitoring a group of raucous U.S. teenagers.

"Seppi? Jerry (Spitz) is stuck out behind the Sagebrush (hotel)," I said excitedly on the phone as I woke up our coach at 11:00 p.m.

"Wot you say? Jerry he stuck on a sag-e-brush? How he

stuck on a sag-e-brush, huh?", was Seppi's broken English reply.

"No, Seppi. He's stuck in the mud behind the Sagebrush Hotel. We need to have you pull him out, okay?" I said as I tried to make myself clear.

Seppi came and we got Jerry out of the mud and in the effort succeeded in covering ourselves in the stuff you make adobe bricks out of. All went well until the hotel manager at the Taos Inn, where we were staying, called Seppi at 3:00 a.m.

"Mr. Olmi?"

"Si...yes," Seppi replied.

"This is the Manager. Your kids knocked a huge hole in the wall in their room. You're going to have to pay for this damage, you hear?" the angry manager said as he called from our room. The hole occurred because the wall was flimsy dry wall and I went through it when one of the guys pushed me off the bed. There weren't even any studs in the wall.

"Hey you Mister Manager, de kids. De not my kids." and with that Seppi hung up the phone and turned out the light. His "kid sitting" days in N.M. were over. We would have to find a new coach. Surprisingly there were two others vying for the job. Who would be so lucky as to take us to Sun Valley?

John and I were the first two skiers on the team picked to go to Sun Valley for the Westerns States Junior Championships. There were eleven states that would be represented plus British Columbia, which was ably sponsored by the American Legion. Our other team members, who were all from Santa Fe, were John Brennand (who was then a freshman at the University of Colorado) on a skiing scholarship. John Kinsolving, Jim Jordan and Mary Lind. Ernie Blake, who was the manager of the Santa Fe Basin, was the likely candidate to be our coach since everyone on the team, except myself, was from Santa Fe. Only one problem. The Santa Fe contingent (and most of the parents) didn't want Mr. Blake to take us on this one week trip. They wanted Buzz Bainbridge and his wife Jean (who managed La Madera) to accompany us to Sun Valley. Someone had to tell

Ernie that the team voted in favor of Buzz. Big, brash Buster was the designated hit man. I remember the phone call I made from the Dendahl house all too well.

Ernie was furious. His crusty, hard-nosed Swiss-German disposition lashed out at me as he used a number of Teutonic words I never heard before. He was nasty, which was precisely why he was voted out. Even I was intimidated. Ernie never forgave me. Hell, I was only the messenger, but it's usually the deliverer of bad tidings that gets shot.

I was actually competing in two incompatible sports at the same time. Track practice had begun in late February which was also the high season for skiing. I was very forthright with Coach McDavid. He knew my dual role. I won the javelin throw in the first three meets prior to departing for Sun Valley the last week in March.

"I'll miss two meets, Coach," I said to Pete McDavid in his office at the gym.

"That's okay, Buster. They're just dual meets. The big ones come in April and May. You'll have plenty of time to get ready for them. Just don't break a leg...or something else while you're up there," Coach said, probably trying to reassure himself as much as me that I would return in one piece. Unfortunately, his words were prophetic.

Our group posed for a team photograph. (Tellingly, my face was removed from this photo in Blake's biography.) Buzz had purchased white turtleneck sweaters with a large, red embroidered "Zia" on the front. The "Zia" is a Native American symbol representing the sun. It is also the flag of the State of New Mexico. I got an inkling how our team was perceived by our competitors when John Brennand, who had competed that season for the University of Colorado against all the western schools, wouldn't wear his Zia sweater or hang-out with his teammates. We were an embarrassment. We were snow bunnies playing in the snow amongst a pack of timber wolves. Either the unaccustomed, hostile and difficult trails or our savvy, mountain tested opponents would eat us alive, so it seemed.

But, I had something else other than no fear that my teammates didn't have. I was by now an experienced and an aggressive competitor in several sports. I would never accept defeat without a battle—even against long odds—and they were even longer than my 7'3" (220cm) Northland downhill racing skis. Ridicule by the Colorado, Utah and California teams made me angry and raised the bar. As the kids say today, we were "dissed." They had the technique. They had the experience. But, were they competitors? I was out to prove them wrong. I tried to rally my teammates but I could see trepidation in their faces and you can't race scared. You can't ski stupid, either.

The three day competition was comprised of downhill, slalom and jumping. Our jumping experience was limited to forty or fifty feet off an improvised jump on "suicide" at La Madera. Hardly a preparation for the 50 meter (165 feet) jump that we found ourselves staring out on Rudd Mountain. Standing at the top and looking down, the jumper couldn't see his landing area. The landing slope was much steeper than "Suicide" at La Madera. Sid Cutter, my buddy from AHS who made the team the year prior, had given me his "jumpers" (special skis for jumping). As adventurous and crazy as Sid was, he never intended to use them again.

I had a flashback to six years prior when Dad and Uncle Bob took Terry and I to Ishpemming, Michigan, to watch the jumpers soar like eagles off a scaffolding jump. They appeared to us youngsters, huddled below the landing, like Superman sans his cape.

Downhill had to be a piece of cake compared to the jump. I was pretty nervous prior to my first leap. My form was horrific but I landed feet first and didn't fall. After a couple more jumps, trepidation turned into excitement. The big test was behind me and my teammates. We could now practice our slalom technique on "Half Dollar" mountain.

"That's Stein Ericsen!" John Brennand shouted to all of us as we herring-boned (climbed) up the practice slalom course.

We all watched in amazement and awe as Stein, who was a gold medal winner from Norway at the past Olympics, skied down past us.

"Look at the reverse shoulder'," Buzz said, describing Ericsen's unique style that was as foreign to us and all U.S. skiers as the Bogners (stretch ski pants) he wore. He was handsome. He was magnificent. Even if he was Norwegian (a Swedish lament.)

John Dendahl had the best slalom technique. He was small in stature, had excellent coordination and used short skis. I was trying to get my 7'0" skis through the tight gates with limited success. The gates were large, round, wooden poles about the size of a (appropriately) silver dollar planted deeply into the hard-packed snow. They were intractable obstacles. If you hit a gate with your shoulder you could dislocate it. If your uphill skis caught the gate you would undoubtedly spin out and hit the snow and be out of the race. A far cry from today where the slalom racers, equipped with helmets and face guards, boldly take a direct line and run over the hinged gates on short 158 cm skis without fear of being pummeled by the gates.

"Let's go swimming," John suggested after our first day of practice. "The pool is 90°, it's like a huge whirlpool bath," he added.

And, swim we did. And, snowball fights. That was "rare." What us bush leaguers from New Mexico didn't know was that a couple of hours in the steamy, hot pool was a prescription for trouble. It softens and relaxes your leg muscles. Not proper preparation for a grueling mile-and-one-half downhill race. But, what did we know?

With Buzz's assistance we had scoped out the Olympic downhill run section by section. It was nearing the end of our last practice day before the competition began for real.

"Okay, guys," Buzz said as we stood near the Roundhouse at the top of the Olympic run (Mary was considered one of the guys) "I want you to take the run all the way down to the finish. No stops. Run it as if you're in the race tomorrow. If you fall, get back in the race as fast as you can. I'm going ahead of you. Brennand will lead, of course, followed by Dendahl, Jordan, Kinsolving and Quist. Mary, you follow Buster. Okay?" Buzz asked us as he took off down the run. I was last which I preferred.

As soon as John Kinsolving was near the "catwalk" I aggressively poled away from the starting gate. All the other teams had already taken their runs and were back at the top probably "yuking" it up watching us.

216

The catwalk was narrow and had a series of washboard-like bumps that seemed to be designed to rattle your teeth and catch an edge if you weren't paying attention. I was closing on Kinsolving who didn't schuss the entire slope before the catwalk. A sharp right turn was directly ahead. We couldn't go off the "springboard" because there wasn't sufficient snow on the face of this nearly vertical drop. I edged hard to slow to make the turn. Kinsolving was blocking the narrow turn. Miraculously, I missed him and continued full out over the long traverse heading into the real scary part of the course. Jimmy Jordan fell but was back on his feet. I passed him. My weight was propelling me down the trail at breakneck (an appropriate choice of words) speed. I reached the final turn that would take me to RiverRun and the finish. I heard Buzz yell, "Great run, Buster."

I went into a full racing crouch position to cut down the wind drag. I was moving from sunlight to shadows as it was nearing the end of the day. My thighs and calves were burning as I squatted down in my crouch. The hot swimming pool had sapped my muscles. In my exhilaration and anticipation of a spectacular run, I failed to see the last major mogul and drop off just above the turn into River Run. I missed my pre-jump. I was airborne! The light was flat. I couldn't see. My legs were gone when I hit the bottom of the transition. My knees hit me in my chest as my skis hit the snow. I went over my tips going 60 mph. An "egg-beater!"

One, two, three careening bounces off the hard packed snow. I lost count. I was in preservation mode protecting my head from the sharp edges of my skis when suddenly my right ski, on one of my end-over-end bounces, buried tip first almost up to the binding. My body kept going downhill. Something had to give. It wasn't the ski. It wasn't the binding. It was me. My right ankle snapped like a twig on a falling tree.

In 1953, there really wasn't a true safety binding. In fact, during races we tightened our bindings so the ski wouldn't come off. And, it didn't.

My ankle burned and throbbed but I never even thought that it was broken. I had this illusion after surviving numerous "egg-beaters" previously that I was indestructible. Stupid but true. Jimmy Jordan and John Kinsolving skied on by. By the time Buzz came by I was on my feet, retrieved my hat and goggles and was carefully making my way down to the lift. Sure, the ankle hurt, but I was pissed that I screwed up a great run. I would be ready for that bump tomorrow. I returned to the Roundhouse to meet my teammates.

"That was one hell-of-a spill, Buster," Buzz said. "I didn't think you'd ski away from that one. You were flat-out flying. You sure you're okay?" he added.

"I better take my boot off and find out. I think I've got a pretty good sprain," I surmised.

I removed my boot and stocking. I watched my ankle swell up like a puff adder (a snake that increases in size when aroused or in danger). I couldn't get my boot back on. I had a problem. The ultimate indignation for a racer. I had to take the lift down. John took me to the emergency room.

"You've shattered your tibia in five pieces, son," the doctor said.

"What's that?" was my natural reply.

"It's the bone near the ankle. It's going to require surgery. I'll put a cast on it to immobilize the area but you must see a doctor as soon as you get home, okay?" the doctor advised me.

"How long will it take to heal?" I asked beginning to think about track for the first time.

"It all depends. Could be six to eight weeks. I've seen this type of break not heal for six months," the doctor added.

"Awe geez n' plutz," I said as I almost cried thinking of Coach McDavid's last words to me.

Worse, gone was my dream that I would surprise everyone and finish in the top ten or twenty in the downhill. My bravado and my ego was bruised but one thing was still intact. I was there to compete. I wasn't intimidated by the likes of Buddy Werner and Max Marolt, who would both make the U.S. Olympic team in 1960, nor the run called Olympic. The real success story was my close friend John Dendahl, who changed the image of ski in New Mexico by also making the 1960 Olympic team after competing on this slope three more years.

As a postscript to this adventure, I have to add that I fell down the stairs at the Challenger Inn not knowing how to descend with crutches, aided by a mixture of pain killers and Coors beer, and had to return to the hospital for another cast. And, to put the finishing touches on this whole humbling experience, on my plane flight home, the DC-3 landing in a snowstorm in Farmington, NM, ground-looped on the icy runway causing my over-abused right leg, that I had elevated across the isle, to crash to the floor. I had taken the plane home, of course, to avoid further injury. I was comforted by a gorgeous stewardess (now known as flight attendants) but it didn't ease my physical and emotional pain. Mom and Dad met me at the airport. Mom vacillated between the extremes of anger and sympathy as she wrung her hands. Dad brought a copy of the *Albuquerque Journal* that had a lead in the sports section:

"Quist breaks ankle in Idaho"

The *Journal*, appropriately, highlighted the short article in bold, dark print. Appropriate because my boldness caused a dark day. The article went on to say, "Buster Quist, AHS athlete is through with the interscholastic sports competition for the season." To everyone's surprise, including my own, the death knell was a little premature.

I had an appointment at Doctors Forbis, Simonds and Boyd the next day and within a few days Dr. Boyd surgically wired all the five bone fragments of my ankle together like stringing popcorn on a wire. Glo visited me at St. Joseph's Hospital.

"I guess the good news is that you won't be traveling much now. At least I'll get to see you, even if you can't dance," Glo said, both pleased and chagrined at the same time.

"I'll be able to walk in a couple of weeks. If I can walk, I can dance, for sure," I answered Glo who, fortunately, was still wearing my "A" pin. The last couple of months had been a real test for our relationship but we had both been true blue. Neither of us had dated anyone else. Glo had the patience of Job and was as faithful as Lassie. (Not to imply that she was a canine.)

Within a couple of days I was back at school. Dad dropped my sister Joanie and I off on his way to his new office, which was now located on Lomas Boulevard near the University. Glo and I were having lunch in the cafeteria. I was holding court while the kids stopped to sign my cast. It was all light-hearted until Coach McDavid came in. He approached me with his usual engaging smile and swagger and put his arm around my shoulder.

"Tough break, Buster," he said, trying to humor me with his play on words.

"Geez, I'm sorry Coach. I never should have gone to Sun Valley. I've screwed up the track season and I..." I couldn't continue. I broke down and cried. Right there in the cafeteria. Right there in front of Glo and a whole bunch of kids. It was the first time that I had cried. If Coach hadn't been so nice and understanding and forgiving I wouldn't have broken down. He was counting on me for first place in every meet and I let him down. It was a tough moment. Glo clasped my hand and gave me a big hug. I think that she understood, probably for the first time, what athletics meant to, not only me, but to all the boys. Our image of self worth, our value to our school and our coaches was inexorably tied to our performance on the field. An injury, no matter what the circumstances, diminished our value. Glo never again complained about equal time. She understood. She was "terrif."

On Saturday, April 26th, the District III Track and Field Championships would be held at Zimmerman Field at the University. It had been only three weeks since my surgery. I now had a walker on the bottom of my cast. On Wednesday before the meet I showed up at practice with my sweatsuit on.

"Hey Coach! I can throw the javelin with my cast on," I said to Pete McDavid who stood there, clipboard in hand, shaking his head.

"Buster, I know you want to prove something and help the team but you can't throw...you'll hurt your leg again if you did," Coach admonished me.

"No, watch. I can throw off my right foot and not follow through. I don't have to land on my right ankle at all. I don't need my run-up either," I continued as I demonstrated my new "technique."

"So, you want me to enter you in District, huh? Have

you asked your Mom and Dad," Coach asked.

"Dr. Boyd gave me an x-ray yesterday. He said he could-n't believe how fast my bones have healed. He said I'll be out of the cast pretty soon," I said not really answering his question.

"Well, okay. But I'll check with your Dad to make sure it's okay." And he did. Mom did her usual hand wringing and nail biting. Dad thought I could do it.

The preliminaries were Saturday morning. Each competitor got four prelim throws and the top six would qualify for the three final throws in the afternoon. The top two finishers would go to the State meet the next weekend. At the end of the prelims I was leading! The newspaper article doesn't list my distance but it was around 165'. My two closest competitors, who were from Highland High, Dave Mohar and Stan Bazant, were standing close-by putting on their sweats.

"I can't believe it, Stan. We're losing to a 'frickin' cripple!" Dave said. "That's 'frickin' unbelievable," he added. I laughed to myself. They weren't even expecting me to be throwing, much less leading. It was even more satisfying to prove the prognosticators wrong. My year wasn't over, yet.

Jack, H.B. and I went to the Stromberg's house to grab a bite to eat and relax for a couple of hours before the finals.

"That's amazing Buster. You can throw that far without a run. That means that your run-up doesn't do you any good," Jack said, as he analyzed my technique as he did everything else.

"Geez, you're right. I've got to find out how I can put it all together. Guess it will have to wait until next year," I said as I laughed.

Given several hours to think about it my two competitors from HHS rose to the occasion and bested my mark and I couldn't improve mine. Dave had an excellent throw of almost 177' and Stan threw almost 166' to edge me out for second place. Stan, who would later become a teammate in college, admitted to me several years later that had the finals been held immediately after the prelims (which they normally were) he and Dave probably wouldn't have improved their throws. They were really shook-up getting beat by a crip — standing still no less. God did bless me with a strong right arm.

The 1953 golf team, in the early season when the ever-present winds raised havoc with scores, won matches over New Mexico Military Institute, Carlsbad, El Paso and the UNM Frosh. Three experienced lettermen Bob Matteucci, Richard Bryan and LeRoy Weller returned to form the nucleus of this good team. Alex Miera, Victor Giron, Grafton Berger and sophomore Fred Luthy added depth to the "linksters," and my close friend Jim Harris took up the game seriously and contributed to the team. Unfortunately, however, the Bulldogs finished second to Highland for the State Championship for the second year in a row.

AHS continued to excel at the spring sports and the ˋ53 Tennis Team lost only one meet to a New Mexico school while posting a 14 won and 2 lost record. The team was led by veteran lettermen Bob Sanchez, Don Smiley, Chuck Vidal and brothers Richard and Robert Vigil. Don and Bob won the doubles title. Don Smiley later accepted a tennis scholarship to a Texas school but tragically was killed in an auto accident on his way home from school during the Thanksgiving break.

Continuing a reputation of having the finest baseball program in the state, the ˋ53 team romped to thirteen wins during the season with lopsided scores like 10-4 vs. Roswell, 26-2 vs. Farmington, 15-2 vs. Santa Fe, 17-2 vs. St. Michael's, 10-3 vs. St. Mary's and 4-0 vs. arch rival Highland. The only blemish on an otherwise clean record was a 8 to 9 loss to Carlsbad after the Bulldogs won the first game 7-4. The seniors that were the glue to this outstanding team were Tom Curley, who consistently knocked the cover off the ball and went on to play in the pros, pitchers Royce Ankeney and Mel Sedillo, Ruben Rubio, Bill Gore, Don Miller, Dick Trott, Jack Brown, Jim (Punkin) Elizando and Dave Otero.

The Bulldogs were odds-on favorites to win the state title, but an unforeseen obstacle in the form of the team from Our Lady of Sorrows from Bernalillo upset the "Dawgs" in the District Tournament and the team failed to advance to state. It was truly a major disappointment to this senior group that had played together for three successful seasons.

The girls Tri-Hi-Y and the boys Hi-Y clubs were involved in numerous events. Dances on Friday nights at the "Y," which was only a couple of blocks from school, were always well-attended. The "Y" pool was also a great meeting place to swim until the Acapulco Swim Club opened for the summer. One afternoon both the clubs were going to have a co-ed swim. Since I was not a member of Hi-Y and wasn't in on the "scandalous" affair I must rely on one of my friends, who must remain anonymous, to recount the story. Both the boys and the girls were in their respective dressing rooms. The rooms were pretty basic. One large area for dressing and hooks to hang your clothes.

"Hey," one of the guys whispered to his Hi-Y members, "Did you know there's a hole in the skylight over the girls dressing room?"

"No s...?" One of the members replied. "How do you get to it?"

"It's pretty tricky. We've got to go up the fire escape to the roof. Gotta be quiet or the girls will hear us," the ring leader cautioned as five or six guys followed him out the back door and up the fire-escape to the roof. Sure enough, there was a hole about the size of a half-dollar directly above the girls dressing room. The ring leader had the first peek, then another, then one of the other guys. Most of the girls now had their suits on. Those guys who were waiting their turn got anxious. A little too anxious. Pushing and shoving ensued. The volume of their voices increased.

A shriek! The peeping toms had been discovered. Most of the girls, not knowing who and how long they had been exposed, wouldn't go swimming and dressed over their suits. There weren't any more co-ed swims and the last couple of dances thinned out. In today's parlance, this "scandal" would hardly note a snicker much less an investigation. But, in 1953, this type of behavior was outrageous. The teacher who was in charge of the event apparently was fired.

Just after the Junior-Senior Prom, the tradition was to get as many kids to sign your yearbook as possible. We milled around the patio seeking signatories to our *La Reata* (The Lariat). Sample salutations were:

223

"Lots of luck to a swell guy"
— George Harris
"To a neato and super guy! Best of luck always!
— Judy Minces
"Buzzy—even though I give you a hard time most of the time, I really think you're tops. Stay that way! I'll be seein' ya'."
— Love, Riette Lewinson
"This may sound crazy' however I'm looking forward to having you as a pupil next year.
— F. E. Graham (art teacher)
"It has been a real pleasure to have you in my English III class. You have been a true 'addition',"
— Best of luck, Rhea Miller

The words swell, neato, super and rare were the language of the day. Deanie Stephens used the word "cool" for the first time. It didn't catch on until much later. The most important message, however, came from Glo. It took an entire page.

Dear Buz,

Well, another year is almost over and well, it has held its ups and downs for us. But when we had fun we really had fun. And after all the arguments, the making up meant a lot. Every time we would quarrel, I'd be afraid we wouldn't make it again. We always did and I was glad. I'm sure next year will mean a lot (an awful lot) to both of us. You'll really star on that football field and I'll always be cheering for you all of the way! You know how much you have meant to me all the way through so I don't need to tell you, do I? I've never had so much fun with anyone else, ever! Really! We'll (together) make a hit (a real hit) next year!

I loves ya'
Glo '54' "

I responded by writing:

"GoGo (using another nick-name)

The first thing I'll attempt to do is to apologize for the 'not so good' year we've had. I'm sure sorry but next year if we're still together I know it will be greater. The times we've been together have been the happiest. I'm sure and if I lose my stubbornness it would be a great accomplishment! I'm looking forward to next year if I'm here (serious) and if we both try hard it can be done. Together or apart I know we'll always be the same so bye-bye and maybe we'll see each other this summer—it would be wonderful!

Lots of Love,

Buz "

We were two teenagers attempting to articulate our feelings and our relationship with each other as all kids do. Glo's words were clear and unambiguous. Mine were convoluted. I certainly don't know where I planned to be during our senior year other than at AHS. Green Bay, maybe? Also, I was acknowledging that my stubbornness was a problem while at the same time professing that I'll always be the same. We struggled with our relationship and overwhelming sexual libidos but we didn't have to wrestle with alcohol, drugs, guns, bombs, disobedience and parental interference at our school. A mere decade later the ideal environment that we grew up in would dramatically change. The "Golden Era" would be over.

The Editor-in-Chief of the `53 *La Reata* was Edna Duncan aided by Caroline Maciel and Martha Finn as Associate Editors. A tradition and practice established many years prior, the yearbook was printed entirely at AHS. Not many schools in the U.S. could make this claim. The *Record*, our school newspaper, was headed by Larry Bonaguidi as Editor-in-Chief, who had attended the national Institute of High School Journalism at Northwestern University and he brought a high degree of professionalism to this publication. Sally Erxleben and Carol Bambrook served as Associate Editors. Jerry Ginsberg was Editor of the *Yucca* our magazine which truly exhibited the literary talents of the student body. This writer had not written a line yet.

"Glo, Jack and I were selected to go to Boy's State. Isn't that 'neato'?" I said proudly as I caught up to Glo as she was leaving school to go to work.

"Terrif Buz. I was chosen for Girl's State, too," Glo responded with equal pride.

"Boy's State is at the N.M. School of Mines in Socorro," I said. "Hey, why don't I take you to work? I'm on my way to the doctor's office to get my cast off."

"Great, why don't we go to the Heights (Community Center) tonight for the dance? You will be able to dance, won't you?" Glo asked as she got in our new 1953 Plymouth station wagon. My right foot was bulky and clumsy but I had learned to use my left foot on the brake. Finally the cast was coming off. The itching was driving me nuts and the odor wasn't too swell, either.

The Heights Community Center was adjacent to the field where we played baseball in the summer, which would begin soon. In fact, I would miss the first three games while at Boy's State.

Dances at the Heights were usually cowboy dances. We often had a band. Crowds could be huge and unmanageable. Kids from St. Mary's, Highland and AHS all came together at the Center. Invariably, fights between the rival schools or gangs would break out. This particular night there was a bad one. It got out of control. Glo and I fled to the safety of my car, so we thought, but the fight spilled over into the parking lot. It got real ugly. Within minutes the police were there. I thought they would break it up which they normally did. This time it was different. This time the kids turned on the cops. Someone was really going to get hurt—or killed.

The melee turned the parking lot into a series of whirlwinds of billowing dust with shadowy figures, like armies, flailing at each other. Then rocks, like missiles, pierced the dimly lit battleground. I saw someone pick up a brick or a large piece of concrete from the wall behind my car and hurl it in the direction of the blue-suited peacekeepers who were surrounded. Reinforcements arrived. The fighting subsided but several combatants couldn't rise from ground zero. Their injuries were serious— or worse.

"You know who that was, Glo?" I said as I sat up more erect in the front seat of my car. "The one who threw the brick."

"No. Who was it?"

"It was a guy I know who used to go to AHS," I said, trying to determine the severity of those wounded in the bedlam. "I think it was Bobby Unser. Not sure. But if there's a fight, he's usually in the middle of it," I reasoned.

Fortunately, no one was killed. One policeman was severely injured—hit by a projectile in the head. Bobby and lots of kids were arrested. None of the rocks hit my windshield or the car and I was happy that I didn't have to run on my gimpy leg to avoid the fracas. Bad as the fight was, there were no bullets. No one, except the police, packed a pistol.

This incident was reminiscent of a similar fracas that occurred a couple of years earlier at the same venue. According to Ralph Matteucci the police were "overly aggressive" using their night-sticks on the combatants. Ralph retaliated planting a hard right jab on the jaw of a policeman coming to the aid, of all people, Bobby Unser. While being booked at City Hall, Bobby said to Ralph, "When my dad hears about this he's goin' to come down here and beat the hell out of these guys." Ralph, now realizing the predicament he found himself mired in, replied "When my dad hears about this he's goin' to come down and beat the hell out of me!" Ralph had the misfortune of being the only miscreant over age 18 and therefore the only name published in the newspaper. Maybe his dad didn't relish Ralph's dastardly deed but his mom prominently displayed the article in Ralph's scrapbook.

Bobby Unser, brother Al and the whole Unser clan distinguished themselves not many years later winning the Indy 500 numerous times and bringing great fame to themselves and Albuquerque. They were troublemakers that became heroes. I don't know if their high school experience gave them a spring in their step, but their post high school days certainly did. Ralph not only excelled at football at AHS he also starred at UNM and was inducted into the School's Hall of Honor.

———

Glo and I were hardly the only romance on campus. Mary Ann Bond met Dan Bunten in her sophomore year and they continued dating after Dan graduated in 1951. They were married when Mary Ann was in her junior year and was only age 17. They moved, briefly, to Colorado but she obtained her degree from AHS. Mary Ann vividly recalls her favorite teacher, Violle Heffernan who started the "Moon Watch Team" and they tracked the Russian satellite Sputnik across the evening sky.

Gladys Miller was a Rah-Rah and very popular. She was a member of the Honor Society all three years, as well as the Pepper Club and Tri-Hi-Y (President her senior year). She was also the Leader of the Drill Team her senior year. Gladys also met her beau Frank Blea her sophomore year and their romance flourished. It must have been extremely difficult however for this couple to find time together. Frank, in addition to playing football, worked the night shift at Public Service Company of New Mexico all three years while at AHS. They married while at AHS and both graduated. The fact that Gladys and Frank stayed in school was remarkable in itself but their story was even more exceptional when you consider the times. Their marriage was a "mixed" marriage. Gladys was a Gringo and Frank was Hispanic. Gladys' parents believed they couldn't' bridge both worlds. Both of them took considerable heat from all sides. Frank's grandmother objected strenuously because Frank was Catholic and Gladys was Protestant. Close friends wished them well but privately whispered that the marriage wouldn't last. Gladys was concerned that she would be asked to leave school, but Virginia Sacks and Mary Cole Dixon supported her 100%. Fifty years later, their love and commitment to each other has proven their nay-sayers wrong. Whenever I think of Frank I recall that day in the locker room as a soph when he accepted me into his domain.

Not all student relationships were as positive as these. LeRoy Weller, who was this writer's teammate on the basketball team and an excellent golfer, recalled an incident in Franklin (Pop) Reynolds Drafting Class that dispelled any notions that no hostilities existed at AHS.

"Pop's" class was casual and informal. The popular teacher permitted his students to bring cokes and donuts into the class room. Alfred (Alf) Howden was the biggest kid in school, about 6'6" and approximately 250 pounds. Jack Brown, a star halfback on the football team and first-rate catcher on the baseball team, was about 80-90 pounds lighter.

It appears that someone was usurping other students' cokes that were scattered around the room and several of the students hatched a plan to spike the drinks with a not-so-potable substance to foil the perpetrator. A nasty fight broke out between Alf and Jack when the plan was exposed. All the student spectators as well as Pop removed themselves from the fray as the large drafting tables were becoming the prime victims of the fracas. The mild-mannered Pop couldn't intercede. Finally, the fight was over and the would-be architects and builders focused on reconstructing their damaged desks. LeRoy, now better known as Louis Weller, may not have learned anything from the fisticuffs, but he became a successful, well-known architect.

Another student that attributes his success to one of his teachers is Hunter Geer.

"I was from the south valley. We were country boys, floundering, not going anywhere," Hunter admitted. Fortunately Vioalle Hefferan (World History) took an interest in this "Stomper" and constantly admonished him by saying, "You can always do better." And, Hunter did. He received his BA at UNM and went on to get his law degree there also. He served as an Assistant Dean of the Law School at Loyola University and the same position at UNM for 5 years. In addition Hunter has served as a Probate Judge and Assistant Bernalillo County District Attorney as well as developing his private practice. His brother Otto, was the first Principal at the new Albuquerque High.

"Buster, I've found a solution to your vision problem," Dad said as he got out of his new Chrysler New Yorker in our driveway at Lazy Q. Terry and I were playing catch with a baseball. It was my first day out of my cast. I was testing my ankle. Baseball season was only two weeks away.

"What is the solution?" I asked.

"There's a new invention. They're called contact lenses. Look at the brochure I picked up at the doctor's office. You put these little round plastic lenses right in your eye," Dad continued.

"You gotta be kiddin," I replied in amazement as I scanned the brochure. My poor vision was really effecting my performance, particularly at night, and I wouldn't wear glasses with one of those awkward "bird cages" covering my face.

"I made an appointment with Dr. Carter Haydon. His office is on Vassar near the University. He'll explain the whole deal to you. You will have them ready for baseball season when you get back from Boy's State," Dad said.

I was dying to find out what this new invention was all about, and I desperately needed help if I was going to be the quarterback in the fall. Almost all of our baseball and football games were at night.

Dr. F. Carter Haydon was a neato guy and a real sports nut. He thought that the new contact lenses would be a godsend for athletes. He was right. I think he gave Dad a deal on the cost. I was one of the first in Albuquerque to use them and they were expensive. Obviously, the ones that I was fitted with were a far cry from the tiny gas-permeable cornea lenses that I wear today. These were huge in comparison. I could only wear them for brief moments at first and gradually increased the time each week. Man, I soon found out why I couldn't make those jump shots from outside the arc or hit Jack consistently with a thirty-yard pass. And, the big plus, girls just didn't care for guys in glasses. No matter what they said to the contrary.

The week at Boy's State was really rare. I was honored to be picked to represent AHS. It was easy to understand why Jack was selected; Class President, Honor Society, three sport letterman plus he was well-liked. I got decent grades— making Honor Society, but I really didn't focus on my class work like I should have. Anyways, I got to go. It was a crash course in civics and we got acquainted with kids who we competed against on the athletic field the prior two years and discovered that our sport rivals were pretty neat guys. (That included the "fairies" from Highland.)

The surprise came at the end of our week. We were bused north to Albuquerque 70 miles for a dance with the girls at Girl's State at the University of New Mexico. How "rare" was that? How many guys would have their girlfriend at this dance? Glo and I danced to "I'm Walking Behind You" by Eddie Fisher, "Till I Waltz Again With You" by Teresa

Brewer, "Don't Let The Stars Get In Your Eyes" by Perry Como and other hits. It was our first real unimpeded dance since I broke my leg. Most of the other kids were just getting acquainted. We were definitely an item. It ended too soon. All the way back to Socorro I counted my lucky stars that Glo was there—even though we were never alone.

————————

The summer American Legion Bulldog baseball team had already played three games on the day I arrived at Lincoln Field for my first day of practice, and may have been still smarting from their unexpected loss in District a few weeks earlier.

"Hey! Look who is here?" Mike Saul shouted as I drove up in the station wagon. It seemed like the guys were happy to see me.

"Could ya use another pitcher?" I joked with the guys as I approached them. "Geez, I've heard you guys have lost three in a row. That ain't good, team."

"We almost beat St. Mary's Friday night, Buster," Bob Fink offered kind of apologetically. "Lionel Romero pitched a good game. We're just not getting hits in the right spots to support Bob (Stover). And, we booted a few at the wrong time, too," he added.

We had a new coach, George Foehr, who was filling in this summer for Jack Rushing, who had to fulfill his military obligation with the Naval Reserve. Coach Foehr had assisted Pete McDavid in football that fall and had coached baseball in Kentucky before moving to New Mexico, so he wasn't new to most of us or the game.

"When did you get your cast off, Buz?" Coach asked as he approached the group of us.

"Two weeks ago Coach," I replied.

"Have you been throwing any?"

"Nope. Just playing catch with my brother and my Dad. Dad doesn't want me to throw hard. He missed one pitch and it hit him in the stomach," I added.

"I'd like you to pitch batting practice today, if you're up to it. Don't throw hard, okay?" Coach asked.

After the workout Coach called me over to the bench.

"Buster, we play Highland Friday night. I noticed that

231

you're limping quite a bit. Do you think you're up to starting against Highland? They beat us the first game," Coach asked.

"Geez, Coach, I don't know. I'm out of shape and I haven't thrown since last summer. I could be pretty wild. I'll give it a try if you want me to," I offered reticently.

Sure enough, Coach had me start against our rivals. Some of the same guys I lost to in the playoff last year were on the team. I had some real doubts as I took the mound with new contact lenses, a gimpy right ankle, and little practice. No one, including my teammates, my parents, my Coach nor my opponents could possibly have predicted the outcome. Most of all, myself. It was memorable.

Mickey Miller, the Highland Coach, had a devilish strategy. Bunting! The "fairies" came out bunting! Knowing I had trouble getting off the mound fielding the ball they tested me early. Fortunately, I had Eddie Geis as catcher, George Harris at third base and Mike Saul at first who covered the "pussy" bunts like a blanket. I got mad. I came right at them with my fastball as they squared off to bunt. There weren't any hard hats in those days so the threat of getting beaned was intimidating. My teammates thought the bunts were "chicken s...." There's no doubt that we came together as a team that night. The *Albuquerque Tribune* article said:

Buster Quist hurled a brilliant two-hit shutout over the Highlanders as the Albuquerque Bulldogs took a 3-0 ball game in one of the best seen this year in American Legion action Friday."

The morning paper, the *Albuquerque Journal*, had a feature article that provided more detail:

The Bulldogs picked up their first two runs in the third. Quist drilled a single through the middle and went to second on a wild pitch. First sacker Mike Saul followed suit with a one-baser through the hole between short and third. Bill Gideon then provided the game winning blast with a booming triple over the center fielder's head.

I had to include this piece for the benefit of my teammates who constantly ribbed me for being "all pitch and no hit".

The American Legion season was broken down into three rounds. Oden Motors, which was coached by Jody Villa and the team was comprised of players from St. Mary's High School, won the first round handily. An *Albuquerque Journal* article stated:

The Bulldogs, reinforced by the return of Quist who had suffered a broken ankle, fought back and took the second round of City play and tied the Highlanders for third round laurels.

In a key game in the third round, we faced Oden. An excerpt from the *Journal* summed up the results:

Buster Quist and Harvey Cotton were the Albuquerque stars. Quist tossed a one-hitter to gain credit for the win and Cotton hit a bases-loaded triple in the third inning that sealed the fate for the Motormen.

Cotton also starred afield with several brilliant catches. Quist's bid for a no-hitter was spoiled by Billy McIntyre who socked a triple in the fifth.

That win set up a three way playoff between Oden Motors, Highland and ourselves. Pretty exciting stuff. Oden beat Highland 13-2 in the first game which created a best two out of three series between AHS and Oden for the District Championship.

Coach Foehr nominated me to pitch the first game. I started out a little shaky allowing one run in the first inning, but our guys came back and scored six runs in the second and four in the third and we cruised to a 16-2 victory. For Lionel Romero, the opposing pitcher and a good friend, it was a "bad day at black rock." He was always a tough competitor but this was his poorest outing. Partly out of frustration, perhaps, plus unaccustomed wildness, he hit me in the middle of my back with a pitch. Concerned, he apologized profusely as I was trying to gather my breath. We joked about it years later. He laughed as he said he hit me intentionally!

Bob Stover pitched the second game against Buddy Mader. Again, our Bulldogs ferociously attacked our opponents early, scoring seven runs in the first inning. Oden fought back and closed the gap to 7-5 in the fifth inning and (as I remember) had the bases loaded with only one out. In a rare and unusual move, Coach Foehr sent me to the bullpen to warm up and brought me into the game to relieve Bob who was tiring. I had just pitched seven innings an hour or two earlier, and I didn't know how much gas I had left in the tank, but I came in. I thought Brice Day, who was fresh, should have relieved Bob but Coach went with his gut instinct. He didn't want to go a third game. And, maybe he was saving Brice for the third game in the event I couldn't hold the lead.

Coach Foehr's move proved to be sound. I retired the side without any more damage and we scored five more runs in the top of the sixth inning to seal the deal. It wouldn't be long before Bob and I would reverse roles and he would bail me out of a jam. That's what teammates do. That's what made us such a good team.

The Bulldogs were the 1953 American Legion District Champs. Out of the six teams in the summer league, these three plus Los Lunas, were extremely competitive. Some of our other players who contributed immeasurably to our success were Don Young, our shortstop, who, along with Mike Saul and Bob Fink, were our top hitters. Don's father was "Pep" Young who played in the "Bigs" (the Major Leagues) for the Philadelphia A's so Don had the game in his genes. Brice Day played outfield and was also our third pitcher in the rotation. "Kiki" Saavedra played center field and always was a consistent contributor to our success. Bob Stover, in addition to being an excellent pitcher, was also a .300 plus hitter which made him invaluable. Bill Gideon was our power hitter.

Bob and I got the nod to pitch against Gallup for the regional championship. We had to win two out of three to make it to the New Mexico State American Legion Championship Tournament. Both of us pitched two hitters for easy wins. We were on our way to the big one. Bob and I were a tough tandem.

Included in all the memorabilia is our team picture commemorating our District and Regional victories. Also among the wealth of our family treasures is a Lloyd Manufacturing Baseball team picture taken in 1922 with my Dad in Menominee, Michigan. Dad was 18 in this picture. He had just graduated from high school and was participating in the summer industrial league for his employer. The picture is a classic with the Babe Ruth era uniforms, the rickety, old wooden bleachers in the background spotted with kids of all ages in their bib overalls eager to observe their heros on a weed infested field. Dad didn't make it to the "Bigs" but baseball was also in my genes. I had a 6-0 record up to this point that summer. Coach Foehr said I was almost unhittable — the fastest pitcher that he had ever seen. Was there a baseball career in my future? Did I have the stuff to make it in pro ball? Mike Saul said I threw just like Robin Roberts. That was neato. Events were about to unfold that permitted opportunity to knock.

It was early August 1953 and we were headed to Clovis, for the State Tournament. Our chartered bus made a pit stop in Vaughn, which was about halfway to our destination. (All AHS teams stopped there.) The stop had another purpose. Bill Easley, one of our key players during the school year, was working at the filling station where we stopped. Bill had the misfortune of being a couple days too old to qualify for Legion play. He was overjoyed when we pulled into the station.

"Man, you guys did it! You beat those 'frickin' fairies'," Bill said as he shook our hands and gave everyone a big hug.

"Yep, we did it. Sure wish you could have been there, Bill. We missed you," I said expressing all of my teammates' sentiments.

We stayed as long as we could, replaying the defining moments of the key games. Bill wanted to hear it all first hand from his buddies. His teammates. The team he should have been a member of. It was time to leave. As the bus pulled away we watched Bill as he waved and followed us out onto the highway. Then he covered his eyes with both hands. We could tell. Bill was crying.

It was as if Bill seemed to sense that he would miss a high point in his life as our bus and his team faded into the horizon of the hilly, treeless plains of eastern New Mexico.

Often, if there is some substance to Kathyrn Parker's theory of our high school experience, there's a stumbling point while searching for that "spring in our step." In Bill's case, it was a matter of being born a few days too soon, but Bill shared in the joy of our success.

Clovis was a few miles from the Texas state line. For all practical purposes, we were in Texas. Coach Foehr checked us into the Hotel Clovis located downtown in the small farming and ranching community. As he was handing out the keys to each of us, the desk clerk noticed that Harvey Cotton, our left fielder, who was Black, was carrying his bags up the stairs.

"Hey Coach. Is that 'nigger' on your team?" the clerk asked.

"If you mean Harvey—yes, he's on our team. Why?" Coach responded seemingly not surprised by the question.

"That nigger can't stay here," the obviously overweight clerk stated in a derogatory tone of voice. I don't know why but most of the bigots we encountered were slobs and the clerk at the Clovis Hotel fit the mold to a "T." Coach handled the situation well.

"If Harvey can't stay here, the whole team doesn't stay here," Coach laid out in plain unaccented English. The clerk was unmoved by the loss of almost a week's revenue for our team plus numerous parents and friends that also made the trip including our Principal, Glen O. Ream.

"Hey guys—give me back your keys. We're leaving," Coach said to all of us in the lobby and on the stairs. Some of my teammates didn't immediately understand what was happening, but since I had experienced the discrimination before in southeastern New Mexico, I knew segregation and prejudice was still alive and well in this area of the State.

After several stops, we ended up in a flea-bag dump of a motel on the outskirts of town. We weren't in the motel for more than a couple of hours when Mike Saul was caught leading a battalion of his cohorts in a balloon water fight. Mike almost was sent home and we were close to being thrown out of the only non-segregated accommodation in town. Fortunately, we dodged a bullet on both accounts. I played five different sports and each team had its own personality. The baseball team won the cut-up award hands down. We were a pretty loose, fun loving group of kids. One good reason that we were winners.

The teams in the finals were Hurley, Clovis, Alamogordo, Santa Fe and Albuquerque. It was a double elimination tour-

236

nament. You had to lose twice before your team was eliminated. We drew Hurley as our first game. Coach Foehr picked me to pitch the opener. Our guys jumped on our opponents right out of the box and scored six runs in the first inning, which was becoming a trademark of our team. They made my job pretty easy. I pitched a three hit shutout and we won 10-0.

Bob Stover followed our first game with a three hitter of his own as our team beat Clovis 4-1 despite six errors. We had the enviable position of being the only undefeated team in the Tournament and would have to lose a doubleheader to Clovis (whom we had already defeated) to lose the tournament. I had a couple days rest and was ready to face the locals. Little did I know that the odds were stacked against me and the team. Big odds.

Confident and pumped up for the State Championships game I delivered my first pitch fastball over the heart of the plate.

"Ball!" The empire bellowed. I couldn't believe it. Maybe the ump couldn't see the pitch, I thought. I split the plate again.

"Ball two!" the ump said and signaled with his right hand. I called Eddie Geis, my catcher, out to the mound.

"Weren't those two pitches over the plate, Eddie?"

"Damn sure they were," my catcher replied. "Keep throwin' them down the middle. The 'ump' has gotta call em," Eddie assured me.

But he didn't. In no time flat, the bases were loaded. I was getting hot. Coach came out to the mound. Eddie joined us.

"They're right over the plate Coach. What the hell can I do? I'm really getting pissed," I said.

"I'm going to argue the calls with the ump. You just settle down and keep throwing strikes," Coach said as he turned back towards home plate. Coach Foehr was an easygoing guy and the team had never seen him raise his voice before, but I could see that he was heating up too as he jawed with the umpire.

A few strikes were called but they were tokens.

I started guiding my pitches instead of throwing them. It

took just enough off my fastball that they could hit it. Before you could say Jackie Robinson, Clovis had scored a bunch of runs. (Disgusted, I must have thrown the write up of the game away. I don't have the box score.)

Obviously, the hometown strategy was to unnerve me and get me to blow my cool. What none of us knew until the end of the game (although Coach Foehr knew prior) was that the umpire behind the plate was from Clovis. Not only that, he had the same name (Lanier) as that of their star pitcher, Lindy! Was he the pitcher's dad? An uncle? A coincidence?

We lost the game 9 to 6. It was my first loss of the year and my worst performance. Coach told us to "shake it off" and quit bitching and get ready for the second game. There would be a different umpire and he wasn't from Clovis. A thunderstorm symbolically cleansed the rotten stench from the field as we waited for the second and deciding game to begin. Several of our parents left the field and bought us hamburgers as it was 11:00 p.m. before the game got underway. We were starved. We were also hungry for a rematch!

With Bob Stover shutting down Clovis' batters our team pounced on Don Isham and Lindy Lanier for five runs in the first two innings and we coasted to a 7-1 victory. Clovis committed eight errors to our one. Sure, the field was wet and the game didn't end until 1:00 a.m. but most of us were convinced that it was our opponents loss of their "tenth man" that unnerved them and led to their miscues in the field. Retribution was rendered. The Bulldogs were State Champs! Late as it was and tired as we were, we all had a "spring in our step" as we left the stadium and our moment in time.

There is a postmortem to this smelly episode that is not only revealing but it supports my (and my teammates) claim of being "hometowned."

Clovis and its over zealous support for athletic recognition became the focus of a major controversy just one year later. Bolstered by two superb athletes, Bob Dugan and Milt Barron, the Wildcat football team had an undefeated record halfway through the 1954 season. After an exten-

238

sive investigation[17] by the NMHSAA, it was determined that Dugan's parents lived in Dumas, Texas, which made him ineligible to play for Clovis. Most significantly, Barron, who was as devastating and dominating a running back as ever seen in N.M., was lured from close-by Melrose, N.M., by several Clovis businessmen via a "Milton Barron Personal Loan Fund." Clovis was forced to forfeit all their games won and their two remaining games were cancelled.

Occasionally, community support went over the top. For sports to continue its untarnished tradition, it had to maintain moral integrity. At AHS it certainly did.

A more formidable challenge now faced us. The American Legion Regional Tournament in Nebraska. The final step to the World Series.

Taking a train from Albuquerque to York, Nebraska, via Denver was like booking a slow boat to China. The long trip coupled with being confined to close quarters provided numerous opportunities for mischief for a bunch of zealous and euphoric teenagers. Glen O. Ream, our Principal, and Don Young's dad "Pep," provided added logistic support to our coach. Adding to the mix was a group of giggling, teenage girls who were on a field trip from Albuquerque to Denver. Our sleeper cars were back to back. It was probably Mike Saul who designed the late night sneak attack on the sleeping beauties with their hair up in curlers.

The up and down bunk beds were only separated from the dimly lit aisles by loosely draped black curtains. There was one empty lower bunk near the middle of the car. The diabolical plan was for three or four of us to reach in under the black curtains and simultaneously pinch the girls and

---

[17] "A History of N.M. Athletics" (unpublished) Dan Ford, Page 98.

then retreat to the empty bunk. Carefully we synchronized the first attack.

Three shrieks pierced the silence as the train rumbled through the night. Most of the girls peered out of bunks attempting to find the evildoers that perpetrated this heinous act. No one, of course, was to be found. Soon the protests subsided. Calm was restored. Silence, save the rhythmic beat of the wheels hitting the rails, returned.

Then, a second attack! The shrieks and the protests were louder. Two ladies who were apparently the chaperons took charge. They were determined to find the culprit guilty of this dastardly deed. A thorough investigation was undertaken. It was akin to locating the murderer on the Orient Express. The three of us, crowded into the still undiscovered bunk, were fighting to contain our laughter. The damsels in distress didn't think it was funny.

The chaperons agreed to police each end of the car still thinking that was the entry and exit point of the perpetrator so no one could enter or escape for the remainder of the night! We were trapped. Our carefully conceived plan had no exit strategy. Packed like sardines in the bunk we tried to sleep. Within a few hours from our window we could see the birth of day light. We had to make our move.

Carefully I peered out of the curtain. The "guards" appeared to have abandoned their posts. As I slipped out of the bunk I motioned to my fellow conspirators to follow—quietly. We made a dash for the sleeping car door. The coast was clear! We were out the door and between the two cars. No one was there to impede our escape. Inside our sleeping car we gathered in an alcove near the restroom and surveyed the passageway back to our bunks. Composed and almost giddy with our success we casually strolled around the corner smack dab into—Glen O. Ream, our Principal.

"Hey! Where have you guys been?" Mr. Ream asked, surprised by our sudden appearance.

"Oh, ahh—we've been in the bathroom," I offered sheepishly.

"All three of you?" Mr. Ream continued unconvinced.

"Yeh," we all offered in unison.

"And, you're all dressed at 5:30 in the morning?" Mr.

Ream said questioning the credulity of our story.

"We couldn't sleep," I continued suspecting that our Principal was not buying our fabrication.

"Well (and there was a long pause as Mr. Ream was determining our fate), get back in bed and keep quiet and not wake the other boys. We'll be in Denver in a couple of hours," he said as we breathed a sigh of relief.

I've often wondered what Mr. Ream was thinking. Did he think that we had been in the girls sleeping car? Did he suspect that we had spent the night with some of the girls? He certainly surmised that we were up to no good. Fortunately, nothing more was said. The case of the "mad pincher caper" was never solved. It _was_ a mystery worthy of Agatha Christie.

At Denver the Colorado State Champions (Denver Duffy) boarded the train. It was there that we got a glimpse of their star pitcher, Stan Williams, whose size magnified his reputation as one of the best pro prospects in the nation. Bob Fink, our second baseman and one of our top hitters, recalls how cocky and arrogant the Denver team was as they avoided any interchange with the lowly regarded New Mexicans. It was _deja vu_ all over again. It was just like our ski team at Sun Valley. What was it about New Mexico that fostered disrespect? Why were we "dissed?" Hey! We were good.

This tournament _was_ a big deal for our lightly regarded bunch from New Mexico. Nebraska after all was a hotbed for baseball. The College World Series has been held in Omaha for many years. The small farming communities loved the sport and packed the small stadium in York for this series.

Stan Williams _was_ the real deal. Denver played Hastings, Nebraska, in the first game at York. Stan pitched a one-hitter and struck out 20 opposing batters as the Tournament went to nine inning games instead of seven. We drew Cheyenne, Wyoming, as our first opponent and Coach Foehr selected me to pitch the first game.

Nervous and anxious in the first inning, I walked the first three hitters I faced and allowed one run to score. Coach Foehr and Eddie Geis calmed me down and I didn't walk another batter the remainder of the game. We were down 2-0 going into the bottom of the fourth inning when

Bob Stover (playing in right field because of his strong bat) walked followed by successive hits by George Harris, Mike Saul and Kiki Saavedra. We scored three runs in the fourth inning and two more in the fifth. George Harris had three hits out of four at bats to lead us to victory. I fashioned a three hitter as we opened with a 7-3 win. The York newspaper wrote:

> *Bernie Dunn was the games defensive standout. The Cheyenne third baseman's top effort was a backhand on Quist's hard pop in the third.*

Actually, I hit four hard shots at Dunn that day. He managed to stop three of them. Finally, one line drive went through for a hit and scored a run. We were off to a good start. What happened next can only be described as "bizarre." An incident occurred that very few baseball fans, at any level, high school, college or professional, would ever witness. Adding to the on-field weirdness was Brice Day tripping on a curb while strolling downtown and badly spraining his ankle. Brice had a 5 win and 2 loss record coming into this tournament and we desperately needed him in this, the toughest of a double elimination tournament, if we were to get to the American Legion World Series. He was out. Bob and I would have to pitch all of the games. Nine inning games at that!

Hastings had lost its first game to Denver. They had to beat us or be eliminated. We were amazed when we took the field. Over 2000 fans were in the stands. Those, who were in the majority, from York were rooting for the New Mexicans! Hastings was York's bitter rival. The hometown folks wanted us to win. That was refreshing and encouraging given our experience in Clovis.

Bob pitched a brilliant game taking a no hitter into the fifth inning. The score was 0-0. Then "it" happened. It is best described by Gary Frandsen, the sportswriter for the York newspaper:

> All the trouble started when lead off hitter Ron Gilmore was batting at the plate. Bob Stover, hard-working Albuquerque right-hander, had just set Gilmore down on strikes and Applebee (Hastings' coach) immediately called time to go into a discussion with the umpires on

the sleeves of Stover's jersey.

SENT BACK TO THE PLATE

After a short conference Applebee sent Gilmore to the plate thinking that the Hastings' right -fielder had only two strikes against him. Plate umpire Wal Harbour had chalked up a strikeout but didn't know Gilmore was making a repeat appearance with the bat. Ron then smoked the first pitch for a single and Zuttell moved him to second with a bunt sacrifice.

According to the press box there was only one out since Gilmore made a second appearance, but on the field there were two gone as the New Mexico coach, George Foehr, and the umpires failed to notice the fact that Gilmore had batted twice. Foehr immediately filed a protest after learning of only one down and the dispute was on.

Actually it was Bob Fink who first protested to the umpire.

The problem was that the dispute wasn't settled until the next day after we completed nine innings! Legion officials in Indianapolis ruled that our protest was sustained and the game would have to be re-played from that point in the fifth inning when Gilmore batted twice. Bob, undoubtedly unnerved by the situation, gave up two runs in the disputed fifth inning and four in the sixth when Coach Foehr called on me to finish the last three innings. Bob, up to that point in the fifth, had baffled the Hastings batters. He was in sync. He was in a rhythm. We scored three runs in the last four innings. Bob Fink had four hits to lead the team. Had Gilmore not batted twice and singled after he was out, we could well have won the game. The biggest problem, of course, was that Bob had pitched six innings and my inning count was now up to twelve.

Bob was tired as he took the mound the next day in the fifth inning. He retired the side in the fifth and sixth innings but ran out of gas in the seventh. Hastings scored three runs aided by third baseman Tom Osborne's single. (Yes, the same Tom Osborne who would put Nebraska football on the map.) I pitched one and a third scoreless innings to run my inning count to over thirteen. Bob went into right field after I relieved him and he smacked a towering home run in the ninth inning but unfortunately, we didn't have any runners on base. The score ended 3-1. We would have to face Hastings again the next day.

Coach Foehr had the unenviable task of choosing which of his two exhausted pitchers would start against Hastings. It was do or die. We had to win. Coach went with Bob. We sure needed a fresh arm but we didn't have one. Hastings had three good pitchers and a fourth we didn't know about.

Cal Johnson, who was a towering 6'5", started the game for Hastings. The York paper said that Johnson was "one of the top Legion pitchers seen anywhere." In the second inning, Bill Gideon, Mike Saul and Kiki Saavedra all singled and Harvey Cotten then doubled over the (fourth strike) Ron Gilmore's head and we were up two zip. The York fans were delirious.

Bob, who had a great curve to go along with a good fastball, hit the wall in the third inning and our nemesis Tom Osborne knocked in a couple of runs to tie the game. Coach Foehr called me in to put out the fire and hoped I had enough fuel to go the distance—six more innings.

Disaster struck again! Don Young, our star shortstop pulled a muscle and had to leave the game. Bob Fink moved to short and our catcher Eddie Geis moved to second base (he never played there before). We were a patched up, worn out bunch of kids seeking to accomplish something no one else had done from New Mexico—play in the American Legion World Series.

In the 1950s few coaches or players knew how to effectively change speeds and keep hitters off balance. Today fastball pitchers vary the speed of their pitches, which throws off the hitters' timing and allows pitchers to save their arms. In the "olden" days all I knew was to rare back and throw as hard as I could and fool the batter with an occasional change-up or curve ball (now called a slider).

For three innings I held Hastings scoreless. Then, in the eighth, the zip came off my fastball and our opponents scored three runs. Hastings brought in a fourteen year old Black pitcher who fooled our hitters with an array of slow stuff and we succumbed 5 to 2. The Nebraskans gave us our

244

due in the media:

"It was the consensus of many of the fans that this was the finest New Mexico team to come out of that state in years."

We weren't dissed anymore!

I had lost the biggest game of my high school career. My record was 8-2 for the summer and 14-3 for my two years in Legion ball. I had pitched over eighteen innings in four days. Bob pitched almost as many. We were tired and disappointed and faced a long trip home. There weren't any more shenanigans on the train. It was the 20th of August. Football practice had already started. Time to change uniforms again.

I answered the phone in the den.

"Dad, there's a man on the phone. He wants to talk to you. He says he's from the Chicago Cubs," I yelled to my Father who was in the kitchen at the other end of the house. Dad picked up the phone and listened for a long time without saying a word.

"Listen, I appreciate your call and your interest in my son playing for the Cubs but my son is going to college," Dad said to the scout on the other end of the line. After a few more minutes, Dad hung up.

"What did he say, Dad?"

"He said that you pitched extremely well in York. He said that you have great potential to become a pro. Said that there were many scouts there to see Stan Williams and Cal Johnson and you impressed them too," Dad informed me.

Stan Williams pitched in the majors for many years with the Los Angeles Dodgers and other teams. He still coaches in the "Bigs."

"What did they want?" I asked Dad to elaborate.

"They want you to sign a contract now and start working with their pitching coaches in their farm system. That's not for you. I didn't go to college and I want you to go. You can play baseball after you go to school if you want to but not now," Dad explained.

Dad was adamant. And, he was right. In those days if you played pro ball in any sport you couldn't participate in collegiate athletics. Dad had another reason. He thought pro baseball players were bums. He thought they were uneducated (good players like Mickey Mantle didn't finish high school), beer-drinking, pussy-chasing, bums. The image of Babe Ruth's outrageous lifestyle was still foremost in his mind. Baseball's persona would dramatically change when college became, in effect, part of the minor league farm system. It was memorable moment because it was one of the few times growing up that my Dad actually sat down and counseled with me.

Mom and Dad hosted a big swim party for the team at the Lazy Q. It must have been a doozy. Even today, all my teammates recall the event as vividly as our winning season.

My focus turned to Glo, football and my senior year at AHS—not necessarily in that order.

CHAPTER EIGHT: HAPPY DAYS 1953-1954

MY RETURN FROM YORK, NEBRASKA, on August 20, 1953 was just in time for Joanie's birthday on the twentieth and Terry's on the twenty-second. I missed the first day of football practice. I was exhausted and disappointed with our loss but Mom had some unexpected and uplifting news for me.

"Ralph called last week," she said while I was recounting our trip to Nebraska.

"Ralph? Ralph who?" I asked, still focused on baseball and our great adventure while playing coulda', woulda' and shouda' over and over in my mind.

"Ralph Boan, your buddy from Washington Junior High. Surely you remember him?" Mom asked, almost deriding me for my memory lapse.

"Ralph Boan! Geez. Was he here in Albuquerque?" I asked excited at the prospect that Ralph could be in town. And, why would he be in town?

I grabbed the telephone which was hanging on the wall in the kitchen near the breakfast table and dialed the number Mom gave me.

"Ralph? It's Buster. What brings you to Albuquerque?"

"My folks have moved back. I'm a Bulldog now! I'm goin' to play with you guys again," Ralph, in that very recognizable squeaky voice, said, obviously excited.

"Ah geez, that's terrif' Ralph! Damn I can't wait to see you. I'll be at practice tomorrow. Boy. We can really have a good team with you in the backfield. I can't wait," I said, unable to contain my enthusiasm.

Coach McDavid was ecstatic too. An *Albuquerque Journal* article said after the first day's practice:

McDavid was particularly impressed by Ralph Boan. The ex-Farmington halfback showed plenty of speed and general football savy. 'That boy (Boan) really likes to move,' the Bulldog mentor said.

What Jack and I, nor any of our teammates knew, was how it came to pass that Ralph would return to Albuquerque. It wasn't until many years later that we discovered that Ralph's stepfather was enticed to accept a better paying job in Albuquerque. Turn about was fair play, those who were involved must have figured. Ralph was an exceptional talent. It didn't take long before Jack, H.B., Jim, Ralph and myself became a "fearsome fivesome."

One of our first nights out together we went to the Hitching Post, a cowboy bar which was then a considerable distance west of town on Highway 66. H.B. discovered that we could drink beer there and no one ever checked our I.D. (identification cards). The five of us packed into my Mom's station wagon, which I dubbed "The Green Hornet." The bar had a live band, Dick Bills and the Sandia Mountain Boys. I had seen them on TV. It was a great opportunity for teammates to bond together particularly with Ralph being new to H.B. and Jim.

Ralph had spent the past two years in Farmington, which was developing into one of the country's hottest oil and gas areas. A type of boomtown that attracts some pretty hard working and hard drinking folks. Ralph worked as a roughneck in the oil fields during the summer. An appropriate job description. He opened a new door for us that night. We all got drunk. Remembering the awful scene with Jack Douglas in Flagstaff, I imbibed less than my teammates. I didn't want to get that sick and s... all over myself. Besides, I had to drive.

We had an incredibly fun time. Coach McDavid wouldn't have approved, of course, but we paid a horrible price running wind sprints in the hot sun the next day. H.B. puked his guts out. Apparently Ralph was accustomed to the rigors and pitfalls of drinking and training and it didn't seem to phase him a bit and he was a heavy smoker too.

Years later I remembered that there was a teenager, like us, who was a guitarist and singer in the band at the Hitching Post. He was Dick Bill's nephew. His name was Glen Campbell. He knew H.B. Glen came over to our table that night and told us he was going to Hollywood the next week. Said he was going to be on TV. We laughed. Three weeks later Glen was on "Hollybaloo" and his career was launched. The laugh was on us.

Thirty years later playing in a golf tournament with Glen in Scottsdale, Arizona, I said:

"We have a couple of things in common, Glen."

"What's that?" Glen said with that sly smile and squinty eyes, now so recognizable.

"You had your first 'gig' at the Hitching Post in Albuquerque in the mid 50s when I got drunk for the first time...'just before you went to Hollywood."

"Oh s..., no one remembers that! What's the second?" Glen replied, putting a finger to his lips as he sidled up closer to me so no one could hear my reply.

"We both married girls from Carlsbad," I added. "And, we played in the New Mexico open there back in the 70s."

"Geez (he used that expression too) what do 'ah hafta do to make sure no else hears about that, huh?" Glen replied.

"How about three shots a side for a hundred buck Nassau," I joked.

"Ya got it," Glen quickly acknowledged as we got ready to play. I never took him up on the bet. He'd probably have beaten me anyway. I didn't quite understand why he was so embarrassed about his start at the Hitching Post. Big names or small, everyone has to start somewhere. Guess he thought Albuquerque was nowhere like a lot of people did.

Although I spent most of my time with the "fearsome fivesome" and Glo, I had also developed a circle of friends in our remote section of the North Valley who had diversified interests like hunting and horseback riding. One of my buds was a kid by the name of Rolfe Black. He was a genius — a nerd.

Amongst his myriad of endeavors Rolfe had completely rebuilt a 1939 Ford from the frame up, powered by a V-8 engine. It was an exciting car to tool around Corrales Road and Coors Boulevard. What was really unique about Rolfe's hot-rod was its finish — a deep, burgundy metallic paint job. In contrast it made all other production cars look like dullsville as they would say in L.A. Rolfe had hand-painted his car utilizing a technique formerly only used on stripping and trim on aircraft. It took quite a few years before Detroit caught on.

Rolfe had bought the old car for $500. Completed, the custom job cost him about $4,000 not including his many hours of labor. Unable to recapture his investment in his car by selling it as is Rolfe dismantled his project and sold the custom parts one by one until he almost broke even. Rolfe had a deep love of cars and everything mechanical— including airplanes.

Rolfe's father, Albert, who was a 1929 AHS grad and brother to Ed Black cited earlier, was in those days a rancher. The Black's 7-Bar Ranch extended from the middle of the Rio Grande River west to the Rio Puerco (approximately 19 miles), south to the volcanos and north to the Sandoval County boundary line. This massive parcel of real estate was originally a land grant from the King of Spain. Today, of course, it is densely populated.

Housed adjacent to Coors Road was the 7-Bar Flying Service and Airport. Rolfe learned to fly about the same time as he learned to drive a car.

This beautiful fall day while I was at Rolfe's he said, "Hey Buster? Let's go for a spin in my Super Cub."

"You mean flying? Like up in the air?"

"Sure. I've been working on the Cub. It was a wreck and I've rebuilt it. I need to try 'er out," Rolfe said matter-of-factly.

"Geez Rolfe. It doesn't even have any doors," I observed.

"You won't fall out. The seat belt will keep you in. Come on. Let's go up."

"Geez," I thought to myself, "Rolfe's taking me up for a test drive. What if he forgot to connect something?"

We took off. My first flight. With the wind whistling in our ears and the noisy engine drowning out any conversation we flew south along the Rio Grande. I yelled to my teenage pilot:

"Let's go over to my house."

We circled the Lazy Q. Mom was out in the yard hanging

up a wash. We circled lower. Lower still. We were only 100 feet or so off the ground. Rolfe banked the Cub so that I was looking directly down on my Mother.

"Hi Mom!" I yelled.

She looked up. Startled, she dropped the clothes basket. Losing her balance she fell over bassackwards onto the lawn. Leaving her probably muttering to herself, "You'll be the death of me," we returned to base. Mission accomplished.

Make no mistake about it, however, flying was "hours and hours of boredom mixed with moments of terror." Not long after this episode, Rolfe was in the back seat of a 1939 WACO biplane with one of his instructors at the controls. It was a hot summer day. The WACO was underpowered for Albuquerque's altitude. On takeoff, the engine stalled!

The WACO hit the ground hard, bounced and nosed over into an arroyo at the end of the runway. The fuel tank located above the pilot's head ruptured and exploded. Rolfe, fortunately, was ejected out of his seat by the force of the impact.

Rolfe's father, hearing the sickening sound of the crash and seeing the fireball from the tarmac, ran to the end of the runway. The plane was completely engulfed in flames. Albert knew that he had just lost his oldest son.

Miraculously, Rolfe appeared out of the smoke and dust-filled chaos to fly again. Unfortunately, the pilot was killed in the crash.

Undeterred by this incident, I secured my pilot's license at 7-Bar and a couple of years later bought a Cessna 182 Super Skylane from Rolfe. Given my propensity for adventure and lack of aversion to danger, numerous episodes would follow that would boggle the reader's mind, but that's another book.

Rolfe's business career is a true Albuquerque success story. 7-Bar now operates in Dallas, Sun Valley, Farmington as well as Albuquerque and is one of the largest air medical transport companies in the U.S. SBS Technologies, a public company headquartered in Albuquerque which employs about 400, was founded by Rolfe and others.

As a friend of Rolfe since our days at Washington Junior High, I also remember him as a member of our football team.

Not a gifted athlete, Rolfe worked hard and persisted, earning his letter his Senior year. This gritty determination to excel at an activity where he was not blessed with natural skills, framed the man. It also demonstrated that there were nerds who ventured into the sportsworld too.

"Buz, are you going to be home tomorrow afternoon?" My sister asked as the summer began to fade into fall and we had just finished a Saturday practice.

"Yeah. After church I'm bringing Glo out to the house for a swim," I replied. "Why?"

"Oh, Byron needs a guinea pig for his class in 'psyche,'" Joanie offered lightheartedly. (Byron was in pre-med at UNM.)

"Geez, that doesn't sound like much fun. What do I need to do?" was my guarded reply.

"Well, you have to sit still for an hour or so and answer a bunch of questions. It's an experiment for his class, that's all."

"That's okay. How about later in the 'aft' when I take Glo home," I suggested.

"Sure. Byron and I will be here all day after church," Joanie said.

"I'll fix the lunch, Mrs. Quist," Glo offered as we came in from the pool. "We can take care of ourselves. You should rest."

Mom was still having difficulty physically. Her energy level was extremely low and it was almost impossible for her to lift anything. Glo was terrific. She engaged Mom one-on-one and demonstrated an enormous amount of empathy towards her while fixing her lunch and washing the dishes. Tasks that Mom valued as primary qualifications for a wife.

Glo and I, along with Byron and Joanie, soaked up the rays. Terry had developed a keen interest in guns and hunting and he was target shooting into the bank of the irrigation ditch at the rear of our property.

Dad was in the den watching TV, eating a TV dinner on a TV tray, while Mom took a nap. An uneventful but relaxing day at the Lazy Q. I drove Glo home later in the afternoon and regretted that the swimming season would soon end. I loved to see Glo in her swimsuit. What a "bod."

"This test is called the Stanford Binet Test," Byron indicated as we sat down at the kitchen table after dinner. "Just do your best. There's no right and wrong answers. No pressure."

As I recall there were various aspects or sections to the I.Q. test, but the most memorable portion was the numerical sequence portion.

"I'm going to give you a sequence of numbers, Buz, and then you repeat them back to me, okay?"

"Okay."

"Then, after you repeat the numbers, repeat them backward. Like I say; one, six, five. You give them to me in order then repeat them backwards; five, six, one. Got it?" Byron laid the rules out clearly. "Here we go; two, five, seven."

"Two, five, seven. Seven, five, two," I responded quickly.

"Okay, two, five, seven, six," Byron continued.

"Two, five, seven, six. Six, seven, five, two," I repeated.

That process continued up to eight numbers. "You missed a number, Byron. You missed the six," I observed.

"Whoops, I'm sorry. My mistake." (I think Byron did it on purpose.)

The sequence continued up to ten numbers. I repeated the numbers back to Byron without any difficulty.

"Hmmm," Byron said as he read from his test material. "You're not supposed to be able to do that."

"Why?" I asked not knowing what inference Byron was making.

"Very few people can go to ten and reverse the sequence without making a mistake. I noticed that you had your eyes closed. What were you doing?" My inquisitor asked.

"I was picturing the numbers in a line as you gave them to me," I admitted. "Is that cheating?"

"Heck no. I just wondered how you did it. Have you done this before?" Byron pressed me further.

"Nope. It just came to me," I admitted.

We continued on with the remainder of the test. Byron said that I did extremely well but I didn't attach much significance to what had elapsed until I was in college. I could remember all my friends telephone numbers and I knew I had an excellent sense of direction because I could picture, in my mind's eye, all the necessary landmarks on a route that I had previously seen. I could picture an entire race course while skiing but I had no idea that I had a photogenic memory. Byron had made an amazing discovery but he didn't tell me the importance of what he had discovered or how I could utilize it. It did come to me later.

We were now ready for our first scrimmage or game condition-like contest between our first and second teams. The first team was on defense and I was playing on the line at end. Dale Galaher, who played halfback on the second team and backed me up at QB, dove off tackle. The defense swarmed to crush him. Gene Fox, who was playing linebacker on my side, wore glasses under a thick wire-meshed mask. Somehow in the melee my left hand got entangled in Gene's face mask and as my momentum carried me over the pile of humanity, the last three fingers on my left hand were bent backwards, while they remained stuck in the mask.

"Awe s...!" I yelled as I tried to extricate my hand from Gene's mask. Gene could readily see my plight. My fingers were directly in his face. Blood from my hand was covering his glasses.

"Buster is bleeding," Gene cried out as Coach Rushing came to the rescue. He pulled my hand out of the mask. I yelped like a puppy who had caught his paw in a mouse trap.

"Coach! The bones are sticking out!" I exclaimed as Coach assessed the damage.

"Calm down, Buster. You ain't gonna die," Coach said as he tried to put the protruding bone of my index finger, back in place.

Seeing the blood-stained white bone of my finger sticking out like a chicken bone and realizing that my index finger had shrunk to half its length, I got a little nauseated, but I sucked up enough courage to minimize my pain in front of my teammates.

"We better get you to St. Joe's," Coach said as he asked Sam Blair, our manager, to go get his car.

Fortunately, none of my fingers were broken, but the

doctors at the emergency room put the bones back in place and stitched up the third and fourth fingers. They taped and immobilized the three fingers on my left hand. The problem was obvious. How in the hell would I be able to take a hard snap from center? How could I possibly hold onto the ball with my left hand? The opening game against the Gallup Tigers was less than two weeks away.

Interviewing Jack in 2002 when he was in declining health, I recalled this incident: "'Hah! Do I remember it. You did the damdest dance I ever saw."

"Geez, Coach. It hurt like hell," I reminded the "Tough Guy" who never winced at anything.

Things didn't get off to a good start in our senior year for my two best friends, either—Glo and Jack.

Jack lost the election for President of the senior class. After two successful terms as President he didn't "three-peat." Bill McIlaney, whose parents owned a dairy farm in the North Valley within a few miles of Lazy Q, was elected President. Charlotte Stevens, whose brother Jimmie who was one of my buds, was elected Vice-President. Marlene Ford, who was a "looker," was our Secretary-Treasurer.

The run for President of our class was interesting. Lester Dohner taught the Agriculture Class and was the Future Farmers of America Club sponsor and encouraged Bill to run. He received considerable support from the Stompers and the Vocational & Agricultural Class students. Joyce Campbell's father made a large sign for Bill which was hung over the entrance to the gym. Jack probably was a tad over-confident.

The hotly contested election was a tie! Not between Jack and Bill but Bill and Rosie Olivas. Bill won in a runoff.

Bill's teacher and mentor continued to take a keen interest in Bill's dairy farm long after Bill graduated and paid our Senior Class President the ultimate compliment. When the tough disciplinarian was dying he called Bill to his bedside. His last wish? He wanted Bill to conduct his funeral service. A request that defines both men and their relationship.

I tried to console my best friend. "Just like they told us at Boy's State, Jack. Politicians are like baby diapers. When the voters think its time for a change, they make a change," I said trying to be funny.

"Are you trying to tell me that I stink?" Jack retorted in response to the diaper analogy.

"Geez. I didn't think about that," I said apologetically. I got the impression that Jack wasn't too upset over his loss. Besides we both thought Bill was a neato guy.

Despite Highland High School's drain on our school population, the Sophomore Class of `53-`54 had 1200 students. Montie Cast, whose hair-do was a precursor of Elvis Presley's memorable locks, was elected President. Mary Ellen Derbyshire was elected Vice-President and Tang Ong, whose sister Jane was one of our Senior class friends and classmates, was Secretary-Treasurer.

The Junior Class elected Billy Mann, who was a valuable member of our football team, as President. Neva Jo Weese was elected Vice-President and Sue Coleman, Secretary-Treasurer.

The Student Council, which was responsible for planning activities such as Pioneer Day, Pep Rallies and the Green & White Ball, was headed by Homer Ledbetter as President, Bill McIlhaney Vice-President and Irene Scott as Secretary-Treasurer. All three were classmates from Washington Junior High.

Mr. Robert Thomas shouldered the responsibility to see that the yearbook *La Reata,* which has been invaluable in the production of "Bulldogs Forever," was completed on time. Caroline Maciel was selected as Editor with Betty Ann Rose Associate Editor and Elnora Bowers as Assistant Editor. *La Reata* had a staff of almost thirty students.

The Record, our newspaper which reported all the latest activities on campus and occasional scuttlebutt on who was seeing who, or who was seen with who, had three Co-Editors — Harry P. Moskos who appears later in this chapter, Carol Kutnewsky (who later shared the top spot as Valedictorian of our Class with Jack Stromberg) and Martha Mersman. The *Record* had a staff of seventeen. The article in *La Reata* states that this publication began in 1902 as *The Accident.* That may have been what happened, but the first newspaper was known as *The Occident.* A 'typo' as we often then referred to our oversights.

Glo always wanted to be a cheerleader since junior high, but given her job after school and her desire to keep a straight A average, she never tried out. Encouraged by Arlene Garcia and Joyce Campbell she made an all-out effort as school convened. I saw her soon after the results were announced. She was in tears.

"Buz, I didn't make it," she cried.

"Ginny Shaver, Arlene Garcia and Joyce Campbell made it but I didn't."

"Geez. I was really pulling for you, Glo. It would have been terrif for you to be on the road trips," I said as I tried to comfort my girlfriend whom I'd seen very little of during the summer.

"Gloria (Koenig) got it," Glo added exhibiting an element of surprise.

"Gloria was selected?" I asked not fully grasping the meaning of Glo's statement.

"Sue. Sue Harris made it too. She's cute and she was good," Glo added. "But..."

"But what?" still not comprehending Glo's inner thoughts, I asked.

"I think a lot of the kids mixed us up, since we both had the same name. There were so many trying out it's hard to remember. I can't help but think those who voted were confused," Glo elaborated.

"Geez, I never thought of that, Glo. Sure seems logical to me," I added again trying to comfort her.

Glo was devastated. She thought about it often and it almost always brought tears to her eyes. Damn, she sure would have looked terrif in that short-skirted cheerleader outfit, I thought. It wasn't to be.

During the 50th Reunion of the '53 class, I asked Arlene Garcia, our Head Cheerleader, what it meant to be a cheerleader and was there any resentment amongst the girls in the role they played in the holy trinity of sports:

Whether it was Pepper Club, Drill Team or Cheerleading we girls wanted to do things with our friends. Being in those organizations is something we wanted. They were our goals. Just like making good grades. I charted out what I wanted to do, but we were all very loyal to each other and supported each other's efforts to achieve our goals. We didn't feel that we were doing these things just for the boys.

On another issue I asked Arlene if she experienced any discrimination while at AHS.

"You know Buster, that never even occurred to me."

Arlene was one of the classiest, brightest and loveliest girls at AHS. And, she remains so today.

Riette Lewinson, a party to our conversation joined in:

"The only thing I resented was you and Jack taking that trip to Wisconsin on your own. Our parents would never let us girls do that!"

Jeanne Bennett, who was Head Cheerleader during the `54-`55 school year, added to the chorus:

"I really never thought about the objectives of the Pepper Club. We never questioned our roles and being selected as Head Cheerleader was 'super neato' as we used to say."

A week later and after suffering several painful hits on the end of my dislocated finger, Coach McDavid felt I could handle my chores at Q.B. without too many fumbles. Tony Valdez and our trainer had gerry-rigged an apparatus on my hand to avoid further injury but I still couldn't hold onto the ball.

We overwhelmed Gallup 40-6. They never figured out that we ran all of our running plays to the left side so I didn't have to hand off with my bad hand. The left side of our line, anchored by 205 pound Joe Harris, Kent Bennett and Velma Corley, was our strong side. It was also, as we proudly referred to, our "dark side." All three were Black.

Ralph demonstrated quickly that he was the real deal. Within the first couple of minutes he broke off tackle and ran 56 yards for our first score exhibiting his blazing speed. Jack recovered a fumble in the end zone for another T.D. and I threw a touchdown pass to Jack for one score and Velma for another as our second and third team played most of the second half. I did the punting and Velma kicked the extra points. I was delighted that Coach relieved me of the responsibility for the conversions. I wasn't very good at it.

There was a memorable moment in this, our first game of the year. With all the Tigers' attention on Ralph, I made a quick pitch out to H.B. who scrambled 70 yards down the sideline for a T.D. "H" was ecstatic. It was his first long run for a touchdown. The refs called it back. Holding. Retreating 15 yards H.B. said:

"Who was holding ref?" H.B. asked the man in the zebra shirt.

"Number 79," he replied. We huddled up for the next play.

"Jesus_____ Jim! What the f___ were you doin' holding that end? He couldn't have tackled me no way," H.B., exasperated, yelled out to Jimmy Harris, one of our fearsome fivesome.

"S..., I'm sorry, H. I won't try to block anybody next time," Jim said wryly.

We all laughed in the huddle. I could tell this was a special group of guys. We would make this year, our last year together, a memorable one. In an unusual turn of events, Dick Hyson, the star quarterback for the Gallup Tigers, and I would become friends and teammates exactly one year from this game. But neither of us could possibly have imagined at this point in time where that was going to be.

The 1953 football season marked the first time in New Mexico scholastic history to have playoffs amongst the divisional champions to determine the State Champion. AHS was in the "western" 1-AA division which was comprised of the largest schools in the northern part of the state including Santa Fe, Farmington, St. Mary's and Highland. For some reason Las Cruces, which was in the southern-most part of the State near El Paso, Texas, was also included in 1-AA. There would no longer be a mythical or consensus State Champ. This year would be different. Coach McDavid told us to focus on our conference games. Our next opponent, however, was Clovis, a non-conference tilt.

I was still seething over the home-town job that our baseball team got in Clovis just six weeks earlier. I wanted to beat these guys bad. Conference or no conference.

Al McPherson, a sportswriter for the *Albuquerque Tribune*, trumpeted the strength of our depth-laden experienced, big team and Coach McDavid appointed Joe Harris and me as co-captains. I was now over 180 pounds which was exceptional size for a quarterback. Coach added the option to our play book to take advantage of my size and give H.B. and Ralph an open field on pitch outs from the option.

A crowd of 3,200 fans watched a scoreless game for almost three quarters. Led by a defense anchored by Gerry Nesbitt at linebacker, who was tough as nails, Clovis stymied our running game. Suddenly, Ralph intercepted a pass on Clovis' 28 yard line and ran it into the end zone. Within a minute, Ralph then grabbed Nesbitt's punt on our 31 yard line and raced 69 yards for another TD. Dale Galaher and I alternated at quarterback in the fourth quarter and I hit Charley Salazar, subbing for H.B., with a 33 yard pass and Dale, with H.B. returning, completed a 20 yarder to H.B. for our third score and the Game was over. A shutout, 19-0. A bit of revenge was extracted.

The win made the Friday night dance at the Student Union Building much more enjoyable as Glo and I danced to *No Other Love* and *Don't Let the Stars Get in your Eyes*, both by Perry Como. Saturday night we finally got to see *From Here to Eternity* at the Kimo Theater. We were only eight years removed from World War II. The Academy Award winning picture brought back memories of those days in Green Bay when we were constantly bombarded with events of the war. How could we now forget? Marilyn Monroe, it seemed, was trying to get men to forget the past as her smoldering sexuality on the screen was a new form of bombshell seemingly ready to explode at any moment. *The Kinsey Report* and *Playboy* aroused our sexual consciousness. Glo and I, tough as it was, continued to defuse our own passion. America in the Fifties, was the epitome of sexual repression seeking an outing.

The third week of the season we returned to Artesia, the scene of my broken ribs two years prior. It was also a homecoming of sorts for the Quist family. My grandmother, my two Uncles, Aunt Fre, Cousin Don and Mom and Dad again were all there to watch the game. I don't know whose side of the field they sat on but it didn't make much of a difference. We lost 20-6. Fortunately, it was a non-conference game.

The only good news was that I was able to remove the splints and bandages from my left hand.

Santa Fe was a critical conference game. The Demons were undefeated. Little did we know what was awaiting us as we unboarded our bus to dress at Major Field in Santa Fe. Through skiing I knew a lot of kids at the capitol. I thought I had friends up there. Wrong! Posted on the walls and our lockers were messages like:

"We're going to kill you 'dawgs'."

"You come around my end Quist and I'll break that same leg again!"

"You Bulldogs are going to eat dog s...."

The message was pretty clear. They didn't like us...or maybe it was just me. Maybe it was because of that fight at La Wash with the basketball team? I don't know. Some teams could have been intimidated. Fortunately, we weren't. We got mad—fighting mad. Ironically it was the Demons who were shaken. The post game report said:

"The Bulldogs scored almost at will against the jittery Demons."

Ralph, H.B. and Jimmy each scored a touchdown the first three times we had the ball in the first quarter for a 20-0 lead. Reserves played the entire second quarter and we led, 32-6 at the half. The romp was on. The intimidator was the intimidated. The demoralized Demons fumbled five times; two were returned for TDs by Kent Bennett, a defensive lineman. The first team played just a little more than a quarter of the game. Coach McDavid, who coached at Santa Fe High School prior to coming to AHS, didn't want to run up the score but it ended up 52-12 anyway.

In recounting past athletic events it's easy to recall the heroes, the first stringers, the guys that got almost all of the playing time. Quite often there are ten or 20 players that toil for all three years on a team and never get to play in a game. Coach McDavid made certain everyone got a chance to play. And, did they make the best of the opportunity? You bet.

Noel Baca, who played in Ralph's shadow, scored two TDs. We discovered a new talent in a third string fullback, George Hutchinson.

Bob Stewart, who had grinded it out every year since we

played together at Washington Junior High, had a field day making several long runs. Merrill Rogers, who was primarily a linebacker, also got his chance at carrying the ball as did Bill Easely as we rolled up 343 yards rushing.

A picture accompanying the write up on the game shows me airborne carrying the ball into the end zone on an option keeper (called back due to a penalty). Sprawled on the ground is the Demons' Ray Crews, who missed the tackle. I've often wondered if he was the end who threatened to break my leg? We would later become teammates on the All-Star Team.

The Demons' strategy backfired and it was pretty stupid. But, what if they were determined to get even? What if their Pachucos would attack us as we attempted to board our bus? I told our coaches what had happened at La Wash. They took it seriously. Guarded, we boarded the bus and returned home without incident. John Dendahl and his sister Karen were waiting to greet me after the game. I had at least two friends in Santa Fe. And Karen? She would soon become a very close friend. (This is a different Karen.)

Years after this memorable game took place, I mentioned it to my friend, Jaime Koch, who was one of the standout players at Santa Fe High.

"Yeah. A bunch of us signed the note. Your coach brought it over to our locker room just before the game. Our coach was mad as hell. He benched all of us for the whole first half. And, to top it off, he made us work out for three hours after the game," Jaime relayed to me.

"Served you right, you numb nuts," I retorted. "Even if you guys had played we would have smoked your butts!"

Jaime did not agree.

Over 4,000 fans packed Public Schools Stadium to see the twenty-second meeting between St. Mary's and the Bulldogs. It was an important conference game as well as a great rivalry. Lionel Romero, their quarterback, and I had been rivals in baseball since the eighth grade, and I knew that he and his teammates would like nothing better than to beat us. We had great respect for Lionel's ability. He could pass as well as he could pitch. We expected a wide open, offensive game.

We were leading only 12-6 with time running out in the half. On the last play with only seconds remaining I hit Velma Corley with a 24 yard pass for a score. Velma was a rare talent. He was six feet tall, weighed over 170-pounds, and had blazing speed. But what made him exceptional was his running style. He was a Black version of Elroy "Crazy Legs" Hirsch, who was one of the NFL's top stars in the 50s. Once Velma had the ball in the open field an opponent had two chances of tackling him. Slim and none. His upper body would go one way and his lower body would go another. What a sight to see.

H.B. had probably his best game. He ran for 144 yards on 14 carries, a 10 yard average per carry. The most unforgettable play occurred when Joe Harris, our 205 pound defensive tackle, picked up a fumble and rambled 82 yards for a touchdown. He had an escort of three or four of us all the way down the field. I didn't think he was going to make it, but he did. That turnover spoiled any chance that St. Mary's would catch us and the score ended 32-12. The only sore point was Velma's inability to convert three out of five extra points — a problem that would soon bedevil us. On the plus side, Dale Galaher and I combined to complete seven out of fourteen passes for 105 yards, outpacing Lionel's 91 yards. We were 4 wins and 1 loss entering the toughest part of our schedule.

The undefeated Carlsbad Cavemen were our opponents for homecoming. A cold, windy and of course, dusty day marred the Bulldog Day Parade down Central Avenue. Our Bulldog Queen was Donna Standifer, who was elected by the student body from a field of twelve candidates. Jo Hankins, who was a soul mate of mine from Mr. Graham's art class, was one attendant and Jay Twilley was the other. Jay's good looks reminded me of Karen (Wisconsin-First Love) Markwardt. Homer Ledbetter, Doc's son, our Student Council President, crowned the Queen. Bill McIlhaney, our class President, escorted Donna to the game. Homecoming was a well-honed tradition and ritual in every high school and college in America. Gretchen Stromberg argued that this entire pageant was to praise the male ego but I disagree. Homecoming brought recognition to the girls and others who participated in the whole ball game called "high school." It also provided an opportunity for alums to turn back the clock and relive those days that were so precious to all of us. Homecomings were an event in themselves. We could have had one without the other but they were better together.

I was faced with a difficult problem even before the game began. The sand filled air was creating havoc with my contact lenses. My eyes would tear making it extremely difficult to see. Then my eyes would dry out and the mucus would crystalize on the lens. That, coupled with the fact that Carlsbad, led by the twin Forrest brothers at quarterback and end and the imposing John Wooten at tackle, were a dominant, well-coached team. We were on our heels all night. We couldn't move the ball on the ground, which was our strong game. Throwing into the wind and battling erratic eyesight, I completed only five out of nineteen passes for a paltry 59 yards. We got shellacked 32-7. But, the worst, for me anyway, was yet to come.

I got to the point where I couldn't see out of one eye. Then the pain got so excruciating, I couldn't open my eye. Dad came down to the bench. It was obvious I had a real problem. I took the lens out, but still couldn't see. Dad located Dr. Haydon in the stands and they rushed me to (my favorite place) the emergency room at St. Joseph's Hospital.

At the hospital Dr. Haydon discovered that a particle of sand had lodged between my lens and my cornea and severely cut my cornea. Man, was it painful! Eye injuries are really intense. It took a painkiller and considerable amount of time before I could relax. Worried, I asked Dr. Haydon, "How long will it be before I can see, Doc?" I'll never forget his reply.

"You've got a nasty cut on your cornea. Bad as it is, however, your eye heals faster than any organ in your body. Within a week or so you'll never know that you had this injury," Dr. Haydon said.

"You mean I will be able to see next week for the Cruces game?" I asked hardly able to hold back my glee.

"Yep. You should be okay. You'll be able to wear the lens too...if there isn't another sandstorm," he added.

There was another downside to this whole ordeal, of

course. I couldn't go to the homecoming dance with Glo. She was all dressed up with no place to go. I had let her down again. Knowing I went to the hospital she waited at home. It was late when I was able to give her a call.

"Glo, I've got a bad cut on my cornea," as I related to her all the gory details. We had been through the same scenario with the broken ribs, my leg and all sorts of minor mishaps. I could tell she was, and rightfully so, exasperated with one calamity after another plus my absence on team trips.

"Can't we at least make an appearance, Buz?" was her plaintive plea.

"Glo, it still hurts even though Dr. Haydon put some salve in my eye and...and I've got a gauze bandage and tape over my eye. I look like a one-eyed dip s...," I continued.

"Oh, Buz...it's always something," Glo said as she began to cry.

"You should be dating some egghead and not a jock," I suggested. It wasn't a sarcastic comment. I was trying to empathize with her. She took my comment the wrong way.

"I...I guess I will," Glo said in an unfamiliar tone as she slammed the phone down.. That wasn't the bad part I made matters even worse.

Marilyn Keith was an attractive, perky, strawberry blonde junior, who had caught my eye on several occasions. I guess she had picked up on Glo's rebuffing my attempt to reconcile our differences that following Monday in the patio at school.

"Did you and Glo have a fight?" she asked as I was heading for my Mom's car parked on Broadway Ave.

"Yeah. I couldn't make the homecoming dance Friday night and Glo was really disappointed," I replied.

"Gee whiz. You were seriously hurt. She should have understood that," Marilyn, empathizing with my position, said as she made herself available for a more detailed discussion. I invited her to join me in my car. It was lunch time.

I was down psychologically. Our demoralizing loss to Carlsbad, my injury and not knowing if I'd be fit to play Friday against Las Cruces, a key conference game. Glo's rejection made me a vulnerable target. I unloaded all my woes on Marilyn, who I hardly knew. I took her into my confidence. It didn't take long for the fit to hit the shan.

Marilyn used my plight to advance her own agenda. She told anyone who would listen how non-caring Glo was and that I wanted to break up with her and all kinds of stuff that suited her own designs. If her primary goal was to drive a wedge between Glo and myself she certainly was successful. Glo was furious and rightfully so. She returned my "A" club pin, vowing to never wear it again. I was devastated.

As I mentioned earlier, the greatest lesson learned in high school isn't in any formal class. It's in interpersonal relationships. The experiences can be gut wrenching. We've all been there. I had hurt Glo immeasurably, again. It looked certain that our relationship was over. We had our ups and downs many times over the past three years, but this time the schism was serious.

"Buster? If you need some more medication for your eye, go over and see Red at Highland Pharmacy and he'll take care of you," Tony Valdez said as we were discussing my visual problems. Tony and Red were close friends and the drug store was at the southeast corner of Central and Broadway across the street from AHS and was one of our hangouts. Red Heyman was one of our biggest boosters and a super guy.

"Do you think he has something for 'fecalopia'?" I asked.

"Fecalopia? What the heck is that?" Tony obviously puzzled asked.

"I can't see for s...!"

We both laughed.

I was like Irv Comp, the one-eyed quarterback for the Green Bay Packers in the 40s as I tried to get ready for the Las Cruces game. The shocking loss to the Cavemen had shaken our confidence. We had a new assistant coach, Ed Garvanian. He worked on getting us up as Friday approached. Las Cruces was a long, five hour bus ride. Our mood was sullen.

The Las Cruces Bulldogs (there were so many "bulldog" teams in the state it often seemed like we were playing ourselves) dominated the first quarter but couldn't score. They drove down to our 13 yard line halfway through the second quarter, but our Bulldog-like tenacious defense rose to the occasion and we stopped them. Ralph and H.B. carried the ball to our 25 and a first down. I passed to my buddy Jack for a 13 yarder and another first down.

I was gaining more moxy every game at Q.B. I noticed that our opponents were pursuing aggressively in my direction when I took the ball from center. If I ran the option to the right the defense would immediately move in that direction and split the gaps in our line. We had a play to counter that move which was smothering our running attack. I called 45 slant/reverse as coach McDavid let me call all the plays.

I took the snap from Gene Fox and moved quickly to the right, which resembled an option in that direction. Jim Harris and H.B. moved in the same direction as if to block or receive a pitch. Ralph remained stationary in his position at right half-back. As I moved at an angle away from the line, I deftly slipped the ball to Ralph who took off in the opposite direction on a "naked" reverse. The defense had over-rotated. There wasn't anyone there! Ralph had clear sailing, 62 yards untouched for a TD. Velma again missed the extra point. We held a precarious 6-0 lead going into the second half.

An *Albuquerque Journal* article said:

"Long punts by Quist kept the Crucens out of range most of the evening in the defensive duel which attracted more than 5,000 spectators."

I had four punts for 179 yards. A 45 yard average. In addition, I was able to complete 5 out of 5 passes for 81 yards for one of my best overall games. Las Cruces drove down to our 20 yard line late in the game and our defense again held. We won 6-0 and, more importantly, we were 3-0 in the 1-AA conference. Our team was resilient. We could bounce back from a crushing defeat. Now the Roswell Coyotes were coming to town. They were billed as the strongest team in the state. Even stronger than Carlsbad.

The very first play from scrimmage produced a bad omen of things to come. Ralph carried the ball on a quick opener for 18 yards but was injured on the play. A "hip-pointer." He never returned to the game. Later Jack was knocked out of play and he was replaced by Bill Mann, who later scored his first TD. In short order we also lost Dale Galaher and H.B. AHS was decimated by injuries but that wasn't the biggest problem. Roswell was big, fast and talented.

Lloyd Taylor was all he was touted to be. He scored four touchdowns and carried the ball for 135 yards. He was on the cusp of breaking Tommy McDonald's state scoring record, set only a year earlier, of 151 points. The Coyotes also had a 190 pound fullback by the name of Sherman Pruitt who scored on long runs and Jack Doran, their QB threw for 144 yards. We were undermanned and overwhelmed. Despite my two TD passes, one covering 65 yards to George Hutchinson, we lost 52-26. Little did we know then, a rematch was in the future. To say we would be underdogs, was the understatement of the year.

It was getting to be a bad habit. We would play well in conference games and look like "dogs" in the non-conference contests. Farmington, an important league game was next. True to what was becoming form, the team responded again.

Although Ralph was unable to play against his former teammates, we unloaded on the Scorpions early. I threw three touchdown passes in the first half, two to Velma and one, a screen pass, to Dale Galaher. I never got to play in the second half as we took a 27-0 lead into the intermission. We ran up 448 yards of total offense to only 65 for our opponents. Bill Easely, showing that he could play offense as well as defense, ran 18 yards for a TD. We had three touchdowns called back and were penalized 155 yards, otherwise the rout would have been greater than the 40-0 score. The stage was set for the game of the year. AHS and Highland were undefeated going into the last game with the championship of 1-AA at stake and the opportunity to play for the state crown for the very first time. Without a doubt the biggest game, ever, in Albuquerque High School history.

Highland had just barely edged Santa Fe 20-19, a team that we had demolished a few weeks earlier, but our teams were rated even by the Albuquerque sportswriters. No one could possibly have predicted the outcome of this pivotal game. I thought that last summer's baseball game against Hastings was bizarre. That palled in comparison to what was about to happen. No one who is still alive, who had any involvement whatsoever with high school football in the 50's in

Albuquerque, will ever forget this defining moment.

Getting ready for the big game we had to trek up to Public Schools Stadium, which was about a couple of miles from AHS. Jack had acquired a World War II vintage jeep which relieved me from picking him up every morning to go to school. Jack was late for practice and driving up Central Avenue when he saw George Hutchinson, Kent Bennett, Vel Corley and Joe Harris walking to practice. Jack stopped and waved to his teammates.

"Hey! Jump in guys," Jack yelled to his four Black teammates.

"Ya sure ya got room for all of us, Jack?" Joe asked, hesitating at the curb, like he was uncertain whether or not accepting a ride would be socially acceptable.

"Sure, sure. We can all squeeze in," Jack reassured him.

"Sure appreciate ya doin' this, Jack. We'd be tired before we even practice," Joe added. They all laughed as Jack headed for the stadium.

After practice Jack drove his teammates back to school and the dressing room. While driving down Central he suddenly felt conspicuous and self-conscious with four Black guys exposed to all the traffic in his open-air jeep. He thought to himself:

"Oh, my goodness. What if someone sees me? What will they think? Hell, these are my friends, why should I feel this way?"

Jack worried about it all night. He concluded that he was ashamed of himself for feeling that way. Why should he let society's perceptions and prejudices rule his thoughts or actions? He asked the guys to ride with him the next day. It was the right thing to do. They were teammates. He felt good about it.

Ever since Owen Smaulding graced the scene at AHS in the early 1900s, Blacks played a pivotal role in Bulldog athletics, as elucidated earlier. But, were they an inclusive part of the social fabric of our school? There were only six Black kids in our graduating class of 1954. I regarded Joe Harris, Kent Bennett, Harvey Cotten, Vel Corley and Eugene Agnes as not only teammates, they were my friends.

Eugene, looking back 50 years, offered this valuable insight:

I was born and raised in Albuquerque. My dad died when I was very young and I really only knew my mom and my grandmother. My grandmother was born in Ireland. She was Irish and White. Somehow she met my grandfather who was Black and they married. He was a Buffalo soldier in the U.S. Army—they chased Pancho Villa in Mexico. Racial discrimination was never an issue with me. I always felt that I was accepted at AHS and in Albuquerque. I never knew there was discrimination until I went to southeastern New Mexico with the Basketball Team. I 'hung out' with Joe, Kent, Velma and another Black kid by the name of Harvey Smith, but my best friend was J.D. Metzger, a White kid. We were in Cantata and the Operetta together and we spent lots of time together at each of our parents' houses. I had a great time at AHS. Mr. Ream was an incredible man. He made sure all of us kids had the opportunity to participate in anything we wanted to. There were no limitations on anyone.

"Gene? What about school functions like the Green & White Ball or the prom. Did you feel excluded from any of these activities?" I asked my former teammate. "No. We didn't go because we didn't have a car and we didn't have any money. For me, I didn't have any real interest in dating until I got out of school."

Eugene's recollections were somewhat different than those recorded earlier from the interview with Ken Carson. It's possible that the KIMO and the Sunshine theaters and other establishments may have changed their policy on admission in the four or five years since Ken had graduated. The U.S. Supreme Court decision Brown vs. The Board of Education in 1954 made segregation in schools prohibited by law, thus ending this onerous situation in New Mexico and throughout the U.S.

Many AHS grads will recall Eugene as a basketball referee. Max Shirley asked Gene to referee for his Parks & Recreation program while he was still at AHS. That start became a career. Gene worked for the Western Athletic Conference for 38 years. His traveling referee partner was Mel Otero, acknowledged previously as a distinguished AHS grad.

Prior to their first trip, Mel's wife Georgia warned Gene that Mel snored rather loudly.

"That's not a problem," Gene retorted. "I'll just turn him over and give him a kiss. I'm sure he'll sleep with one eye open!"

In addition to his very visible on-court presence, Eugene obtained his Ph.D. from Trinity Theological Seminary in 1995 and became an ordained Minister for the International Pentecostal Assemblies of the World. He is also licensed and qualified as a Mental Health Therapist/Counselor helping people make the "right call" as he did for many years.

A crowd of over five thousand was on hand for THE game at a cold, wet Public School Stadium. It had snowed the night before and a pile of dirt-infested snow ringed the field like an ice rink. It started badly for us. We were quickly skating on thin ice.

Lynn Parker returned Bill Easley's kick off 47 yards almost all the way for a touchdown to our 27 yard line.

H.B. trying to come back on his injured knee, helped make the tackle, but re-injured it. He was carried from the field. His football days were over.

Parker rammed over for the TD on fourth down but Jack, heroically, blocked the extra point. A very key play.

On our 32 yard line after the kickoff, I attempted my first pass. With a wet ball and poor footing, Tony Gray intercepted my toss intended for Jack and returned it to our 22. Not a good start. Things were beginning to look as bleak as the darkening November sky. Our defensive corps anchored by Tom Nethery, Kent Bennett, Joe Harris, Dale Galaher, Jerry Billings, Bill Easely, and Jack, smothered Highland's offense and we held, but the "fairies" made their second penetration inside our 20 yard line.

The New Mexico High School Athletic Association made the determination prior to the 1953 football season that there would be no tie games. If a game ended with the score tied, the team that penetrated inside their opponents 20 yard line the most would be declared the winner. If the penetrations were tied, the team with the most first downs would be declared the winner. If the first downs were even, the Captains of each team would stand back to back at the 50 yard line, take ten paces and then duel to the death with snowballs! Truth is, I don't know what would've happened if the first downs had been tied. Fortunately, it didn't go that far.

In the second period Tony Gray, who had great speed, returned my kick 33 yards to our 17. Another penetration for HHS and we were in trouble again. But, our defense stymied the Hornets and they failed to score.

Finally, with the second quarter coming to a close we started to click and moved the ball. Charley Salazar filling in for H.B., who was out for the season, made eight yards. I ran for five and then passed to Jack for nine. I then pitched out to George Hutchinson on an option play and he gained 35 yards around the left side. We penetrated Highland's 20 yard line for the first time. Then, one of the most memorable, albeit embarrassing, plays occurred.

Fifty years later, people still remember the spectacle of me being thrown for a 13 yard loss by "Lefty" Thompson in the middle of a muddy quagmire. When I sloshed my way out of the murky mess I looked like the creature from the black lagoon. My green and white uniform was as black as my shadow. The half was history. We were down 6-0 and I changed uniforms.

Coach McDavid told us at halftime that the game would be won by the team who wanted it the most. Pete was not a passionate man. He didn't rant and rave to fire us up. He appealed to our pride and our place in AHS history. He renewed our resolve.

The wet field and the saturated pigskin made it difficult to execute. Both teams traded several fumbles. We had the ball on our own 41 yard line. Time was running out in the third quarter. The defining moment had arrived. We were in a time out.

My Dad took movie film of the entire game. It clearly shows the team huddling around their quarterback during the time out. Using the mud as my chalkboard, I modified one of our plays.

"Highland has two deep safeties guys. Here's our chance. We're going to run 33 A (a pass play with Ralph as a flanker outside Jack's right end position). Jack, you and Velma get down field and go right to the safeties as fast as you can and make them go with you to the sidelines. Ralph, you hold up at the line. Don't take off with the snap. When you see Gray go with Jack, break for the middle. You should be all alone. Hold the rush guys and we've got six," I said as we broke the huddle.

Ralph was, as I had envisioned, wide open. I threw from our 35. Ralph juggled the ball momentarily at the HHS 25 yard line, cradled it in his arms and went untouched 59 yards into the end zone. Our enthusiasm was mitigated somewhat when Velma missed the extra point. A 6-6 tie as the third period ended.

Then strange things began to happen. Jack, who was co-captain with H.B., made his first inquiry to Richard Van Fleet, the head linesman, who was ahead on penetrations. Mr. Van Fleet, emphatically replied, "AHS is ahead." Jack reported his statement to Coach McDavid. Highland and their coach Hugh Hackett, <u>thinking</u> that <u>they</u> were ahead in penetrations, never asked Van Fleet. They kept the ball on the ground protecting against a turnover. Coach McDavid, relying on Jack's report, told me to keep it on the ground and keep the ball myself on the option. He didn't want me to pitch it and risk a fumble.

Dad was beside himself in the stands. Too bad that there wasn't any sound with the film. His criticism of my play-calling would have been hilarious. He, like thousands of fans and all the sportswriters, didn't know what we knew. Only our team and our coaches knew that we were ahead, or at least, knew what the referee <u>thought</u> he knew. Both teams muddled in the middle of the muddy field for the remainder of the game. When the gun went off <u>both</u> teams celebrated their "win." But, both teams couldn't have won, could they? Confusion reigned. Then, the announcement came from the public address announcer in the press box:

"The winner, on penetrations, is Albuquerque High!"

The Hornets and their fans were stunned. The fans in the green and white-dominated west stands were ecstatic! Hugh Hackett, Mickey Miller and Clem Charlton, the Highland coaches, immediately filed a formal protest. The crowd, which in a literary sense is the "Greek Chorus," was dra-

273

matically split without resolution. The army of blue and gold from the east stands were about to attack the green and white. Our team quickly re-treated to our bus to avoid a melee that seemed sure to follow. We were entitled to the Bronze Shoe, the trophy that was to be awarded after the game to the winner. HHS had it in their possession from the previous year's victory. They weren't about to give it up. There was no post-game ceremony.

Learning of Highland's protest, I asked Coach McDavid:

"Coach Foehr (who was with us on the bus) protested a baseball game last summer. Our protest was upheld. Is it possible we may have to play the game over?"

"Buster, whatever happens, happens and we'll deal with it. The officials will make the decisions," Coach McDavid reassured us in a calm, cool manner, reflective of Pete's disposition.

Our bus was surrounded by Highland hecklers. Skirmishes were breaking out between the fans. The police, present because of the natural rivalry, seemed to be in control. We didn't know whether we should celebrate or not. We were subdued as we returned to our locker room at AHS. Glo was there to greet me. She gave me a big hug. She had forgiven me for my indiscretion. It made my day. We had (apparently) won the game and I won back my girlfriend.

The *Albuquerque Journal* ran a play by play account of the game the next day. HHS clearly had more penetrations than we did. The game was replayed on TV and each penetration was clearly marked. Highland had two penetrations to our one (excluding the TDs). Jack and H.B. were interviewed on TV. Jack reported that he not only asked the referee once but "four or five times." He said we were ahead 2 to 1. One Hornet player reported to Coach Hackett that one referee told him that HHS was "way ahead." What went wrong? How could this happen?

Monday morning's headline in the *Albuquerque Journal* made matters worse. In large, bold one and one half inch letters the front page, the lead article read:

"AHS 'TITLE' MAY BE VACATED"

While reading the *Journal* at school Monday morning the rumor, spreading like a raging wind-driven prairie fire, was that an army of Hornets, like locusts, were about to devour our campus. The Rah-Rahs, the Stompers and our Pachuco gangs banded and bonded together. We were ready to defend our honor and our school. All our coaches demanded that the players remain in the locker room, so we could live to fight the next battle—the State Championship—if there was one.

We had some real tough guys at AHS. Harry Owen was one of the Stompers who, after graduation, would become a professional "enforcer." Jerry Vernon, who had jumped me just a few months earlier and we had a knock down fist fight, would later be convicted of the murder of one of our classmates. The Fairies surely didn't want to mess with the Dawgs.

Glen O. Ream, our principal, knowing the mix of his student body, called the police. Three squad cars were dispatched to Broadway and Central Avenue. Ed Garvanian (who was a pretty tough guy also) and the police were able to disperse four hundred students determined to defend our school. The invasion of "locusts" (they kinda look like hornets) never came. A potential riot was rebuffed. But, the Highland protest still hung in the air like a thunderhead gathering for a storm. We practiced Monday not knowing if we were going to play Roswell for the State Championships the next weekend, or not.

U.G. "Monty" Montgomery, executive secretary of the New Mexico Officials Association, as well as executive secretary of the New Mexico High School Activities Association, ruled that the decision made by head linesman, Richard Van Fleet, who was from Los Alamos, would stand. "There is no provision in the NMHSAA for an appeal of the field judges' official account on penetrations," Monty said. Van Fleet would not make any public comment on the matter but a newspaper account indicated that the head linesman had a tape on his pants with two headings; AHS and HHS. The A and the H could have appeared similar and Van Fleet simply marked one penetration under AHS when it should have been awarded to HHS. Someone reported that the wetness and mud blurred the tape. The mystery was solved, but the turmoil, like a witch's brew, continued to stew.

Imagine, for a moment, that this situation occurred in the year 2000. Parents, rather than the players and the students, probably would have led the angry mob. Influential supporters of the Highland cause probably would have filed a lawsuit. School officials and the Public School administration probably would have been cowered and intimidated. A judge would probably have ruled that the NMHSAA didn't have final jurisdiction and would issue an injunction preventing the championship game from proceeding between AHS and Roswell. Possibly, sometime around Christmas, a month later, AHS and HHS would replay the game. Times would change.

An error was made, for certain, but who can say, knowing that we were down in penetrations, that we wouldn't have scored again? We played the entire fourth quarter "defensively." Highland's error was that Coach Hackett or the team captain didn't ask the head linesman where they stood. The time to protest was <u>during</u> the game, not after, or to play to win the remainder of the game, if Van Fleet wouldn't reverse his decision. One thing was clear on Tuesday. AHS was on its way for a re-match with the Roswell Coyotes for the State Championship.

Adding more irony to the situation, the 1954 game between the two rivals also ended in a tie, 7 to 7. This time, however, the officials took extreme care in marking the penetrations and Hugh Hackett personally made certain that Highland was ahead in penetrations. The Hornets were declared the victors and fittingly beat the Artesia Bulldogs 20-0 for the State Championship. At last, Hugh Hackett's turkey dinner (the AHS-HHS game was played on Thanksgiving) didn't taste like sawdust. In another ironic twist, within five years I would become one of Hackett's heros instead of his nemesis.

One of the stars of the 1954 game and the entire season was Highland's running back, Dewey Bohling. Attesting to Dewey's versatility, he not only was a sprinter and a miler, he threw the discus 179' setting a new state high school record. We saw each other in future years at track meets while Dewey attended Hardin Simmons University. Dewey was drafted by the Pittsburgh Steelers of the NFL and also played for the Buffalo Bills and the New York Titans. He was one of Albuquerque's greatest athletes despite the fact that he was a Hornet.

I won back my girlfriend but lost my trusted receiver. Jack injured his right knee in practice and it required surgery. Glo and I made up for the umpteenth time and she and the Drill Squad would be going to Roswell. We were four touchdown underdogs. After all, we had just lost to the Coyotes by that margin a month prior. But, there was an aura of upset in the air.

The day before the game in Roswell many of our team strolled the downtown area in our green and white letter jackets and sweaters. We were an instant target of local ridicule such as:

"You guys shouldn't even be here."

"Yer gonna lose by six touchdowns this time."

And, even more pointed remarks.

A group of us including Lanny Dally, Bob Schnurr (who looked like my twin brother), Mike Saul, Benny Gutierrez as well as Jimmy, Ralph and I holed up at an ice cream shop on the town square. Holding court was our play by play sportscaster, Frank Joyce, who did most of our games. Amidst all the game talk the topic turned to the "Roswell Incident." The now famous purported crash of the alien spaceship north of town in 1947—just six years prior.

Frank worked for radio station KGFL in Roswell at the time that the incredible event occurred. He followed one of the greatest stories of his long news career with keen interest. He mesmerized us recounting that there were four little grey men with large eyes that were taken from the crash scene to the Roswell Air Force Base Hospital for examination. Scanning the room suspiciously, he whispered to us that the Air Force story of the weather balloon was a ridiculous ruse. To this day, I've always been fascinated by the story. I got the feeling that Frank was "encouraged" to leave Roswell. Maybe he knew too much.

On November 22, 2002, months after I wrote the story above, a special TV program entitled, "Startling New Evidence on the Roswell Incident" hosted by well-known personality Bryant Gumbel, revealed for the first time a new "smoking gun" of the spaceship crash near Roswell, in July 1947.

One of the persons interviewed was my old friend, Frank Joyce. Happy to see him alive and well at the ripe old age of 80, I called him to revisit his revelation to us.

"Holy cow! You remembered that?" Frank marveled.

"How could I forget it Frank. I don't know about the other guys but your story intrigued me. Rumor had it that you were fired from your job at the radio station because you knew too much. Was that true?" I asked.

"Hell, that wasn't half the story..."

"What's the other half," I countered, cutting Frank off in mid-sentence.

"After I went out to Brazo's ranch and saw the crash site first hand and saw how frightened Brazo was and talked to a few people, I found out as much as I could. Before you know it, Sheriff Wilcox comes into the station, slaps some handcuffs on me, and in no time I'm on my way to the Veteran's Hospital in Waco, Texas. Hell, they threw me into the "psycho" ward and had the acting head of the hospital, this shrink, trying to convince me that I was nuts!"

"Holy smokes! They must have thought you were 'dangerous'," I reasoned.

"Hell, I think they even tried to poison me. I wouldn't eat my dessert 'cause it smelled funny. The poor guy next to me ate it and he died."

"Good Lord Frank! I guess when the government thinks you're a threat to their secret, you either die, disappear or become damaged goods!" I theorized.

"Yes. I'm fortunate to have survived, got that job at KOB and raised a family," Frank concluded.

The U.S. Air Force initially acknowledged that a UFO had crashed but quickly changed the story on orders from a very high source and fabricated an official account of a weather balloon that had fallen to earth in the New Mexico desert. There is a well-recognized photograph of General Ramey pointing to the flimsy remnants of the balloon that convinced a dubious public that the official account of the incident was not a spaceship. In the General's hand is a piece of paper, undeciphered—until now.

David Rudiak, a computer technician using state of the art equipment, has been able to isolate key words and phrases from the memo in Ramey's hand dated July 18, 1947, such as "disc" and "victims of the wreck" and other information indicating that there indeed was a UFO crash and there were in fact, bodies recovered from the craft. Another Air Force officer, who was involved in the covert cover-up, Colonel Dubose, has admitted that the weather balloon story was a fraud. Numerous other military personnel like Moe Cox who aided in the transport of the aliens and the spacecraft to Ft. Worth, Texas, have now come forward to reveal the true facts.

The newly elected governor of New Mexico, Bill Richardson, who served in the Clinton administration as Energy Secretary, was also interviewed on the two hour program and called for a complete investigation of the Roswell Incident. John Podesta, who was also a high-ranking official in the same administration, demanded on the tape that the U.S. Government release all of the data, heretofore zealously guarded, concerning the incident including photographs and autopsies of the aliens, if they exist.

This incident, though relegated to a lone page in this memoir, could be the most significant "defining moment" in world history. The discovery that we're not alone in the universe should be the most fascinating and thought-provoking revelation in the history of mankind yet it escapes its significance to most of our species. Only an alien (ET) interview with Larry King on CNN will seemingly convince the public that there's another world out there and in the whole scheme of things a war with Iraq, or a collapse of the stock market or the need to revamp social security is considerably less relevant.

It didn't go unnoticed to this writer or probably to the producers of this TV program, that November 22, was the date chosen for "Roswell" to be released. The date of the assassination of John F. Kennedy—another U.S. Government cover-up on a scale equal in its hubris and effrontery to the American public.

In the cramped locker room before the game Coach McDavid raised the expectations of his team. "They will be overconfident," he reminded us over and over. He also used the old cliche, "They put their pants on just like you do...one leg at a time."

Sitting on the locker room bench I stretched both of my legs out in front of me and preceded to pull the pants of my uniform on both legs at one time. Ralph, witnessing my contrarian approach to dressing, did the same thing. Several of the players snickered. Then everyone laughed. Then everyone put their pants on two legs at a time. It broke the tension. We were loose. We were ready. A telegram from Chuck Hill, an AHS icon, (of which I have a copy) said, "Play inspired football Bulldogs. The City is behind you."

We won the toss of the coin and Coach McDavid told me to tell the officials that we wanted to kick off. That was strange. Almost every team would choose to receive the ball at the opening of a game—particularly a "Big Game." But, Pete had a bold, surprise plan.

Bill Easley squibbed an on-side kick through the unsuspecting Coyotes. Playing left end I picked up the loose ball and carried it down to Roswell's 36 yard line. The bi-partisan fans and the Coyotes, to a man, were shocked! They should have gotten the message right then and there. This wasn't going to be a cakewalk. With Dale Galaher and I carrying the ball I punched it in for a score. Only two minutes had elapsed. Unfortunately, Velma missed the extra point. 6-0. The "underdawgs" were on the board. The Coyote faithful sat in stunned silence as if one of those grey alien creatures had landed on the 50 yard line.

Lloyd Taylor, Roswell's star halfback, was acclaimed "as the finest running back in the state." He had gained 1800 yards in ten games and scored 138 points. Roswell, recovering from the shock of being behind, drove 65 yards to our 20 yard line. Jack Doran hit Taylor with a pass and the versatile back not only scored, he kicked the extra point. We were down 7 to 6.

In the second quarter, Taylor broke loose and scored on a 46 yard gallop, and it looked like we were going to be victims of a track meet with Taylor sprinting all over the field.

Resilient, we grinded out a 56 yard march of our own with Dale Galaher and Charlie Salazar making short gains. Not risking a hand off, I attempted to sneak over for the score.

Like a pack of their namesakes, the Coyotes scratched and clawed at the ball to force a fumble as I tried to fight my way into the end zone. With my head down someone's fist hit me smack in the mouth. (No face mask of course.) Angry and spitting blood, I forced my way into the end zone. As it had plagued us all season, Velma again failed to convert. The half ended 14 to 12.

Inspired by the defensive line play of Joe Harris, Benny Gutierrez, Gene Fox, Jerry Billings and Tom Nethery, we stymied Taylor and Sherman Pruitt in the third quarter. We held them to only 34 yards. The 5000 "natives" in the stands were getting restless. The four TD favorites were being out-played by a decimated team that didn't deserve to be there. Then, we gave the hometown fans something to really worry about.

I hit Bill Mann, ably substituting for Jack at right end, for a couple short passes. Dale Galaher, Charlie Salazar and Bob Stewart filling in for Ralph who was hurting, moved the ball to Roswell's one yard line. Stewart rammed it in and Velma made the extra point and the Dawgs were ahead 19-14. Mom and Dad and my Artesia family were thrilled. Our small contingent of fans who made the 200 mile trip whooped it up to the dismay of the locals who were cata-tonic. Jack, in his hospital bed listening to Frank Joyce's play by play, was more nervous than he would have been sit-ting on the sideline. We could feel it. The fans sensed it. An upset of gigantic proportions was in the making.

Time and time again, in the fourth quarter, we stopped the vaunted Coyote attack. Jack Doran punted out of bounds once at our one yard line and again at our three. Playing in the shadow of our own goal posts, Coach told me to keep it on the ground. We played conservatively. As the game was winding down I punted and the ball was downed on Roswell's 43 yard line. The heavily favored Coyotes faced a do or die situation. They would have to score on this pos-session or lose the game. They moved the ball to our 43.

Taylor picked up five yards on two carries. The newspaper account implies that it was third down and two yards to go for the first down. Our recollection is that it was fourth down and two to go. Doran handed off to his big, bruising fullback, Sherman Pruitt, and he smashed into the line. Our defense, steeled with Bulldog-like determination, met Pruitt head on. He didn't make it! We held the Coyotes on downs. We could now run out the clock. AHS, the team that virtually no one gave any chance to win, would be 1953 State Champions. But wait!

A referee threw a late flag! He said Tom Nethery had "piled on." It was an outrageous call. A 15 yard penalty gave Roswell a first down and new life. Our opponents worked the ball down to our 11 yard line. Time was running out.

I was playing left defensive end. I sensed that the defining moment had arrived. Jack Doran took the ball from center and rolled out to my side as if to run. It was the same play that they had scored on in the first quarter. It wasn't a run. I recognized the throwback pass play. I yelled:

"Pass!"

I threw one blocker aside and made a mad rush for Doran as he stopped and planted his right foot to throw back to the opposite side of the field. I was inches from his arm as he released the long cross field pass to his intended receiver. Jimmy Harris, who over-rotated in his zeal to assist against the run, didn't see Ken Wright who slipped behind him and was all alone in the end zone. The Coyotes scored! We were crestfallen. With only a minute remaining my attempt at a long "hail Mary" pass was intercepted. We couldn't muster a threat. Our once-in-a-lifetime chance at glory slipped from our grasp. Exhausted and disconsolate we drug ourselves into the miniature locker room.

Coach McDavid was in tears as he told us what an incredible effort we made and how proud he was of this team. He told us to keep our heads up and don't get our "Dobbers" down. We could leave DeBremond Stadium with pride. All that was true, of course, but coming close only counts in dancing and horse shoes, as the well-worn saying goes.

There is another saying in the sports world—statistics are for losers. Maybe losers seek solace in the numbers to validate their near victory, but in this case they are remarkable not so much in the total but for those who were responsible for the "Stats."

Ralph, hampered by an injury to the same hip pointer, had zero yards rushing in four attempts. Dale Galaher and I carried the ball for fifty and fifty-one yards respectively while Charlie Salazar added thirty-one and George Hutchinson twenty-four as we rushed for a total of 199 yards to Roswell's 216 despite Lloyd Taylor's 135 yards. Jack Doran and I were just about even in the passing game. What was remarkable, of course, was that the Bulldogs matched the vaunted offense of the Coyotes with Ralph, H.B. and Jack on the sidelines and I was the only starter in the backfield. Our underrated defense, which held the potent Roswell attack to it lowest output of the year, deserved rave reviews.

Glo was there to console me after the game. I couldn't kiss her with my swollen and cracked lip and blood stained teeth. She and I had arranged to ride home in my parents' car after the game.

Looking back in 1960, after all of our college athletic days were concluded, our performance in the title game was even more remarkable. Lloyd Taylor went on to become an All-American running back at Texas A&M. Sherman Pruitt became a star performer at the University of Colorado and Jack Doran, the Coyote quarterback, also played in college. Numerous other Roswell players played college football with varying degrees of success. The 1953 Roswell Coyotes did have, indeed, college material.

In contrast, for almost all of our AHS senior team members, their high school football experience and the All-Star Game would be their last hurrah. H.B.'s knee injury prevented him pursuing an athletic scholarship at the University of Texas. Jack's second knee surgery prior to the North-South All-Star game made it impossible for him to compete in interscholastic sports. Kansas University aggressively recruited Ralph but his grades were woefully inadequate for the Big Eight Conference. After one short year at Ft. Lewis Junior College, Ralph never played football again. Jimmy played for a brief time at the University of New Mexico but did not continue past his sophomore year. Velma, who didn't attend college, got a try-out with the Dallas Cowboys but unfortunately didn't make the team in their first year. Jack, Velma, Jim, Kent Bennett, Joe Harris and I made the North All-Star Squad.

What happened to me? That's part of another story. But, for someone who was only selected for the All-City second team on offense and was recognized solely for honorable mention on the All-State team, college, athletically, was an unexpected surprise. In fact, as a high school senior, I was not heavily recruited. To the major schools, I was probably considered a good all-around high school athlete but didn't have any specific skills to excel at the college level. Fortunately, that perception was wrong.

Yes, given, the level of the talent on our Bulldog team, our inspirational effort in the championship game was truly remarkable. Moral victories can put a spring in your step.

Interviewing Coach Rushing as the final seconds ticked down slowly marking the end of his life devoted to teaching and inspiring kids like me, he said, reflecting on the past:

"The 1950s were the 'golden era' of coaching. You kids did everything you possibly could to do what we taught you. You didn't bitch or create a problem. You just did it. Ten years later, it wasn't any fun for me anymore."

To lighten up our last meeting together, I said:
"Except when you told me to 'stop trying to strike out everyone'."
We laughed our last laugh together.

Jack's wife, Theda, who met Jack when they were school kids in Oklahoma, paid me one of the best and most meaningful compliments that I've ever received.

"Buster, you had more presence than any boy that we ever knew. You immediately commanded attention the moment you walked into a room...and still do. We admired you so much and we wanted you to know that."

Thanks to Pete, Jack, Tony, George and others, I did have "a spring in my step." It was visible to those who cared. Those who helped me find it.

"I can't practice basketball for another month, at best," Jack said to me as we sat in the "A" Club meeting room above the gym floor. Jack's surgery had left a large scar on his right knee and rehab took several months. Today, players have their knees "scoped" and are back in action within weeks—and, no scars.

"I wasn't going to go out for BB, Jack, but I've got a good chance to get a letter and end up my senior year with five. P. G. Cornish is the only athlete who has done that at AHS...at least in modern times," I relayed to my friend who was stretching his leg. "And, Coach Caton said I should play so..."

"Five? How will you get five letters?" he asked.

"Football, basketball, skiing, baseball and track," I offered in response.

"S.... You're not going to Sun Valley again, are you?"

"Nope. But, I can qualify for the team and get my letter," I replied.

"Well, there's no question that Heinsohn could use you. I think he's still pissed at you, though, for skiing," Jack added.

"Yeah, but with H.B. out too, Coach is shorthanded. Plus, with my contacts I can see so much better. I'm going to give it a shot." And, with that I went to the locker room to change for my first practice.

We lost our first warm up game to the alumni by two points as Dick Trott and Tom Curley came back to extract some revenge on Coach Heinsohn. We then beat one of the smallest schools, Estancia 53-44, but six straight losses would follow. Coach asked H.B. to come to his office for a private meeting. "H" was mystified. He certainly wasn't able to play. Why did he want to talk to him?

"H.B.? You've got a lot of savvy. The guys look up to you. I've got to ask you something?" Coach said as he shut the door to his office.

"Sure Coach, what's up?" H.B. asked.

"Tell me, what do you think I'm doing wrong? I mean, I'm frustrated. We're losing to teams that we shouldn't lose to. I don't know what to do," Coach said as he obviously was searching for an answer.

"Hell Coach, I don't know. Most of the guys say that all the plays and stuff are too complicated. They're thinkin' instead of playin'," H.B. said in his direct, no nonsense manner.

"Hmmn, that's interesting. Do the kids dislike me?" Coach Heinsohn asked somewhat reluctantly.

"Hell no, Coach. The guys all like you. That ain't the issue. Hell, I couldn't shoot with my left hand like you wanted me to but that didn't make me dislike you," H.B. added.

"Thanks H.B. I appreciate your comments," Coach Heinsohn said as he left to conduct practice.

I got sporadic playing time at center behind Mike Padilla, my ex-teammate from "La Wash." Jack didn't return until January.

We went to Hobbs to play the Eagles, who later would have one of the most successful high school basketball programs, under Ralph Tasker, in the nation. Hobbs had Ron Wilder at center who wasn't tall but weighed 185 pounds, was first team end All-State in football and was a rugged guy. He dominated the area under the basket. He was grabbing rebounds and scoring with ease. No one could stop him. I got the call.

"Buster, Wilder's killing us inside. Your job is to keep him off the boards and cover him like a blanket." Coach, giving me my instructions, sent me into the game.

I was several inches taller than Ron but we weighed the same. We battled 'mano y mano' the remainder of the game, banging each other pretty good. I shut him down but the game was lost in the first half. We lost by twenty points. Walking off the floor after the game, Coach put his arm on my shoulder and said:

"Great job Buster. You really fought that Wilder kid. You did exactly what we needed." It was the first time I had ever received a compliment from Coach Heinsohn. I guess I should have thanked him and left it at that but I responded:

"I could be doing that in every game, Coach," obviously referring to my lack of playing time. I didn't say it in a disrespectful or mean manner and wasn't trying to be a wise-ass. I simply thought that I had enough game to play. Coach took it the wrong way. I moved to the end of the bench. My chance for a letter was slim and none. Time to head for the mountains, again, for the third year in a row.

The basketball season ended horribly for my close

friends Jack, Mike Padilla, Lee Daily, Bob Fink, Allan McNamee, Eddie Geis, Eugene Agnes, Roger Montoya, Billy Barela, Sam Gardipe, Ambrio Villareal, and George Harris. The Bulldogs won only four games and lost nineteen. I discovered that there was only one thing worse than playing on a losing team. It was sitting on the bench and not playing on a losing team.

Remarkably, Coach Heinsohn was selected as an assistant coach for the North-South All-Star game in August. The 'bio' in the program said:

"...Albuquerque High hired him [Coach Heinsohn] the past three seasons during which he got the most out of the material at hand and despite a series of injuries to key players and some <u>disciplinary suspensions</u>."

Basically, the message for publication was that our team had no talent and I (and others) were problem children.

Ironically, it was Coach Heinsohn who was fired the summer of 1954 for "disciplinary reasons" coupled with his unsuccessful coaching record. But, what followed was more instructive and the primary reason for telling this story.

The next season, George Foehr, who had filled in for Jack Rushing the summer before and led our team to the State Baseball American Legion Championship, became the new Head Basketball Coach. His 1954-55 team lost their first five games then went on to win thirteen in a row and a trip to the State Championship. Remarkably, a coach with very little basketball experience and with arguably a talent pool at least equal to our last season, Coach Foehr turned the AHS program around in one year. Coach Foehr's assistant was Jim Hulsman, an AHS grad, who became head coach in 1968.

Jim's 49-year tenure at AHS, which has become legendary, began as my Assistant Track Coach in 1954! In Jim's 34 years as head basketball coach (retiring in 2002) his teams won 660 games and lost only 223—a 75% winning percentage. They also won 13 District Titles, and seven State Championships and Jim, deservedly, was New Mexico HSAA Coach of the Year five times.

More significantly, perhaps, Jim brought discipline and pride to a program in the late 1960s when young people in

*America were trashing traditions and institutions. Jack Rush-
ing was quoted earlier as saying "Coaching wasn't fun anymore," in that era. Jim persisted and has received more accolades than space allows. Geez, it would have been great to
play for this guy.*

The senior class of 1950 donated a statue of a Bulldog,
which was prominently and proudly displayed on a pedestal
near the Administration Building in the patio of our campus.
Our permanent mascot had suddenly and suspiciously disappeared in the spring of 1953. The statue was bolted down
and probably weighed several hundred pounds. The mystery,
of course, was who stole our namesake? Rumor was that the
Highland "fairies" had lifted the statue. Another arrow loaded
into the quiver of revenge against our hated rivals.

Jack, H.B. and Jimmy joined Coach Tony Valdez on a
deer hunting trip near the fabled town of Cimarron, New
Mexico, where Tony was born. (An area as legend goes fre-
quented by Billy the Kid and other desperados). For some
reason I didn't make this trip which confirms my innocence
in this sordid caper.

Several days of climbing the rugged mountains produced
no bounty. With Tony returning to Cimarron and, as
sunlight was about to be extinguished, a buck ran directly in
front of Jack's jeep on the drive to Albuquerque. One shot
from the moving vehicle felled the unfortunate critter. Faced
with the prospect of encountering a game warden with their
illegal kill, the three miscreants loaded the animal into the
jeep and headed for Albuquerque. Their deception, despite
the foul odor permeating through the jeep, was successful.
But, it was mandatory to gut and clean the buck immediately. Jack, trying his hand at creative writing says:

> We hung the buck up in H.B.'s garage and set about
> to gut and clean the carcass. The first cut of the knife
> produced an explosive blast and the inspiration of things
> to come.

I thought that the smells and sights were so repug-
nant that their rightful home could only be Highland
High, and deservedly so. H.B. recalls that the guts were
laid (symbolically) at our rival's doorstep. I thought that

288

they were dumped in the principal's office. No matter, the Bulldog appeared to have its revenge for being abducted from his pedestal. At first we three musketeers viewed the caper as a crime of sorts, and with mixed emotions scanned the morning papers (beginning of course with the headlines). When no news appeared the mood shifted from disappointment to deep understanding. We ultimately concluded that the atmosphere up there was so putrid that no one even noticed what was in effect more of the same. The question thus remains to this day. Did our beloved mascot, which was indeed returned to its rightful place in January 1954, receive true justice?

In the spirit of truth and fairness it must be revealed that the HHS Hornets were not responsible for stealing our Bulldog! Harry Moskos, who was co-editor of *The Record*, recalls an article written in the school newspaper by Charlie O'Bannon '52, in 1954 entitled "I Stole the Bulldog" where the writer admits that he swiped our beloved mascot! (And, returned it.)

"Why would one of our own guys steal the Bulldog?" I asked my friend who was one of those kids that successfully bridged the gap between the Nerds and the Rah-Rahs.

"Charlie didn't like the 'jocks.' I think he knew Highland would get blamed for stealing it and he could really add fuel to the fire," Harry responded adding: "You know there were lots of kids that resented the athletes, but I really got along well with the coaches and the jocks."

Without question, there were many students who didn't buy into the holy trinity that was the central religion of the Rah-Rahs. Charlie, I learned from Janet Barnes, was also the culprit who attached the "nipples" to our mascot. Charlie was born too soon. In 2000, during a class of '52 reunion, O'Bannon and some cohorts repeated the nipples prank on the statue at the "new" Albuquerque High School. Thirty years after graduation he could have helped Bill Gates launch Microsoft from Albuquerque. Gates was here but couldn't recruit enough nerds and capital and he left for Seattle. True story.

About the same time period, Jack, Glo, myself and others who attended Boys and Girls State, were relating their experience of the past summer to an assembly of all the students. Dick Wilson, who was the first person I had met at La Wash four years prior, was the Master of Ceremonies. Our image as model students was not sullied by the "guts to the fairies" caper.

"Next Monday, your practice teacher will be here from UNM," Mr. Graham announced to our art class. What he said next was a big surprise. "Your teacher will be Joan Quist."

There was a buzz in the class. Everyone looked at me.

"My sister? My sister is coming to AHS? In my class?" I asked, still not believing the incredible turn of events. Yep, my sister was going to be my teacher.

Mr. Graham's art class was a blast. I vividly remember our room with all its artsy stuff plastered all over the walls and my friends Lee Daily and Jo Hankins. Odd as it may seem, I was a serious art student even though Mr. Graham was probably the most "fun" teacher at AHS.

More than 1250 entries and 2000 pieces were judged in the annual Scholastic Arts Awards Contest held in El Paso. Jo received five gold keys, Lee received three and Barbara Wilber, Gene Chavez and I one gold key each. Our paintings were later exhibited in the National Scholastic Art Show in Pittsburgh. I received a $200 scholarship to the Chicago Art Institute which I considered an honor, but athletics were my focus and interest.

I also served on the *Yucca* staff (our school literary magazine) with Jo, Lee, Alan Vermillion and Harvey Jean Peterson. Alan and Harvey Jean were Co-Editors. Lee and I were the Art Editors. I wasn't into writing then but there's little doubt that our sponsors, Mr. Lacour and Mr. Graham, were influential in opening a door of opportunity and enjoyment for me later in my life. One thing was certain. My parents had little concern that I would get into trouble. I had no time to.

Trouble was loosely defined as cutting classes, chewing gum in class, smoking, hanging out with the "wrong" crowd or, heaven forbid, drinking beer. Cheating on a test meant immediately being expelled from school. The biggest trouble any of us boys could face was getting our girlfriends pregnant (we called it PG). To the girls getting PG was not only a big emotional and logistical problem it also meant being expelled from school. And, worse, getting a "rep" (reputation) for doing "It" or sleeping around meant social disgrace. There were good girls and bad girls. Doing "It" with more than one guy made the transgressor a "bad girl." Our parents told us over and over again, "If you get a girl pregnant it will ruin your life." The Sword of Damocles hung over our heads on every date. Boy howdy, would that change by the Sixties.

Harry Moskos, who knew exactly what he wanted to do when only in junior high school, worked for the *Albuquerque Tribune* while he was at AHS. Exhibiting both inside political prowess and journalistic skills early in life, he was successful in securing first page space for our Bulldog Day Queen, Donna Standifer and her attendants Jo Hankins and Jay Twilley. Harry, who would become, at age 26, the youngest Associated Press Bureau Chief in the United States, had several newsworthy stories to tell.

Sitting adjacent to Harry in his senior English class was an Hispanic kid who came to school almost every day in a suit and tie (which was quite unusual in 1954 for any student). Harry was impressed by his maturity and presence and they often exchanged their thoughts on their future dreams and ambitions.

"One day," Harry's friend said, "I'm going to set you up with your very own newspaper. You 'betcha.' You're going to be a famous newspaperman."

Harry relished the thought of owning his own paper, but how could his friend do that? Where would he get the money to buy a newspaper? His friend was so positive and reassuring and he appeared affluent.

Not long after this conversation took place, Harry was at work at the *Tribune* and reading the edition that had not yet hit the street when his eyes fixed on a headline:

"High Schooler Wounded in Undercover Drug Bust."

Harry's dreams of becoming a young entrepreneur newspaperman went down with the drug bust. What is remarkable about the story is that the term "drugs" only meant a prescription to us kids at the time. Was it Marijuana? Co-

291

caine? Heroin? Don't know. Drugs were as foreign to us as a trip to Europe, but I suspect that drugs were a part of the sub-culture then. But, like homosexuality, adultery, abortion, racial discrimination and other social taboos they were purposely shuffled under the rug and not topics for discussion. As young adults, we lived in an age of innocence. Our parents knowing these conditions existed were into denial. To a few, we lived in an age of hypocrisy. To most, it was "The Golden Era."

In the good old days, despite occasional fights between various gangs and social groups off campus, security at school was not a concern. The person in charge of security at AHS was a diminutive, middle-aged man by the name of Victor Juarez, who was the head janitor. His weapon of choice was a scissors. Victor believed, as everyone in the administration did, that kids should be clean cut. That meant no long hair! His favorite target? Pachucos and others with "duck tails." Violators had their choice. Get their hair cut or Victor would do it.

Harry recently chronicled this remembrance in the *Albuquerque Journal* under the heading,
"Our Kids Won't Believe Us."

One of Harry's most memorable experiences came when he decided to try his craft as a thespian. Stan Rarick, one of our most remembered and loved teachers and the drama instructor, had Harry audition for a minor role as a policeman in the play *Craig's Wife.*

Harry diligently rehearsed his fourteen words preparing for his first audition. Mr. Rarick must have been favorably impressed. Harry not only secured a part he got the role of the male lead, Mr. Craig! Fortunately or unfortunately, Harry pursued a career in journalism and had the good fortune to be the only print journalist at work at Midway Island on Christmas Eve in 1968 when the USS Pueblo crew was released by the North Koreans. It was a scoop of a lifetime.

Now at the age of 80, Stan Rarick was one of the few teachers from the "Golden Era" still available for a live interview. His recollections of the Fifties are enlightening:

"I came to AHS in 1948. I felt very fortunate that Mr. Milne hired me. Teaching at AHS was the best opportunity available. I taught History and Drama and my classroom was in the basement. I taught at AHS until 1961 when I became Principal at Ernie Pyle Junior High School for six years and then served as Assistant Superintendent of the Northern District of APS for several years until I retired in 1985."

"What do you recall most about the Fifties?" I asked Stan, who often wore colorful suspenders ala Larry King;

"I was awed by the institution. Not only the size and grandeur of the school but AHS was a 'different place.' Mr. Ream was a marvelous man. He supported any activity any of us teachers wanted to provide to our students. I wanted to introduce the kids to real drama and Mr. Ream never denied any request to buy materials that I needed to stage the plays. Some of my most outstanding students were those who built the sets. Jackie Barnes was an excellent actress in her teens. Mary Ann Hartline was one of my brightest students. I had so many good kids. I wish I could remember them all."

"AHS certainly had a number of incredible teachers like Doc Harrington, May Klicker and others and their classes seemed to have all the best students. I remember that I couldn't get into Mr. Slocum's math class with Jack Stromberg and algebra in college was very difficult for me," I offered:

"Well, there was a 'caste system' at AHS. The good teachers did get the brightest students. It was not a defined system per se but we all knew how it worked," Stan relayed to me.

Earlier in this book I opined that the mid-Fifties marked the beginning of a major societal change in America and that perhaps nowhere was it more apparent than in the schools. "Do you remember the film *Black Board Jungle?*"

"Oh yes. All of us (teachers) did," Stan remarked adamantly.

"What did you see happening in the schools in the late Fifties and Sixties?"

"Disciplinary problems. You know, when Mr. Ream was here we didn't have those problems. He ran a real tight ship. I think the Pachucos for one became a major problem. Mr. Ream and I were very close friends and in the Sixties and

Seventies, I would drive him all around the state. He would tell me the history of virtually every place we visited, but he constantly was grieving at the decline in our schools. We both could feel the change but we couldn't do anything about it. Your comment about what Mr. Ream said about his 'era was over' and the transfer of power from the administration, the teachers and the coaches to the students and the parents is quite remarkable," the popular teacher concluded.

Yes, 1954 was a pivotal year. When someone writes the history of AHS from 1954 to 2004 the perspective may be totally different. One thing is certain. There will be much more drama in the new era.

Hands down, the most interesting subject to me, was Dr. Harrington's physics class. Dr. Harrington, with his lazy right eye lid, looked the part of the absent-minded professor, but had the ability to make the abstract comprehensible and enjoyable.

Arthur (Burl) Humble was very close to Doc. He learned how his teacher acquired the lazy eye lid;

Doc was raised on a farm in Kansas near the turn of the century. The cattle ranchers were at war with the farmers who were to them "sodbusters" who destroyed range land. One day a group of ranchers raided the farm. Doc's mom, fearful for her son's safety, tossed him frantically into his bed. Unfortunately, a pin was in the bedding and it lodged in the young boy's eye. The accident left is mark but it did little to deter this man from his genius.

During his "dawn patrol" which met at 6:00 a.m. (or earlier) he would conduct some of his experiments. One was memorable.

Early one morning before any of the other students were awake much less at school we stood on the roof of the Main Building three stories above the ground. We had a twelve pound steel shot put, a baseball and a steel marble. Half of the class was below us on the grass lawn. The question to resolve was, dropped at the same time, which object would reach the ground first. Logic said, of course, that the heavier mass of the shot put would fall the fastest.

By then, however, the class was wise to Dr. Harrington. We knew that he was into defying logic and dispelling conventional thinking. We guessed correctly. We all learned that all three objects fell at the identical speed— 32'/second/second, if my memory is correct. A good example how impressionable and how enjoyable our education was at AHS. Unfortunately this year 1954 was Dr. Harrington's last at AHS. A 1920 graduate and a teacher for 30 years, he was a Bulldog forever.

The so called "minor sports" produced some great athletes who went on to achieve national acclaim. Clarence Bass is one of the most notable.

Gordy Modrall set a State record in the Pentathlon the prior year and received his trophy during a Student Assembly. Clarence Bass, then a sophomore, was moved by the adulation Gordy received from the student body. That moment, Clarence said, "Set the pattern for my whole life. I wanted to be the Pentathlon Champion the next year." Setting goals and achieving them became Clarence's mantra. He won the State Championship in 1954 and broke his mentor's record. He still continues to win championships.

There's another interesting and instructional aspect to Clarence's story. He began lifting weights at the age of 13. Tony Valdez, like all coaches in that era, told him not to lift weights because "you'll become too muscle-bound." Today, athletes in all sports including women golfers "pump iron" as a necessary component to their workout regime. Clarence, who has had a measured body fat as low as 3% in his Fifties, was truly ahead of his time. Readers of all ages should view Clarence at www.cbass.com. It's never too late to shape up.

No information in *La Reata* accompanies the picture of the 1954 Wrestling Team, and Coach Rushing missed the photo shoot so there isn't much to record for posterity in "Bulldogs Forever," other than the individuals that I can recall. Bill Sandlin, Kerby Landis, Merrill Rogers, Joe Schupla, Bob Stewart, Ray Johnson, and Bob Lucas were seniors and all good friends who participated on the team which had 40 members.

The swim team suffered an ignominious fate. The team was omitted from *La Reata* altogether. What happened? The minor sports always suffered from lack of recognition and exposure. Within a mere decade however, wrestling, golf, tennis and swimming would take center stage.

Skiing, like track and field was an individual event. You either posted your mark in time or distance or you didn't. There was some subjective involvement in the outcome in particular situations but primarily you either did it or you didn't do it. Skiing also wasn't part of the holy trinity team concept. Winning or losing was up to the individual. I loved the competitive nature of skiing. Risking another injury I wanted to climb another mountain.

John Dendahl and his buddies from Santa Fe came to Albuquerque for one of the last qualifying meets for the New Mexico Ski Team. John bunked at the Lazy Q.

Saturday was practice time for Sunday's race. The officials had concocted a new trail for the downhill. Starting from the top of Foster Murphy the trail wound its way through the trees to an area above tower number five at La Madera. Dropping down out of the trees into a small bowl-like feature, we were challenged to make a sharp, left turn in order to stay on the trail and cross the tow line in order to continue the lower portion of the trail down El Diablo (the devil in Spanish).

We were faced with several major challenges at tower five. One, the trail rose up steeply at the place where it crossed the tow line, and two, skiers, riding the T-bar, could be on the trail at the wrong moment when a racer was attempting to cross their path. The biggest problem, however, was the massive amount of large trees and debris that had been bulldozed and cleared to make the trail and piled directly to the right of the race trail. Normally that wouldn't come into play, as skiers would stop at the tow line and then continue on down El Diablo. A racer, however, would never stop or even slow down appreciably to cross the tow line, lest his speed and momentum would be lost.

I dropped down out of the trees into the small bowl at a high rate of speed. I had trouble staying high and left on the trail. The incline at the tow line was directly ahead. I was too low on the trail. When I hit the tow line I was airborne! The trail went left. I flew straight and into the mountain of debris!

On the fly I hit a large tree lying perpendicular to my

flight—in the stomach! Then my momentum carried me over into a pile of thorn bushes that ripped and scratched my sweater, my hat and my face like long fingernails on the hands of the devil. The impact expelled all the air out of my lungs. I couldn't breathe. Another log crushed my racing goggles and knocked me half unconscious. The right side of my head swelled up like yeast in a baking pan.

John was there in a matter of seconds. Bob Nordhaus, riding the tow, witnessed my crash and responding to my cries for air, came to my rescue. They had to remove their skis to reach me in the log pile. I was a mess—to say the least.

Nothing appeared to be broken—not even my skis. My racing goggles, which were a hardened plastic or rubber and covered a good part of my forehead and temple as well as my eyes, probably saved my eye from serious injury, but the thorns took their toll on my face. I retreated to the lodge to count my lucky stars. There were many. I could still see them.

John drove me home. Mom met us at the back door.

"Buster! Oh, my Lord! What..."

"Buzzard (John's new nickname for me) had a bad spill, Mrs. Quist. I think he should see a doctor," John advised.

Then, in one of the most memorable and confounding confrontations in my life:

"I don't care what you do with him! I don't care...I don't care," Mom shouted as she slammed the kitchen door in our collective face like we were Fuller Brush salesmen.

John was dumbfounded.

"What do you want me to do?" John asked as I tried to determine which pain was the greatest. My injuries or my Mom's anger and rejection.

"Let's go over to see Dr. Andrews. He lives on Guadalupe Trail. He should be at home," I suggested.

John took me to the doctor's house. His son, Bill and I were classmates. He examined me and cleaned up my face.

"You're pretty lucky, Buster," Dr. Andrews said. "I'd lay off the skiing. If you start coughing up blood, call me, okay?"

Mom refused to talk to me. John and I confined ourselves to my room. We fixed our own dinner.

"I'll just take my car up to the run tomorrow, Buster," John said as we got ready to turn off the lights.

"Whataya mean, John? I'm going up tomorrow."

"What? You're going to race?" John said with a look of incredibility on his face. "Your Mom will kill you if you don't first," he added.

"Got to do it, John. It would be chicken not to," I said, bravely trying to convince myself probably more than my buddy.

Stealthily we left the house early before I could encounter Mom and her wrath. Mr. Nordhaus and all my competitors chiming in unison, thought I was crazy to race. I had to admit, El Diablo scared the s... out of me. A confrontation with a devil that had demonstrated its dangerous designs would have that effect on anyone.

As I moved into the starting gate, the demons of El Diablo flashed before my eyes. I thought about my year ahead in track and baseball and my promise to Coach McDavid. I had been lucky. Would my luck run out? Would I be too tentative? I wasn't going to go to Sun Valley anyway. Why in the hell am I doing this? I asked myself.

"Three, two, one..." the starter shouted.

I was off down Foster Murphy. The adrenalin kicked in a mega-dose. Whipping through the trees I tried to erase the demons of destruction. Within thirty seconds I was above the bowl. My wax was better. My speed was faster than the day before as I dropped down towards tower number five. My heart was beating like a tom-tom. I was going too fast for the incline, again! There were skiers on the T-bar. "Oh s...! It's *deja vu* all over again!"

I summoned all the courage I had to sublimate the fear that was blinding me like a white-out. I pre-jumped the lift line, missed the skiers but I was airborne. I was off the trail — but, I avoided the pile of junk! I made it! I was on my way down El Diablo. No one, not even the dastardly demon of destruction, could catch me now.

The rest of El Diablo was a wax race. I was much heavier than my competitors. I remained in a racing crouch all the way to the finish. A great feeling of relief swelled inside my aching stomach as I crossed the finish line.

Mom never asked if I skied Sunday. She did read the following article that appeared in the *Journal* the next day and she added it to the scrapbook:

"QUIST PACES DOWNHILL-SLALOM LA MADERA EVENT."

Buster Quist, who made last year's N.M. Junior Ski Team that competed at Sun Valley, won the downhill-slalom events Sunday at La Madera...others who placed in the combined events Sunday were John Dendahl and John Kinsolving of Santa Fe, Dick Nordhaus, Albuquerque, and Steve Cheney and Herb Wilson, Santa Fe.

I was chosen for the 1954 team but, keeping my word, I declined to participate. John remarked to me, almost fifty years later, regarding that memorable weekend:

"Your Mom couldn't decide how to take you. She didn't know whether to admire you or be completely exasperated with you."

John had it figured out right and there was more of both ahead.

———

The big spring social event was the "A" Club-Pepper Club dance. Glo and I nearly missed another "major." All through high school I had often attended the Sunday evening youth group at St. Paul's Lutheran Church. There I had met Lani Wachernagel, a sophomore, who attended Highland. Since Glo and I were not going steady at that particular moment, I accepted Lani's invite to a dance the evening prior at Highland High. Big mistake.

Lani was gorgeous and gracious but the sports rivalry that had grown in intensity during the past three years was always omnipresent. I was in hostile territory. The hassling and heckling ruined the evening but worst of all, Glo knew all about it the next morning. She was cool and aloof as I picked her up Saturday night.

"Did you have fun last night?" Glo asked as she got into my Mom's new white 1954 Ford station wagon.

"Nope," I replied, wondering how in the heck she knew that I had a date on Friday.

"Why not? I understand that your date is really cute," Glo continued with an air of indignance.

"Lani is neato but the guys really gave me a hard time.

They're still really pissed about the 6-6 tie game. I felt sorry for Lani. We finally had to leave the dance," I elaborated.

"Are you serious about her?" Glo continued.

"Geez, Glo of course not. I met her at church. I've known Lani for a couple of years and this is the first time we've been out," I added.

"Buster (when Glo didn't call me Buz I knew she was upset), first there's Karen who you saw all summer in Wisconsin and spent the night with in L.A., then there's Marilyn Godfrey, and Marnie, that girl in Santa Fe, and Dianne who was only a freshman at Jefferson and now Lani. I think you should play the field. You're really not interested in one girl, are you?"

"Glo, you're my girl. I would never go out with anyone behind your back. When I have a date with someone else, it makes me appreciate you more. It convinces me more that I love you," I responded sincerely.

Surprisingly, for once, I said the right thing. Glo didn't say anything for quite a while. Then, she slid over next to me, and I put my arm around her. Her "glo" had thawed the ice.

As we danced to Doris Day's hit song, *Secret Love*, Glo asked:

"You don't have one, do you?"

"A secret love? Heck no. Besides, how could I keep it a secret from you? You've got spies everywhere!"

"If you take your date to The Castle you're not going to keep it a secret from anyone," Glo added.

We both laughed.

Rosemary Clooney (*This Ole House* and *Hey There*) and Eddie Fisher (*I Need You Now*) were the top pop artists at the moment. Eddie must have been dedicating his song to Elizabeth Taylor as he unceremoniously dumped Debbie Reynolds for Liz.

One of our favorite places to go for a date was the Cactus Drive-In Theater. Drive-ins were referred to as "passion pits" and other unprintable expressions. Everyone will be able to recall those cold winter evenings at the drive-in where the speaker and a heater were attached to the window of the car. It was difficult to see the screen. The windows always fogged up—from the heaters, of course.

The jukebox was the centerpiece of many of our dances at the "Y" and other venues. At a cost of a nickel we could select our favorite song and you could get six for a quarter. At the "A" Club—Pepper Club dance, Homecoming, the Green and White Ball and other major occasions, we danced to the music of a band. We had amongst us a very talented group, the Ortez Trio, led by our classmate Virginia (Ginny) Ortez. The group was popular in Albuquerque in the 50s and went on to gain notoriety on the national scene as recording artists. Reunited, the Ortez Trio, played for our 40th Class Reunion in 1994.

"And, for this next number, I'm going to do something I've wanted to do all my life," Ginny announced to the large number of us then fifty-eight year olds. "I'm going to ask Buster Quist for the next dance."

I was surprised—and delighted. My wife was gracious as she always is.

Ginny, still perky and bouncy as she was at AHS, extended her hand as I joined her on the dance floor to the approval of our classmates who applauded.

"I've always wanted to dance with you, Buz. I've had a 'crush' on you since we were sophomores," Ginny whispered to me.

"Why did you wait so long to tell me, Ginny? I always thought you were a doll."

"I didn't think you'd be interested ... and you were always going steady with Glo," she replied.

As we slow danced Ginny squeezed my hand. Hers was trembling and clammy. When she looked up at me (I was almost a foot taller) she had tears in her eyes. As I kissed her on her check and held her tightly, I sensed that there was something very defining in this moment. There was. Shortly after this emotionally charged instant that spanned so many years, Ginny succumbed to a long battle with cancer. She chose to have one of her last dances with me. A tear comes to my eye and a tightness grabs my throat as I write this line.

———————

"Dad? I don't know what to do. Throw the javelin or

pitch. Both Pete and Coach Rushing really want me on their team."

"Well, why don't we go to school and talk it over with both of them so you can decide what to do," Dad suggested.

So, we did.

Coach Rushing remembered our meeting well, forty-eight years later.

"We would both like to have you play for us," Pete said as we sat in his small office next to the locker room. "Jack and I will work our schedules out so that's not a problem. You've got one heck of an arm, Buster. We don't want you to get hurt or throw it out," Coach McDavid added.

"I'd like to try it," I concluded after considerable discussion.

What was neato was that my coaches had my interest at heart. The decision was mine. Dad agreed.

It didn't take long to discover that throwing javelins and pitching baseballs were a tough combo but I was committed to both. One hard throw of the spear was probably equivalent to pitching a full inning. Most noticeable was the effect on my pitching. I lost considerable zip on my fast ball and I simply wasn't as overpowering and effective as I had been the previous summer.

I was scheduled to pitch a Friday game in Santa Fe against those same Demons that plastered our locker room walls with that note a few months prior, and then throw in a track meet at Ft. Sumner the next day.

The game went well. We had a big lead after five innings and Coach Rushing took me out so I would have some arm left for the next day. John and his sister Karen came to the game. So did Marnie (Margaret Woodward) who had been to a game I pitched against Belen and spent the weekend at the Lazy Q a month prior. Marnie was beautiful but there wasn't a spark that would ignite a fire. Her smoking was a big negative. She was the only girl that I dated that smoked. Glo was on hold.

Dad drove me to Ft. Sumner to join the track team. It was a couple hundred miles from Santa Fe. It gave us ample opportunity to talk. Strangely, Dad had very little to say, except "small stuff." I always wondered what he was thinking about. It took years to find out.

Throwing in a cow pasture, I won the javelin with a mediocre throw of 172'. Bob Schnurr starred and won both the hurdles. Joe Harris set a new Ft. Sumner relays record in the discus and Velma Corley set another in the broad jump. Carlsbad beat us by eight points. That margin would have been eclipsed if Ralph Boan had won the 100 and 200 yard sprints. But, Ralph wasn't there. Ralph was getting married. His girlfriend, only a junior, was pregnant.

The rumor, circulating throughout the church prior to the wedding, was that Ralph's bride-to-be was going to be kidnapped in order to prevent the ceremony that was as untimely as the baby. Ralph's cousin, Dan Bunten, foiled the plot and the child bride and bridegroom were married—for a brief period.

Marriage was the only option. Abortion was unthinkable and unavailable. Society and its conventional code of conduct mandated that the baby's parents be wed. It was obvious that the couple were no longer in love. The bride would have preferred to have been kidnapped. The bridegroom would have preferred to be running on the track for a record but was running from responsibility. My picture of love, marriage and the joy of life was clouded by this experience. I saw what was happening but didn't have the wisdom to understand.

Ralph never graduated from AHS. He moved to Farmington and after one semester at Ft. Lewis College at Durango, Colorado, he sowed his oats in the wrong pasture. He departed Farmington under the cover of night in order to avoid another irate father.

About 14 years later, I received a call from my bud. He was in Albuquerque to see his daughter. I invited Ralph to join me for lunch at the Albuquerque Country Club. He insisted that we talk in the parking lot. His low esteem and self image didn't permit him to enter what he perceived was a world of affluence. We spent those last precious moments together recalling the good times and how we almost won the "big one." Ralph, possessed by the demons of drink, died much too soon. Maybe our parents were right. The admonition, "If you get your girlfriend pregnant it will ruin your life."

resounded in my mind. And, what about Kathleen Parker's theory about "those who consider themselves successful in high school have a spring in their step throughout their lives no matter how dismally they may perform later."

Ralph must not have considered himself a success in high school. To me and the fearsome fivesome, he was.

The last week in April 1954 presented a unique challenge. The District 1A Track and Field Meet would be held on Saturday afternoon and the District Final Championship Baseball game would be played that same evening.

My usual routine was to practice with the baseball team for an hour or so and then walk on over to Public School Stadium and work out with the javelin. Most of the AHS tracksters had already finished their practice when I began throwing the javelin prior to the big weekend. For some reason Dick Wilson was watching me practice. I uncorked a good throw.

"Damn, you really got into that one, Buz," Dick said as he paced off the still visible ten yard lines on the football field.

"How far was it?" I yelled to my friend, who we called Chief.

"It's sixty yards plus ten feet...about 190'," Dick shouted back.

"Geez," I said as I took off down the field anxious to see where the spear had penetrated 'new ground.' "That's my best throw ever, Chief," I said enthused over my breakthrough to a higher level. Seeing Coach McDavid working with Joe Harris at the north end of stadium at the discus area, I yelled.

"Coach, I just hit 190'!"

Coach, with his ever-present clipboard in hand, jogged to the south end of the stadium to inspect my feat.

"Great throw, Buster. I knew it was just a matter of time before you got it out there. You're peaking at just the right time," Coach said with his engaging smile.

Peaking at the right time just prior to the big national meets would, in the years to come, be a trademark. Even though I won my event in the District Track meet handily, my outing in the finals of the baseball tournament that evening was not successful. We lost to Lionel Romero and St. Mary's. Fortunately, however, both teams qualified for the State Tournament at, of all places, Clovis, the next weekend. Would it be *deja vu* all over again? Would Mr. Lanier be the umpire as we would face the host team again as we did the past summer? We went to Clovis with a 14 and 2 record and the favorites to win the title.

Clovis, still proudly practicing its segregation policy, mandated that our team register at the same flea bag motel at the edge of town. Unaffected by the social and political ramifications, our baseball team focused on winning our second State Championship.

Ranked number one in the single elimination tournament, we faced the number eight team, Gadsden-Anthony, a small town near the Mexican border. Coach Rushing, rightfully so, chose Bob Stover to pitch our opening game.

Gadsden's pitcher was a short, wiry, Hispanic kid who probably weighed no more than 130 pounds. He was as unimposing as a fly weight boxer in a ring against a 250 pound heavyweight. His fastball had about as much zip as a fast pitch softball but—man, did he have an assortment of "junk." Curveballs, change ups and sinkerballs. We were a good fastball hitting team but we couldn't hit the slow stuff!

Bob pitched a two-hitter but not only did we not score, we couldn't get runners on base. All of our guys were baffled by the junk. Gilbert De La Cruz, a sophomore who hit over .500 during the season, got our only hit. Sal Gonzales, who was touted as the greatest all-around athlete in the state since Tom McDonald, hit a homer with a man on and we lost 2-0. The game was over in only 55 minutes. Our high expectations were deflated and we failed to repeat the last summer's success.

Bob Stover, our star pitcher and team leader, became high profile professionally in Albuquerque, but not a person anyone would want to confront in the line of business. Bob's strong right arm extended beyond his baseball days to the position of Chief of Police from 1973 to 1980. He then was elected Bernalillo County Sheriff and served from 1982 to 1985 and returned to his position of Chief of the Albuquerque Police Department from 1990 to 1994, when he retired from his career in law enforcement.

In retrospect it was quite apparent that virtually all of our athletic teams in these three years did not measure up to the Bulldog teams of the past. Without much question, the opening of Highland diluted the talent pool, but with the AHS enrollment at 2500 many athletes never had an opportunity to compete at AHS. The next year Valley high School opened and those students in the North Valley, including my brother Terry, matriculated there, further sapping the strength and dominance of the once-mighty Bulldog.

"Jack! Did you see the paper this morning?" I asked as I rushed to see him and H.B., who were sitting in the patio before class with the *Albuquerque Journal* in hand. It was May 5, 1954.

"No...what happened?" Jack inquired struck by my display of enthusiasm.

"An English runner just broke four minutes in the mile," I informed my mates.

"Wow! Who was it?" H.B. asked.

"Some guy named Bannister...Roger Bannister."

"Damn...never heard of him. Boy, that's a milestone...get it? MILE STONE?" Jack said laughing at his own clever play on words.

"Yeah, I get it. What I didn't know was that the previous six world records were held by Swedes," I added.

"Guess that's a big f... deal if you're Swedish," H.B. responded in his typical fashion.

It was a 'big deal.' Psychological barriers were there to be breached in all areas of endeavor. More were to come.

In a remarkable sequel to this historic event, Jack competed on this same track five years later.

My pal Jack was truly "the real deal" after his tenure at AHS. Jack attended Dartmouth College where he graduated *Magma cum laude* and then spent two years at Oxford College in England as a Rhodes Scholar. He received his law degree from Stanford and after a short time in private practice, he became in-house counsel for Bechtel Corporation in San Francisco. He ultimately became President of Bechtel Financial and a member of the company's Board of Directors, which is one of the world's largest construction firms. Jack was one of those rare students that could bridge the divide between the jocks and the nerds.

The New Mexico State Track and Field Championships were held the next weekend at Zimmerman Field. Without the rigors of double duty I felt the strength in my arm returning. On Tuesday before the big week, I again reached a personal best in practice. On my last throw, however, I felt a sharp pain in my upper back and my excitement turned to dismay at the prospect that I had pulled a muscle.

I spent the balance of the week in the training room with Jim Hulsman getting rubdowns, using heatlamps and sitting in the whirlpool trying to relieve the pain in my back. By Saturday, the pain was minimized but my effort was far below expectations. I managed a first place in the javelin with a throw of only 168'3," but my hopes of challenging Ben Garcia's record of 190' was out of reach.

The Bulldogs finished a strong third losing by only 2½ points to second place Carlsbad. Highland was State Champ again with 101 ¼ points. Our other medal winners in 1954 were:

Bob Schnurr	1st	Low Hurdles	20.4
	2nd	High Hurdles	15.3
Ralph Solether	3rd	Low Hurdles	
Joe Harris	4th	Discus	145'
Velma Corley	4th	Broad Jump	21'3"
P. Cruz	5th	Broad Jump	21'½"
Jack Stromberg	4th	High Jump	5'9"
	3rd	880 Run	
Harold Faire	5th	Javelin	146'11½"

In addition our teams placed third in the 440 Relay, fourth in the 880 Relay and second in the Mile Relay.

Given my mediocre performance in the javelin all three years at AHS, few, if any, would have predicted that I would become a two-time NCAA All-American, a member of four U.S. Track and Field Teams and a gold medal winner and record holder in the Pan American Games over the next ten years. And, throwing almost 100' beyond my high school mark. Unfortunately the injury bug bit me at the pinnacle of my long career but that's another story.

According to Grafton Berger, who lettered all three years

as a member of the golf team, "The 1954 Bulldogs had a .500 season in its matches. Nothing exceptional. But we had some good players. Alex Miera, Gilbert Lovato and Vic Giron were our top three golfers and they could shoot in the middle to low 70s. Fred Luthy and I were fourth and fifth on the ladder."

The Hispanic kids were exceptional golfers. Many of them observed and learned the game as caddies at the Albuquerque Country Club. The club was closed on Mondays and the boys got to play as much golf as they could physically handle. In addition, Tommy De Baca, the Club's head professional, taught many of them the fundamentals of the game and made certain that the boys had the necessary equipment before they reached AHS.

Ten years later this writer would take up the game. My coach? Tony Valdez, of course. Tony and I played at least once a week and the AHS coach played the game well into his eighties before he died, as a result of a tragic accident.

Chuck Vidal was the sole standout performer returning to Coach Valdez' tennis team in 1954. *La Reata* did not post the team record for the year, so little can be recorded here. Relying primarily on memory which is not a reliable source fifty years removed from the time in question, this writer recalls that those in addition to Chuck who lettered were: Jim Major, Walter Darr, Simon Santileanes and Don Daily.

Senior week was the most joyous moment in time in my high school experience. Sadness, like an approaching fog, seemingly hadn't enveloped any of us as yet. No studies, no exams, no slips for tardiness. We were free to mill around the campus visit with our teachers and most importantly, exchange salutations for posterity in *La Reata* (our yearbook). Some of them were:

"Buster _____

"I can't quite put in words what I want to say. I think you're great Buster and I've enjoyed our friendship. I know you'll be very successful because you've got what it takes. Lots of Luck to you, Buz. — Riette (Lewinson)"

"To a really swell guy who I'll always think the world of. Hope your college years are as successful as your high school years were. Be Good, — Sally Chase"

"The very best of luck to one of AHS' greatest athletes, — George Harris"

"Buster, AHS wouldn't have been the same without you. Best Wishes, —Harvey Jean Peterson"

"Buster, you have been an asset to us. We will miss your athletic ability & AHS will miss you, but I'm looking for great things in college from you. — Jewell Brown (Counselor)"

"When you become important and successful don't forget all the grey hairs I got helping—gee it will be quiet in 314 now! — Frank Graham (Art Teacher)"

The longest and most meaningful message came from my love of over four years.

"Dear Buz—Gosh, it is gonna be hard telling you all I feel in words. No one, not even my closest of friends has been as sweet & thoughtful so consistently as you. You don't know how much it meant to me every time you took me out to your house & I immediately became just 'one of the family.' Guess it's just me but every time you mentioned Karen or Lani or Marilyn my blood would practically boil from just plain ol' jealousy. But I suppose you know that every time you did say something about `em I tried my darndest to be real sweet and well, like you wanted me to be.

"That party at the Rose's was the most wonderful one we ever went to and I don't think I ever had such a great time with you. You don't know how much I'm looking forward to Sr. Week with you and on Commencement we'll really set the world on fire—ok?"

"Don't ever sacrifice that crew-cut, Buz, it's your trademark, and I love you with it. Don't let some babe at C.U. talk you into letting it grow out— you just wouldn't be you anymore. When we come home at Xmas time we'll have to see each other every nite, cuz I'm going to miss you like everything till then."

"Don't guess there's much more to say except for one thing: You know how I feel about you, Buz & don't you ever doubt it for one minute! To quote a friend of mine: 'Words can't express how <u>wonderful</u> it's been.'"

"I'll NEVER, NEVER forget my Buz. — 'Glo'

Almost fifty years later Glo's sincere message is as touching today than it was in 1954. My reply was written after our prom night.

"Dearest 'GoGo:' I really don't know if I can express myself as well as you did but you know I feel the same about you as you do about me.

"It has almost been 4 years now & although we've argued & disagreed the fun we've had far surpasses the disappointments! For instance last night, it was the mostest to say the leastest! We were together all night & the following morning—a practice to be kept in the future!"

"The best to you in college next year and the time we're apart will be hell for me but when we come home & see each other it will be so nice, won't it?"

"I'm looking forward to this summer with great anticipation for everything will be perfect, I know——"

"The best to my 'baby doll.' You're the greatest gal I've ever known & I'm hoping someday you'll be mine! Love, — 'Buz'"

I was right. I didn't express myself as well as Glo did. The senior prom and what followed after clearly articulated our relationship and defined our moment in time.

As we jitterbugged to *Sh-Boom* and slow danced to *Make Love to Me* and *Little Things Mean A Lot* the lights began to dim on our wonderful high school experience. To some of the kids, it was a time for celebration. School was over. To us it was a time for reflection. Glo and I both felt a sense of loss. A loss of friends that we may never see again. A loss of a world and its surroundings that we knew and were comfortable with. Maybe, even a loss of innocence in a more adult world that we would soon encounter. We laughed and joked with our friends at the dance but like an undertow at the ocean's edge, the unknown kept tugging at us as we floated on the surface of the moment.

After the prom we cast off the formal trappings of dress that were as traditional as homecoming. More comfortable in our casual clothes Glo and I as well as most of our gang headed for The Castle.

The guys gathering together around the pinball machine talked about cars and girls—probably in reverse order of priority. There were only a few custom "hot rods" that could "peel out" or "lay rubber" on Central Avenue. The ultimate act of machismo or macho was a drag race way out in the "toolies" on Juan Tabo Road. But, none of our gang was into it. Our modest modes of "transpo" were in-line straight sixes with automatic that could barely meet the challenge of a duel in the desert. Jim, H.B., Jack and I preferred it that way but listened intently to the James Dean or Bobby Unser types who earned their "rep" behind the wheel. That would all change within a year when the Chevys and Fords came equipped with feisty V-8s and stick shifts.

We never lost a close friend in a car wreck all through junior and senior high. Jimmy Dean died less than a year later in his Porsche Spider.

"Hey! How many of you guys are getting laid tonight?" asked one of our friends who graduated in the class of `53. "This is the big night. Lots of virgins bite the dust tonight, you know," he added.

"Why tonight? I know prom night is a big deal and all but why is it any different?" I asked, while all of us waited anxiously for insider information from someone who had been there.

"Awe s... got a tilt!" (The pinball machine shut the game down due to excessive manipulation to control the movement of the ball.) "Oh, I don't know. The girls start thinking and talking about marriage and stuff. You know, it's like school's over and they're not kids any more and they're thinking about raising a family. It's like it's ok to do 'IT' now. That's what happened with me. Believe me, attitudes change when high school's over," our older and wiser buddy reflected as he held court.

"Geez. I never thought of that. Guess a lot of things change now," I added.

"Of course it helps a lot if you add a little booze to those cherry cokes they're drinkin', too," our experienced sage positioned.

Jack, H.B., Jimmy and I all looked at each other, wondering about the validity of this theory. The Castle was about to close. All of us were going to meet at Jimmy's parent's house in the South Valley for breakfast but we had several hours to be alone with our dates. Fortified with new knowledge we waved goodbye and each of us headed in various directions to our favorite place to "park." Our place was off Juan Tabo near Bear Canyon. The view of the city lights below was magnificent—and romantic. A perfect setting for our first night together.

"Glo? When do you think we'll get married?" I asked as I positioned the station wagon at the crest of a hill overlooking the Rio Grande Valley.

"I think we should wait until after our freshman year in college, Buz. We're both going away to school and we won't see each other until Christmas vacation. I'm going to miss you terribly but I know we'll feel stronger about each other when we get home in December," Glo replied as we cuddled up together. The cool mountain air invaded our nest. I suggested that we get into the back seat so that we would have more room.

The excitement and intensity of our intimacy was heightened by our solitude with only the stars as our witness. Our breathing replicated the heavy beating of our hearts.

"I want to make love to you Glo. I love you so much.

"We can't Buz...we promised. We can't," Glo said, agonizing with the dilemma that was our constant companion of four years.

"It is different now, Glo. Everything's changed. We know that we're getting married," I reasoned with the assistance of my newly acquired knowledge.

"I promised my Mom and you promised your Mom...on a Bible. I couldn't face your Mom or mine if we did it," Glo said, fighting back the tears that seemed always to stain these moments.

Glo was right. We couldn't violate the trust we had in each other and the trust that our parents had in us no matter how difficult it was. A cool breeze calmed the passion within. Our focus turned to our past and our future. Our solitude became solemn. The realization that this wonderful time in our lives was over, overwhelmed us. We held firmly onto each other as if to not let go of the past. But, those times were already a memory even though we possessed them in the present. Enmeshed deeply in each of our own thoughts as well as each other, we fell asleep.

As the desert birds began to announce a new day that hadn't yet arrived, I recalled that first day of kindergarten in Green Bay, waking up my sister, at 6:00 a.m., anxious to open a new door in my life. This whole childhood school experience was truly like opening and closing a series of doors.

We all entered that first door that day as five year olds with the ambivalence of fear and excitement both tugging at our hearts and our minds. At each grade we grew more confident in ourselves as we developed our friendships and became familiarized with the environment around us.

At the end of our sixth year, one door closed and another opened. Some of the same anxieties were renewed and in time relinquished. High school had double doors. Our sensibilities were more acute, more complex like those that Glo and I were presently dealing with. Some of us would now leave our homes, our parents, our friends and the familiarity of the city we loved for the great unknown. We had reasons to be frightened but no one should know it.

Sunlight, rising behind the Sandias, lightened the moment as it lit up the sky. We were soon at Jimmy's house. We had emerged from the ocean's undertow and were swimming at ease on the surface again with our closest friends. Everything was so comfortable talking about the small stuff.

Those magnificent and magical doors at AHS had now closed behind us. Some of us had found that "spring in our step" and would use it to propel us to new heights. Some would find theirs much later. Some, unfortunately, never found it at all but we all still are and will always remain "Bulldogs Forever."

www.ingramcontent.com/pod-product-compliance
Lightning Source LLC
Chambersburg PA
CBHW031943090426
42739CB00006B/72